Personality Assessment

Personality Assessment:
A Fresh Psychological Look

QAMAR HASAN

Foreword by
D.M. PESTONJEE

GYAN PUBLISHING HOUSE

New Delhi 110 002

Personality Assessment: A Fresh Psychological Look
[*Psychology*]

ISBN : 81-212-0533-6

Published in 1997 in India by
Gyan Publishing House
5, Ansari Road
New Delhi 110 002

Laser Typeset at Akshar, Delhi
Printed at Mehra Offset Press, New Delhi

Contents

Foreword 9

Preface 11

1. PERSONALITY: ITS MEASUREMENT AND ASSESSMENT 15

Definitions of Personality: Variations, Allport's definition, Pervin's definition
Units of Personality: Traits, Types, Habits
Traits: Classification, properties, identification, implications of properties for measurement
Types: Definition, identification
Habits: Definition, case against traits—correlational evidence and behaviouristic assessment
Measurement and Assessment: Nature of measurement; distinction between measurement and assessment, kinds of assessment methods

2. OVERVIEW OF PERSONALITY ASSESSMENT 41

Historical Resume: Personality assessment in ancient time, pseudo scientific disciplines, advent of scientific assessment, important events
Contribution of Military Selection Programmes: German, British (WOBS), American (OSS)
Other Living-in Assessment Programmes: Institute

of Personality Assessment and Research (IPAR), Veteran Assessment Project

Correlational and Factor Analytic Studies: Contributions of Burt, Thurstone, Eysenck, and Cattell

Other Multiphasic Questionnaire: MMPI, EPSS, PRF

Research in Personality Assessment: Comparison of strategies of construction of questionnaire, Clinical versus statistical prediction, problems of prediction—base rate, selection ratio, utility, and gain

Use of Computer in Personality Assessment: Computer based test interpretation (CBTI), evaluation of CBTI

Personality Assessment in India

New Trends in Personality Assessment

Immoral use of Assessment Devises

3. RATIONAL-THEORETICAL APPROACH *69*

Nature of the Approach

Steps in Developing Rational Theoretical Instruments: Defining the construct, editing and improving language of items, determining item homogeneity, selection of internally consistent items

Evaluation of the Approach

Rational-Theoretical Scales: Study of Values, Edwards Personal Preference Schedule, Jodhpur Multiphasic Personality Inventory, Tri-Guna Personality Inventory, Cope

Substantive Approach: Loevinger's view point, Personal Research Form

4. EMPIRICAL STRATEGY OF CONSTRUCTION OF PERSONALITY QUESTIONNAIRE *99*

The Strategy

Procedure for Developing Empirical Scales:

Criterion groups, items selection, cross validation, reliability and validity
Evaluation of the Empirical Approach
Empirical Scales: MMPI, PGI Health Questionnaire No. 2

5. FACTOR ANALYTIC APPROACH TO PERSONALITY ASSESSMENT *129*
Factor Analysis: Assumptions
Steps in Factor Analysis: Correlation matrix
Choice of method of analysis, estimation of communalities, factors to be retained, rotation of axes, interpretation of factors.
Factor Scales: Guilford's, Thurstone's, 16 PF-comprehensiveness, construction, scales, reliability and validity, use in prediction and diagnosis, evaluation of 16 PF and Eysenek Personality Questionnaire

6. EVALUATION OF PERSONALITY MEASURES *163*
Importance of Item Analysis
Methods of Obtaining Item Statistics: Indices of discrimination, correlational Indices
Reliability: Definition, sources of variance, Cattell's view regarding reliability, methods of determining reliability
Validity: Nature, content validity, concurrent and predictive validities, construct validity, procedures of construct validation

7. SOURCES CONFOUNDING PERSONALITY ASSESSMENT *193*
Response Styles: Acquiescence, deviation response style, extreme response style
Response Set: Social Desirability, faking
Dealing with Response Distortions: Improvement of Test design, detection of response distortions, suppression of response distortions

8. CROSS-CULTURAL ASSESSMENT OF PERSONALITY *223*

Need and Purpose
Culture-alien and culture-syntonic measures
Imperative of Cross-cultural Assessment: Reasons for using foreign tests
Equivalence: Importance, Kinds, emic-etic distinction, Obtaining culture-specific items, importance of translation in cross-cultural assessment, strategies and errors in interlanguage communication
Purpose and Methods of Translation: Criteria of good translation, adequacy of good translation.

9. UTILIZATION OF PERSONALITY DATA *253*

Importance of transformation of scores
Norms: Standard scores, ordinal position norms, normalized scores
Expectancy tables and charts
Profile Analysis: Salient features of a profile, the D Statistics, coefficient of profile similarity
Actuarial Prediction: Developing actuarial system
Multiple Prediction: Selection of predictor variables, stepwise analysis, stability of regression equation
Moderator Variables: Nature, identification
Suppressor variables: The unwanted baggage

Bibliography *283*

Index *305*

FOREWORD

It is not only difficult but even embarassing to venture to write a Foreword for a book. The Foreword should be able to introduce the author as also the book. Dr. Qamar Hasan, Professor and Chairman of the Deptt. of Psychology at Aligarh Muslim University, Aligarh is known to the discerning public as an author of considerable repute. He is known for his diligence and thoroughness. The present volume bears adequate evidence of both these characteristics.

Interest in the measurement of human personality dates back to ancient times. Starting first as an interest in prediction of personal life events and gradually culminating in potential for action, effort and results. The main fillip to the fields of personality measurement came to the West with need for large scale recruitment. Very soon similar endeavours were required to be repeated in India. In some measure an effort to provide scientific information about non-cognitive aspects of human behaviour was made by publication of the three *Handbooks of Psychology and Social Instruments*. Dr. Qamar Hasan's volume is distinct and unique in the sense that it is extremely 'user friendly'.

The volume gives precise scientific information about salient effort made in other countries and their possible lessons for the measurement movement in India.

To the academically inclined students of human behaviour, the present volume will provide very large pool of information on personality measurement. There is hardly any other source material which is so rich.

Many times need to use psychometric instruments in organizational context is felt by the line managers and HRD experts. Both these, face insurmountable difficulties as there is no single source which they can turn to. The present volume is going to serve this long felt need. It is here that one can find the necessary technical details and choices. The present volume has the right mix of technical details about construction and standardization of instruments. It also gives helpful hints on identifying the type of instrument to serve specific needs of the users.

I am sure that this will prove a valuable text and guide.

D.M. Pestonjee

L & T Chair Professor in
Organizational Behaviour
Indian Institute of Management
Ahmedabad - 380 015
May 28, 1996.

Preface

There has been growing realization that a person while doing a job is not only involved to the extent of his capabilities that are directly relevant to doing the job he is rather totally involved in the job and the network of the organization which hired him to do the job. With this realization and the realization that simple questions regarding family background, the school attended, and details of extracurricular activities would not provide the data that would be sufficient for selection of most suitable candidates for doing certain assignment, personality assessment has become an integral part of selection process. Personality assessment helps in obtaining the information about the way a person was behaving in past situations of the kind that he would encounter in his present assignment. However, we have to realize that the comprehensiveness of personality assessment is to be related to the complexity of the job the person would be doing. A candidate who is being considered for the job of taxi driver is not to be assessed as thoroughly as the person who is to be a secret agent or a business executive.

Though the use of scientific method of personality assessment has been introduced in the present century, from the beginning of civilization attempts have been made to select most capable personnel. Moreover, we want to know about our destiny and make the world predictable for us. For this reason a number of pseudoscientific disciplines were originated in the absence of standardized assessment devices and the data relating individuals' scores with the probability of doing certain kind of assignment successfully.

Even after the advent of scientific assessment devices, it is imperative that only those who have sufficient expertise should venture in personality assessment. Eysenck has observed that psychologist get foothold in an established organization through catastrophic breakdown of traditional procedures but after devising an assessment programme they are displaced by influential laymen of the organization, who believe that once experts have laid down the programme, the power of making decision about the fate of the candidates should be restored to them as they as organizational bosses have right to hire and fire the employees.

While different media and a variety of methods can be used for personality assessment, personality questionnaires are the most popular instrument for knowing about a person. Words arranged according to the syntax of the language which one speaks are the main vehicle of human communication. However, we are often not fully successful in communicating to others what we want to communicate. This may happen when an oral question-answer session or a set of printed questions is being used for such specific purposes as doing market survey, forecasting election outcome, doing public opinion survey, or collecting personality data. Foddy (1995, p. 17) has pointed out that four steps must occur in a successful question-answer sequence:

(a) The researcher is aware of nature of information required and is able to encode a request for imparting information;
(b) The respondent decodes the request in the way the researcher wants him to decode;
(c) The respondent encodes an answer that contains the requested information;
(d) The researcher decodes the answer as the respondent intend to be decoded.

While developing personality questionnaires one has to

ensure that the four steps go smoothly. In addition to that he has to assume that the respondent has required information (has self-awareness), he is willing and is motivated to give frank answers despite his concern for being penalized for being frank. Sometimes the respondent may feel hurt for being asked to answer questions involving invasion of his privacy.

The present book is an attempt to provide a comprehensive account of problems of personality assessment. To a layman personality assessment through questionnaire is as simple task as preparing a list of questions and asking the client/applicant to answer by choosing one of the given alternatives. While more and more organizations are making use of personality assessment for personnel selections and man power planning, it is necessary to familiarize the people at the helm of organizations with nature of personality, units of measurement, and important developments in the field of personality assessment. The first chapter is, therefore, devoted to explaining connotations of the terms personality and the distinction between the measurement and assessment. Chapters 3, 4 and 5 are concerned with different approaches to personality assessment. It is explained why one should and why one should not prefer this or that approach. In chapter 6 the procedures for item selection and that of determining different kinds of reliabilities and validities are explained. The sources which confound personality assessment are discussed in chapter 7. This chapter explains different kinds of response distortions and what can be done to minimize their confounding effects. Due to a number of reasons questionnaires developed in one country/culture are to be used in other countries/cultures. While doing so one should be concerned with the equivalence and problems of inter-language communications. Chapter 8 is devoted to the discussion of problems of cross-cultural personality assessment, in regard to the importance of emic-etic distinction and conceptual and translation equivalence. The last chapter deals with methods of proper utilization of personality data. The data which are obtained after painstaking effort is to be utilized for diagnosis, prognosis and the prediction of job performance. No one can claim to have knowledge of the field of personality assessment without knowing what he should do with the data.

I have to acknowledge the encouragement and support given by colleagues and students for completing this work. Professor Afzal Kureshi has gone through certain chapters and suggested improvement. Dr. Saeeduzzafar also helped me in improving the script. My students Saeeduzzafar, Ms. Anisa Waheeduddin, Ms. Sayeda Humaira Siddiqa, Ms. Hina Siddiq and Mr. Mohd. Majazul Huque helped me in different ways and I have to express my gratitude to them.

April 1996 **QAMAR HASAN**
Aligarh (Uttar Pradesh)

1

Personality: Its Measurement and Assessment

It is difficult to tell what is personality. The difficulty is not that we know very little about the personality, but it is due to the fact that we know much about it. Knowledge about an entity creates difficulty when the contributors to the knowledge do not agree with the importance assigned to its different aspects. The situation is more or less like that of an elephant described by the blind men. The legend is that the four blind men touched different parts of the elephant and depending on their limited knowledge described the elephant like a pillar, snake, fan, or rope.

Personality is not like an animal such as an elephant or like an object such as a ball. It is a concept to be used to recognize stability and consistency of behaviour across different situations, uniqueness of the person and individual differences. Putting aside the controversies regarding the definitions of personality, let us try to make clear some of the important shades of meaning of the concept. In his classic work on personality, Allport (1937, p. 26) stated that originally persona denoted theatrical mask used in Greek drama. The legend is that a popular actor had to put the mask so as to cover some cosmetic defect. During the course of time the word assumed so many shades of meaning. Cicero (106-43 B.C.) found that the word has the following four meanings of persona (Allport, 1937):

(a) As one appears to others (but not really is);
(b) The part some one, e.g., philosopher, plays in life;

(c) An assemblage of personal qualities that fit a man for his work;

(d) Distinction and dignity (as style of writing).

Allport gave fifty different definitions derived from the different shades of meaning of the term. We are not going to discuss all the meanings of the word. It is sufficient to mention that there are theological, jurist, sociological and psychological definitions of personality. All the meanings can be arranged on a continuum, ranging from external (false, mask-like) manner to true self. Even psychological definitions of the term reflect hues of the derivatives of persona. In between the two ends of the continuum, external (mask)—internal (player) lie the popular, biological, sociological, jurist, philosophical, psychological, and theological definitions. In sociological definitions, personality is regarded as subjective side of culture; at the most it is the integration of traits which determine the role and status of a person in society. Personality is, therefore, equated to social effectiveness.

The philosophical definitions of personality take note of internal aspect of personality. Two philosophical definitions quoted by Allport (1937) are being reproduced here for the sake of example: (1) "substance gifted with understanding", (2) "Individuality which became object to itself." In jurist definition a person is a free citizen; he is bearer of fundamental rights. A united community living a coherent life is also a person legally.

Psychological definitions of Personality

Personal qualities are the most common reference point of the psychological definitions of personality. In accordance with their emphasis the definitions can be placed into five categories (Allport, 1937):

1. *Omnibus definitions.* This category of definitions make use of a list of personality characteristics. The list is followed by such expressions as "sum-total", composite of "aggregate of", "ensemble of" etc. This kind of definition is illustrated by Allport by reproducing Prince's definition:

"Personality is the sum total of all the biological innate dispositions, impulses, tendencies, appetites, and instincts of the individual, and the acquired dispositions and tendencies — acquired by experience".

2. *Integrative definitions.* In this category are included those definitions which emphasize the organizational aspect of personality. One of the definitions as quoted by Allport (1937) to illustrate this category is, "The pervasive super pattern which expresses the integrity and the characteristic behavioural individuality of the organism" (Gesell).

3. *Hierarchical definitions.* Such definitions regard personality as a pyramid like structure with innermost self in the commanding position at the center. Thus personality is regarded as, "Levels or layers of dispositions with a unifying or integrative principle at the top".

4. *Definitions in terms of adjustment.* Such definitions regard personality as the whole organism in interaction with the environment in the interest of survival. Thus, personality becomes equivalent to an individual's mode of coming to terms with the demands of environment.

5. *Definitions in terms of distinctiveness.* These definitions advocate that there will be no personality if all the individuals behave in the same manner. Marking of any member of a group from others in terms of his system of habits, dispositions and sentiments is collectively known as personality.

Allport's definition of Personality

Allport (1937) did not find biosocial formulations and omnibus definitions of personality to be useful. Distinctiveness, adjustment and growth are the elements which Allport (1937) found useful in defining personality: "Personality is the dynamic organization within the individual of those psychophysical systems that determine his unique adjustment to his environment" (Allport, 1937, p. 48). Elaborating his definition Allport presented the following assumptions regarding personality:

(1) Personality is a self-regulating system which is constantly changing and evolving.

(2) This organization entails the operation of what is known as mental and what is known as physical.

(3) Personality is not the manifest behaviour or impression which an individual makes on others. It is something behind the manifest behaviour; it does something when an individual is aroused to make a response to the impinging stimuli or to meet environmental demand.

(4) Allport assumes that not only every individual's mode of adjustment to the environment is different qualitatively, but there is also quantitative variations in respect of common traits.

(5) Though personality gives distinctiveness and identity to the individual, its role is not confined to making the individual distinctive. It also serves a useful purpose by making an individual to behave in the interest of his survival. Later on, Allport (1965) revised his definition of personality. The revised definition contains the word 'characteristic' for 'uniqueness' and words 'behaviour and thought' in place of 'adjustment': "Personality is a dynamic organization within the individual of those psychophysical systems that determine his characteristic behaviour and thought" (p. 28).

The substitution of "unique" by "characteristic" is the realization that personality is to be studied by ideographic as well as nomothetic methods and that acts and concepts which an individual shares with others are ultimately individualistic and idiomatic. The replacement of "adjustment" by "behaviour and thought" is acknowledgement of the fact that in addition to dealing with the demands of survival created by environmental situations, one grows in accordance with the psychological system that comprise personality.

Although it is not possible to discuss various definitions of personality, we are referring to Pervin's (1970) definition because it has implications for the purpose of research and measurement. It integrates three different aspects of existence: biological (*Umwett*), world of relation with others (*Mitwett*) and the mode of relation with oneself (*Eigenwelt*).

The definition is reproduced below: "Personality represents those structural and dynamic properties of an individual or individuals as they reflect themselves in characteristic response situations" (p. 2).

The above definition recognizes the importance of parts and their relationship as the constituents of personality. It implies that personality is to be ultimately defined in terms of behaviour and that consistency within a single individual, consistency across all the individuals and consistency along the group of individuals are the salient features of personality. Since the purpose of offering a definition of personality is to put forward one's viewpoint, Pervin's definition also contains his views regarding the nature of personality. The views are mentioned below because they have far reaching implications for the assessment of personality:

1. Man is unique among species. Unlike other species, man is less dependent on biological needs for motivation of his behaviour. He has the capacity to symbolize and he can represent to himself past and future. He can think about himself as he can about other objects. He is influenced by symbolic communication.

2. Human behaviour is complex. His behaviour may be determined by a large number of factors. Individuals may construe the same event in different ways and for this reason they may behave differently in relation to the same event. Conversely, the same behaviour may have different roots.

3. Human behaviour is not always what it appears to be. Antecedents of a specific behaviour are not fixed. We have to know about the individual and the situation in which he behaved so as to understand an individual's behaviour at different occasions. On all occasions behaviour is to be understood from the perspective of behaving individual.

4. We are not always aware of the factors determining our behaviour. A lot of our behaviour is unconscious. If asked to explain the cause or reason of our behaviour, we may not be able to report the real causes. People are often found to behave contrary to their expressed desires.

Units of Personality

One of the important reasons to have the concept of personality is that we want to describe an individual as an integrated behaving unit. However, when we have to measure or assess a complex entity like personality, we have to answer the question—what aspects of the complex whole are to be the target of assessment? The situation is same as that of a building which is an organizational whole but which cannot be assessed unless the aspects of information are to be specified. Allport (1937) has mentioned the following proposals for the analysis of personality:

1. Practical and a priori considerations in dividing personality into units.

2. Analysis of personality in terms of uniform nomothetic elements such as needs, traits, etc.

3. Studying personality in terms of stimulus-response elements. According to Allport (1937) the first proposal lacks theoretical relevance, the second ignores uniqueness of the individual, and the third makes little allowance for the generality and complexity of personal dispositions.

Traits, types, and habits are the three general units of personality which are found to be useful in assessment of personality. These three units differ in respect of chunk of behaviour encompassed by them as well as assumptions regarding generality and consistency. Let us consider these units one by one:

Traits

Guilford (1959) regards trait as the aspects of whole personality abstracted for the purpose of comparison between individuals. According to him "A trait is any distinguishable, relatively enduring way in which one individual differs from others" (p. 6). This definition puts stress on three aspects and their presence for the identification or existence of a trait: (a) a quality with respect to which people differ; (b) this quality should be recognized to be different from other qualities; (c) the quantity must be found to have consistent manifestation at different occasions.

Allport (1937) regards traits to have more than nominal existence; they have neuropsychic basis but they are to be discovered empirically. Allport's definition of trait is as follows, "A generalized and focalized neuropsychic system (peculiar to individual), with the capacity to render many stimuli functionally equivalent, and to initiate and guide consistent (equivalent) forms of adaptive and expressive behaviour" (p. 295).

In every language there are a large number of trait names but it is not necessary that every trait name corresponds to an existing trait. However, the list of trait names may be used for the discovery of traits. Carr and Kingsbury (1938) have suggested a logical scheme which helps us to understand how we have idea of a trait and its name. We begin with making observation of behaviour of a number of people and come to know that they differ in what they do and the manner in which they do it. We note that there is some quality common to different behaviours exhibited by an individual though its magnitude may vary from situation to situation. This leads us to use adverbs pertaining to the action. We tend to say that the person behaved confidently, intelligently, or cautiously and so on. The second step in the logical process is that instead of the action the individual becomes the focus of the description because actions are transitory; they become matter of history as early as they are finished. The 'doer' remains and he becomes the focus of attention. This gives rise to the tendency to use adjective to describe him. With the opportunity to observe an individual behaving in different situations and finding that he can be described with the same adjective in different situations, we are likely to move to the third logical step. The third step involves separating the quality from the individual. The quality becomes a thing in the possession of the individual; it is now denoted by a noun.

The above scheme is a good description of the process which may be used by a layman as well as by a psychologists for the discovery of a trait but there are certain formal methods which are to be used for the discovery of trait.

These methods are: laboratory observations, time sampling, statistical method and clinical method.

In the laboratory, traits can be discovered by presenting to the subjects different task sets and observing whether the tasks are responded to in a uniform way. The observation of equivalence of stimuli and responses lead to the identification of traits. Ratings obtained from a panel of judges in respect of a number of characteristics can be compared and used for the discovery of traits. The method of starred rating, in which the raters are not required to rate every individual on the same characteristics, is useful for the discovery of individual traits. In this method the raters have to make a star on the characteristics which according to them are of dominating importance in the individual's personality (Allport, 1937, p. 301).

Time sampling is the method in which a number of observers observe the behaviour of the individuals in the natural setting. The total time is divided into periods of small duration, e.g., one minute. The agreement among the observers regarding the frequency of occurrence of certain form of behaviour leads to the inference of common or individual traits.

The statistical method which helps in the discovery of traits is correlation. It can be used for determining the reliability of a scale developed for measuring an abstracted trait. Subjects' responses to the items included in a scale can indicate the existence of a trait if the items are consistently responded.

Intercorrelations among the items are not considered to be sufficient indicators of presence of a trait of unitary nature. Traits discovered on the basis of intercorrelation can be, at the most regarded as surface traits. Cattell (1950) defines a surface trait as, "a collection of trait-elements, of greater or lesser width of representation, which obviously go together in many different individuals and circumstances" (p. 21). Source traits can be identified with the help of factor analysis of the matrix of intercorrelation of surface traits.

The clinical method is useful for the discovery of individual traits. In this method a particular individual is studied for some duration. On the basis of personal acquaintance and making use of all kinds of information available to him, the investigator is able to say what traits are outstanding in the individual. The clinical method is self-validating; it depends on a single mind, the clinician's, and stands next door to common sense.

Classification of Traits

Different classifications of personality traits have been suggested on the basis of different considerations. Allport (1937) made a distinction between common and unique traits. The distinction is based on the criterion whether a particular trait is not shared by a person with others or it is common to a large number of persons, almost every one. Considering the number of situations, instead of number of persons, distinction is made between general and specific traits. General traits can be identified with the help of factor analysis of matrix of intercorrelation among the responses of individual in different situations related to the elicitation of the same trait. Specific traits are indicated by the residual which cannot be accounted by common factors. Specific traits are given less attention in the psychometric assessment of personality due to the following reasons: (a) Their number is very large or perhaps unknown; (b) they are of little practical importance, and (c) for either of the two reasons instruments for their measurement are not available.

Cattell (1950) made a distinction between constitutional and environmental-mold traits. The distinction is based on the criterion, how a trait is imprinted on personality. As it is difficult to separate the innate and external sources of influence on an individual, Cattell (1950) preferred to use the term 'constitutional source traits' for denoting the patterns that spring from internal conditions and influences such as alcohol, hyperthyroid states, appetitive conditions, etc. The external sources of influence on an individual such as punishment and disapproval by others give rise to environmental-mold traits which are indicated by covariation of a group of habits.

Looking at personality from different standpoints, a distinction among traits based on the modalities of their expression is suggested by Guilford (1959). The classification is as below:

1. *Morphological traits.* People differ with respect to a number of external somatic characteristics such as weight, height, foot size and other aspects for which physical anthropologists have devised measuring tools.

2. *Physiological traits.* People differ with respect to organic functioning such as heart rate, blood pressure, body temperature, basal metabolic rate, EEG, etc.

3. *Needs.* Needs are manifested in desires for certain conditions such as being known, exercising influence over others, etc. Biological drives such as food, water, activity are also included in this category.

4. *Interests.* Interest traits are expressed when individuals are given an opportunity to make choice, individuals express their preferences by indicating likes and dislikes and willingness to indulge in certain activities such as making a painting, thinking, talking, etc. Interests can be defined as desire to indulge in certain activities.

5. *Attitudes.* Attitudinal traits have to do with the readiness to behave in positive or negative manner in relation to certain social objects such as a political party, issue or ideology is known as attitude.

6. *Temperament traits.* Traits which cannot be included in any other modality, the 'left overs', belong to this category (Guilford, 1965). Temperamental traits have to do with the manner in which action occurs; they refer to individual's disposition such as the tendency to be cheerful, insecure, self-confident, etc.

Properties of Traits

In order to understand the problems of personality assessment we have to consider some of the properties of traits which have direct bearing on the procedure of assessment.

1. *Scalability.* When it is possible to visualize variation in traits forming points in close proximity so as to make a continuum, we speak of scalability of trait. When a trait is scalable, we can place an individual anywhere on the continuum and assign him a numerical value. The cues that enable us to locate a person on a continuum are frequency of occurrence of a trait indicator, its intensity, vigorousness of action in behaving, emotional manifestations, and range of behaviour.

One can think of such non-scalable traits as colour blindness, having or not having a phobia, having or not having a conditioned response. However, it is to be pointed out in spite of underlying continuity, individuals can be clustered at the ends of the continuum in the form of bimodal distribution. One can make an effort to find appropriate trait indicators of the variation in the magnitude of traits which appear to be non-scalable.

2. *Unipolarity and bipolarity.* Some traits can be considered to be ranging from 'absence' (zero) to extremely high magnitude. Ability traits are of this kind. However, we can also visualize that zero is located somewhere between the two ends of a trait which can be represented by polar opposite qualities such as ascendence-submission. It is to be noted that zero may not be located in the middle of the continuum because a trait may not have same range of variation on both sides of zero.

3. *Functional fluctuation.* When an individual is measured by administration of a trait scale at different occasions he is not expected to get different scores because he is the same person. But variations in individual's scores are likely to be observed if measurement of different traits are administered on an individual, he is likely to show fluctuations in respect to every measure but the range may not be the same.

4. *Universality.* This property of trait has to do with the number of persons in a population who have the trait. Some traits are applicable to only a segment of population such as children or elderly people, some traits are unique to the

individuals but there are some traits which can be used for describing almost every person.

5. *Generality.* A trait is generalized to the extent that different situations encountered by the individual are rendered equivalent. Honesty may be a general trait in the case of those individuals who regard a large number of situations to be the situations which require a particular type of behaviour. Generality of a trait also depends on the frequency of opportunity to express the trait. For instance, the trait of endurance can find expression when there is a situation requiring perseverance.

6. *Organization.* Strength and pattern are two aspects of organization of a trait. This property has to do with the relation between a trait and its indicators. Considering aspect of strength we can distinguish between poorly and well organized traits. A poorly organized trait (e.g., punctuality) is the trait which is not expressed consistently in all the relevant situations. There is low correlation between expression of punctuality in different situations (like being in time for a meeting, submitting a report in time, turning up at agreed time for dinner, etc.). Sociability is an organized trait because its different indicators are highly correlated.

7. *Durability and flexibility.* This property has to do with long term changes or absence of changes in an individual's score on the trait continuum. It is to be pointed out that this property is different from the property of functional fluctuation which has to do with changes in short duration. Developmental studies are required to discover changes in trait position over the span of life. We may be interested in trend of changes for a population or for an individual. The questions related to this property are: At what stage in life the trait emerged?; What is the duration and age of its remaining unchanged when it declines?

Implications of Properties of Traits for Measurement

1. It is almost impossible to locate a zero point on a scale. The mean value of population which is most popu-

larly used as reference point (z=0) does not coincide with zero even in bipolar trait which is supposed to have neutral point between the two polar opposites. The mean of population may be located on either positive side or negative side of the meaningful zero in the case of unipolar trait.

2. Functional fluctuation implies that measurement of some traits should be done again and again at different periods of time depending upon the evidence of fluctuation. Durability/flexibility of trait has also implications for the practice of repeated measurement. If the variations in trait scores at different stages of life are observed we have to have norms for different age groups. If the growth or decline of trait is not the same for different groups (e.g., male, female, ethnic groups) then in this case also we need norms for different groups.

3. The property of generalization of trait has to do with the availability of trait indicators to be used in the development of measurement device. If a trait is generalized, many trait indicators will be available and a choice among them is possible. The practical implication of this characteristic is that a general trait can be used for the prediction of many kinds of criteria. Individual differences in generality of trait are worth assessing because it would enable us to know the area of behaviour to which an individual's trait is extended.

4. The characteristic of independence and organization of traits have implications regarding the desirability of the study of intra-individual variations. Some trait indicators may be more useful for the estimation of a trait in the case of one individual, another set of trait indicators may be more useful for the estimation of trait score of another person. The same total score, say 10, may be arrived at by the combination of different indicators. This underscores the desirability of obtaining more information other than that contained in the total if we want better prediction of behaviour.

Types

Type is a complex and wider unit of personality assessment. The type description has been popular from the days of Hippocrates and Galen. The division of temperaments into melancholic, choleric, phelgmatic, and sanguine types is the oldest typology.

A typology is based on the selection of some important characteristics and using their combination as a prototype to match and categorize individuals into homogeneous groups of those who resemble the prototype and those who do not. The selection of relevant characteristics for making the prototype for the development of typology makes it possible that the same person is assigned to different types depending on the set of characteristics under consideration. There are three senses in which the concept of type is used in contemporary psychology (Cattell, 1950, p. 6).

Continuous types. When typology is based on the coexistence of a set of normally distributed traits and the persons who are located at the opposite poles of each of the characteristics, we have continuous types. For example, each one of the characteristics used for classification of people into introvert and extrovert types are normally distributed. The characteristics are: gregariousness, intrusiveness, adventurousness, etc.

Species types. When typology is such that an individual can be placed in either this or that category and there are few or none intermediataries, we have species types. It is to be noted that in this kind of typology objects or individuals assigned to different categories may have similarity in some respects but there is no overlapping pattern. Male and female sexes, automobiles of different make, animals of pure breed are the examples of this kind of typology where similarity in colour, height, weight, etc. may be observed between those who belong to the same type.

Discontinuous types. These are hybrid. Such types have characteristics of both continuous and species types. In this type, the pattern of distribution of characteristics is not different or discontinuous but there is no overlap in single variable. This kind of typology is of little significance (Cattell, 1950).

Methods of Identification of Types

To evolve a typology we have to begin with the identification of patterns of concurrent trait endowments which are most frequent (Cattell, 1950). Three methods are possible for the identification of types: prescribing arbitrary standards, the clinical method, and the statistical method. In the first method we take some real or fictitious person as the ideal and then search those which resemble him in the characteristics which the ideal has or is supposed to have. This arbitrary selection of an ideal person has some practical utility. When we are in need of personnel similar to those whom we found to be good, we can make use of this kind of typology. The clinical method relies on those who, by their profession, have the responsibility of helping the persons suffering from physical and psychiatric ailments. The professional people have the opportunity to form impression as to what symptoms or behaviours are frequently found together. It can be expected that the observations on which the impressions are based are unbiased and also that due to good memory no important bit of information is ignored or distorted. The typologies developed by the practicians of clinical method, as one can expect, are confined to pathological types because they have more opportunity to observe and study abnormal persons. When it becomes difficult to rely on memory for the identification of a pattern of covariance, one has to take help of statistical methods. Cattell (1950) has rightly observed that statistical methods help a psychologist in the same way as a microscope helps a biologist. Correlation methods, factor analysis, cluster analysis, methods for determining profile similarity are used for the discovery of types and allocation of individuals to different types.

Habits/S-R Units

Specific S-R units are suggested to be better units of personality because evidence is furnished to the effect that traits are not satisfactory and useful units of personality and for this reason are of little value in the prediction and modification of real life behaviour. S-R units are claimed to provide more specific description of personality when factors which are important for maintaining the contingency between the S and R are to be recognized. One can draw attention to the fact that because the purpose of measurement is to reduce large number of observed events to a small number of variables, it would be negation of the purpose of assessment if innumerable specific S-R units are preferred over limited number of generalized personality traits. However, we should not forget the fact that if events to which the concept refers cannot be bound by the concept and the concept is of little use for the prediction of future behaviour, we have to put aside the requirement of encompassing the events to a limited number of general concepts.

Case against Personality Traits

The essence of criticism against the concept of trait is contained in the following observation: "There are no broad, general traits of personality, no general form of conduct which, if they existed, would make for consistency of behaviour and stability of personality, but only independent and specific stimulus-response bonds or habits" (Thorndike, 1903). The main point of criticism against the use of the concept of trait is that trait presumes consistency of behaviour across the situations and stability over a period of time but a lot of evidence is furnished to show lack of consistency across the situations. Mischel (1968) who led the assault on the concept of trait reported that his search of relevant literature could not furnish evidence that coefficients of correlation indicating consistency in measures of personality traits exceeded 3. Even this value was found on few occasions. Mischel (1968) presented following arguments in support of his demolition of the concept of trait:

1. The correlational evidence furnished to establish construct validity of measures of traits is weak because the correlation between the one paper-pencil test of personality and other similar test can be accounted in terms of: (a) social desirability values of the items of both the tests; (b) tendency

to agree/disagree with items; (c) greater contribution of method variance than that of trait variance to the correlation; (d) many personality tests are found to be correlated with the measures of intelligence and the intercorrelation may be due to their common association with intelligence.

2. Five stable factors that are reported to be identified in a series of studies employing diverse samples are not to be regarded as structural features of persons. They are attributes employed by the raters rather than ratees' traits. Human beings due to their limited capacity of organizing information (5+2 or 7+2, Mandler, 1968; Miller, 1956) simplify incoming information by assigning labels and codes and the stable factors are manifestations of the tendency to construe stable personality consistencies analogous to perceptual consistency.

3. Assessment of personality trait is of little practical utility. Mischel (1969) reported that, in most cases the availability of such diagnostic data could not bring about any change in the kind of treatment to be given to the client. Moreover, there is not much improvement in the accuracy of prediction and classification of cases over that of base rate when information given by the test is also taken into consideration. This is technically known as lack of incremental validity.

4. The concept of trait emphasizes the role of internalized structures in determining individual's behaviour. This leads to disregard of the role of situation and environmental factors in an individual's behaviour. The concept of man that comes from trait-state concept is such that man is shackled by his infantile history and unchanging rigid dispositions. The trait approach is to be rejected if the adaptiveness of man and his ability to modify his behaviour according to the situational demands is to be recognized.

5. When manifest behaviour is explained by attributing it to some trait not much information is forthcoming. The explanation is of the nature of ghost in the machine; it does not provide knowledge about the antecedent of behaviour.

It is to be pointed out that the criticism against assessment of personality in the form of measures of traits is associated with the emergence of the techniques of behaviour modification based on the principles of learning. These techniques make no attempt to make a person well adjusted by helping him to resolve intrapsychic conflicts because they are not interested in dealing with what can be modified with the help of proper schedule of reinforcement. Behaviour therapies have evolved their own procedures of assessment which are distinguished from the traditional methods in the following respects:

(a) The behavioural tools contain items which are sample of behaviour instead of signs of underlying personality trait;

(b) In behaviouristic assessment the prediction of the criterion is direct because assessee's responses are not first linked with some underlying personality trait before being used for the inference of behavioural manifestations of the trait. As mentioned earlier, the instrument itself contains items which constitute sample of behaviour from the content domain of the criterion and as such there is no use of postulating personality trait as the mediator between test responses and the criterion.

Behavioural assessment is focused on four types of variables such as situational antecedents, organismic variables, response dimensions, and consequences. Goldfried and Sprafkin (1974) have employed acronym SORC to refer to the variables attended in behavioural assessment. Situational variables that are to be considered in assessment are specific stimuli which elicit a particular response and also the discriminative stimuli which serve as cue for the person to behave in different ways. The organismic variables have to do with such aspects as physiological makeup as general energy level, hormones and chemical imbalance, and psychoactive drugs within his/her system. Cognitive variables, e.g., cognitive sets, are considered in this category. Response variables are actual samples of different kinds of behaviours which are assessed in terms of frequency, strength, duration, latency, etc. Because behavioural assessment is theoretically based on learning, both positive and negative consequences of behaviour are of much concern in behavioural assessment. Any attempt of modification of behaviour can not be indifferent to the consequences of behaviour because by bringing change in the consequences of behaviour we can bring change in the behaviour.

Measurement and Assessment

Is personality assessment different from personality measurement? If not then why two different names for the same thing? According to Kelly (1967) the term originally referred to such money matters as apportioning of taxes, determination of contribution to be made by members of a club and so on. In psychology the term was introduced by the staff of the Office of Strategic Studies (OSS) in 1942. Though terms assessment and measurement are used interchangeabily in common parlance, it is better to understand the distinction between the connotations of the two terms.

Measurement is defined as assignment of numerals to objects and events according to certain rules (Campbell, 1938). What is to be measured is decided by the subject matter of the science, the theoretical system to which one subscribe, and the application to which the measurement would be put. The first step toward measurement is the identification of the property to be assigned numerical values. We know that every object has many properties such as weight, colour, length, breadth, etc. Though basic physical properties seem to invite immediate attention, many properties remain unidentified until they are considered relevant or constructed. Statements about the property are existential statements since they communicate what is observable by senses or extension of senses through certain recording devices (Lorge, 1967). There will be no measurement if there is no communication of observation. Private experiences have no place in measurement because reproducibility of observations is a basic requirement of a measuring device.

In order to ensure the reproducibility of observations we have to define the property so that every one knows what is being talked about and which of the common feature shared by a set of objects is to be considered. A property may be simple or complex. Health and size are complex properties which are to be reduced to different dimensions otherwise we would find it difficult to devise measuring instruments. We can describe size in terms of height, length and breadth.

Having identified the property, we have to assign numbers to the objects having that property according to certain rules. While assigning numbers to the variation of an identified property, we have to take care of isomorphism between the properties of numbers and the property of the objects. It is essential because numbers have three properties: identity, order and additivity. We can make use of any of these properties depending on the isomorphism with the property we are measuring. The assessor is expected to be aware of the fact that the concept of a property may recognize differences in degree or amount. The difference may or may not be such that we can or cannot arrange objects in a definite order so that the sum of any two would be equal to a third. In the case of the former we have intensive magnitude and in the case of the latter we have extensive magnitude (Lorge, 1967). The distinction between intensive and extensive magnitude is as below:

Intensive

1. Recognizes order.
2. There is no fixed zero; it is arbitrary.
3. Have some, but not perfect, relation with external criterion.
4. The sum of two substances of different values is not equal to that of a substance with the value of the numerical sum of these values.

Extensive

1. Definite order.
2. Fixed zero.
3. Invariant relation with an external criterion.
4. The sum of two substances of different values is equal

to a substance of value equal to the numerical sum of these values.

While measurement is always quantitative, assessment may not involve the use of numbers. Lowell Kelly (1967) noted that, "In common use, assessment has become a very broad term that is applied to all of the following: any judgement regarding one's fellow man; the evaluation of application forms; the writing and evaluation of letters of recommendations; the selection interview; the assignment of grades in schools and colleges; the testing of achievement, knowledge, or skills; the intensive clinical study involved in the diagnosis of an individual suffering from mental disorders; and the use of any one of the hundreds of psychological tests which psychologists have developed to measure human abilities, aptitudes, natures, needs, attitudes, interests, and values. Thus the term includes a variety of methods of assessment and even greater range of attributes or characteristics by which a person may be assessed (p. 1). The preceding description of assessment is much wider than what may be regarded as the scope of personality assessment. For example, one can readily exclude assignment of grades in school from the scope of personality assessment but exclusion of other psychological characteristics referred in the excerpt requires delimitation of the meaning of personality. It is the reliance on judges for the generation and combination of data that makes assessment different from measurement. Judges can be used as instrument of data collection when they are trained to assign numbers according to certain rules. However, the use of judges in assessment goes beyond this restricted use of human being; it is extended even to the impression formation about other person, for example, the impression of a friend formed by a common man. The fact that psychological measurement is distinct from assessment can be made explicit by considering the following points (Tallent, 1987):

1. Psychological testing is physicalistic. With its emphasis on quantification, psychological testing relies on physi-

calistic framework. Rosenwald (1965) observed that the application of physicalistic principles is neither appropriate for the description of personality nor it is helpful in understanding needs of the client. The dimensions of personality traits which can be isolated from tests are not as many as we can attach to people. Tests are inadequate to the tasks assigned to them.

2. Assessment is more encompassing than testing. Assessment is not as much simple as determining what numerical values are to be assigned to responses to a set of questions. Assessment is a problem solving process which cannot be reduced to a finite set of rules. It is a variable process which depend upon the question asked, the person involved, time commitments, and many other factors (Maloney and Ward, 1976). It can never be reduced to A means B type of thinking because the same score can have different meanings and that the same meaning can be conveyed by different scores. (Schafer, 1949, p. 331).

3. Assessment is a multiple and complex interaction. Tallent (1983) presented an assessment scheme which places psychologist at the center of complex process involving interaction between the reason of assessment, raw data and frame of reference. The process of assessment cannot be indifferent to the reason as to why the assessor is asked to collect information about a person. Unlike a tester, an assessor can never ignore the referral question, the purpose, and the context of his assignment.

Understanding the importance of the role that a psychologist plays at the center of the process of assessment, Allen (1981) noted that all concepts that are employed to understand the therapeutic relationship (alliance, transfer; counter-transfer) are central during the testing phase of assessment. An experienced therapist is in the best position to make diagnostic use of these phenomena (p. 251).

4. Psychological assessment is an integrative task focused on the individual. Making use of quantification, quantitative relations, norms, probabilities etc., testing procedures give little importance to the role of assessment psy-

chologist in the integration of information about a person. In assessment, a psychologist is expected to play an important role in non-linear integration of data by selecting the theory that best describes the data. He has freedom to make use of whatever theory he considers to be suitable for understanding the individual client who has specific problems. He can even take the liberty of mixing several theories in making sense of the information available to him (McCoy, 1977).

5. The term measurement lacks the connotations of utility and social relevance while assessment is always socially useful. According to Lanyon and Goodstein (1970), personality assessment includes gathering and organization of information about an individual with the purpose that it would lead to a better understanding about the person; an understanding that would lead to prediction about his future behaviour such as possibility of his success in a variety of areas. The implication of assessment for decision in person-society relationship is stressed by Sundberg, Snowden, and Reynolds (1978) who defined assessment as examination of individual characteristics used for decision in person-society relationship.

Kinds of Assessment Methods

Any method that enables us to improve our understanding of personality more than what we come to know about it by common sense, cannot be excluded from the purview of personality assessment. Thus there are so many methods of personality assessment that it becomes difficult to present a classification that would satisfy every one. Different criteria of classification are suggested. On the basis of the kind of material used in assessment devices, Rosenweig (1948) made a distinction between subjective, objective, and projective methods. This distinction overlaps with Super's (1959) classification based on the level of personality functioning: observational methods, projective methods, and self-descriptive methods. Zubin (1950) suggested that level of personality in which an assessor is interested can be either outwardly reportable or it may not be reportable; it may be inwardly accessible to a person (he may be aware of it) or it may not be inwardly accessible to the person (he may not be aware of it). The combination of communicability and awareness leads to the following levels of assessment which may be considered for the classification of assessment methods: conscious, suppressed, overt, and repressed. There can be as many as seven different criteria for the classification of tests (Eysenck, 1952):

1. *Nature of stimulus.* The degree of organization of stimulus used for obtaining the responses leads to the distinction between structured and unstructured devices.

2. *Nature of responses.* The kind of responses obtained from the subjects for the purpose of personality assessment lead the distinction between verbal (written, spoken), autonomic, and motor methods.

3. *Mode of response.* We can make distinction between selective and creative methods depending upon the fact whether the subject is required to choose from listed alternatives or he has to formulate responses.

4. *Methods of scoring.* We can classify methods into objective and subjective categories.

5. *Nature of interpretation.* We can classify assessment devices into symbolic and non-symbolic according to the nature of interpretation.

6. *Mental mechanism used.* Depending upon what mechanism is relied upon for obtaining individual's responses we can classify the methods into projective, identification, reaction formation, and regression devices.

7. *Method of administration.* The consideration whether the device can be administered individually or in group leads to the distinction of individual and group tests.

Classification of measuring devices can be done on the basis of the medium used for obtaining information about personality. Such a classification is suggested by R. B. Cattell (1957) who mentioned the following three media of assessment: L (Life), Q (Questionnaire), and T (objective tests). The L data includes all the behaviour of an individual from birth to death. However, records of behaviour of all kinds are not maintained. Every society keeps record of only a small segment of behaviour of its members such as school grades, work history, police records (of those who are habitual criminals). Baby books, if maintained by parents, can also be available. If one is willing to rely on memory of those who happened to know the person for some time, one may use behavioural ratings (BR). In addition to the problems of memory failure and lack of equal opportunity available to the raters to observe all the ratees in different situations of life, ratings suffer from errors of leniency, central tendency, and halo effect.

The questionnaire medium rely on verbal responses of the subjects to a set of self-descriptive statements. Depending upon the fact whether the responses given by the subject are treated as honestly revealed facts or as only responses without the implication of being true or false, factual or fictitious, a distinction can be made between Q1 and Q2 data. Q1 refers to the questionnaire data in which responses are treated as factual; Q2 to the data in which responses are treated as responses without the implication of their being true self descriptions. The Q1 data may not be reliable and its independent verification is not possible. Moreover, we have to assume that the individual knows about himself and is willing to communicate honestly what he knows about himself.

Instead of observing a person in real life situation, we can observe him in a standard situation created for this purpose. When we do that we obtain T data. The distinctive features of the T medium are: it is portable in the sense the material used for its recording and the situation created can be created anywhere at any time; the subject is not able to fake because he does not know the meaning of his response and is also unable to alter his behaviour even if he tries to do so. However, T data requires more effort and expenditure for its collection and the subject is not as much motivated to behave as he is in real life situation.

The distinction between the three media of assessment

is important from the point of view of the contribution of method in the variance of personality data. Campbell and Fisk (1959) have drawn attention to the fact that the instrument/media/or method used for obtaining personality data always contributes certain amount of variance to the data in addition to individual differences and other sources. With the realization of importance of variance contributed by the method we have to recognize that personality assessment through questionnaire will definitely contain the variance contributed by the method and this is likely to be reflected in the correlation among questionnaire measures of personality.

2

Overview of Personality Assessment

The purpose of this chapter is to make the readers familiar with the field of personality assessment. This purpose would be served if a historical resume of the emergence of the field is given, some important researches in the field of personality assessment are discussed, and new trends are outlined.

Historical Resume

The field of personality assessment emerged from concern about oneself and others so as to know what can be expected from oneself and others. Knowing about a person is related to the prediction of his future behaviour. The prediction of future behaviour is important from the point of view of determining how good he would be in doing a given assignment successfully, nurturing talent, and deciding what kind of interpersonal relations we can have with him.

The fact that there would be no emergence of personality assessment without the utility of assessment for making some critical decisions about a person or using his capabilities for some social purpose, is evident by the fact that even in ancient writings we come across the discussion of human characteristics and their relationship for different kinds of assignments. *Arthashastra* written by Kautilya 400 years before Christ has an elaborate description of background and personality characteristics of high officials, selection procedures, training, incentive systems, and other aspects of executive development programme (Sharma, 1977). Plato's discussion of problems of individual differences and the use of the endowment for the selection of persons for military career is also an example of realization of importance of assessment. Historical records show the existence of a programme of selection for civil services in China during Han dynasty (200 B.C.-220 A.D.). The candidates were assessed with the help of a battery of tests for competence in law, military affairs, agriculture, revenue, and geography. The selection programme evolved into an objective multistage screening programme by the time of Ming dynasty (1368-1644 A.D.).

Early attempts to know about the fate of a person include astronomy, palmistry, phrenology, and search for other physical signs. Astronomy originated about twenty-five centuries ago in Mesopotamia. It is based on the belief that stars have an effect on the life of an individual and that the personality of each individual and causes of events in his life are determined by his horoscope, the configuration of stars at the time of his birth. Matching horoscope of young boys and girls for deciding their suitability as marital partner is still a must in arranged marriage among Hindus. Palmistry existed as early as 3000 B.C. It uses lines on the palm of the hand as well as swellings between lines to forecast events an individual would encounter in his future life. The claim of success by ardent adherents of palmistry may be attributed to making trivial predictions that can be applied virtually to any person; a phenomenon which is labelled as "Barnum effect" by Meehl (1956) and "Aunt Fanny error" by Tallent (1958).

Phrenology was introduced by a German physician Franz Joseph Gall in the late eighteen century. It is based on the assumptions regarding the localization of cortical action. It is reasoned that since different brain functions depend on the development of certain regions and that the size of these regions would determine the external shape of the head, measurement of skull and study of different protrusions would give information about the characteristics of the person.

An incident at the Greenwich observatory in 1796 gave

impetus to the study of individual differences. Kinnebrook was found to make a consistent error of one second in recording an stellar event and he was dismissed for this error. In 1816 Bessel came to know about this incident from historical records of the observatory and started experiments using fellow astronomers. The experiments were about the speed of reaction to visual stimuli. Consistent individual differences observed in the experiment were called 'personal equation'.

In the early decades of the nineteenth century Belgian mathematician Quetelet made an important contribution with his discovery of applicability of mathematical theory of probability to the measurement of human mental and physical traits. This was followed by Galton's contribution to the science of handling such data. In his work on inheritance of physical and mental characteristics, Galton obtained measures of parents and the offsprings and he approached his statistician friend Karl Pearson to develop an index which can represent the relation between the two sets of measures which could replace the graph of relationship. Thus the Pearson Product Moment Correlation (r) was introduced which is the most important statistical method for the development of assessment devices. Galton established an anthropometric laboratory in London and devised some new methods of his own such as the Galton whistle for determining sensitivity to high pitches, and the breakfast table test for determining imagery. He was the first person to use word association test for the measurement of individual differences.

James McKeen Cattell was an American student in the laboratory of German psychologist Wundt in later half of the nineteenth century. Unlike his teacher, who treated individual differences as error and tried to minimize them by dealing with average of the group, James McKeen Cattell became interested in individual differences. He was the first to use the word mental test and is therefore regarded as the initiator of mental test movement. Other contemporaries of James McKeen Cattell who contributed to the measurement of individual differences were Kraeplin (1895), Ebbinghaus (1897), Gilbert (1897), and Sharp (1899).

Though Galton began the use of word association test, the standardization of the procedure was done by Carl Jung (1910). He prepared a list of 1000 words to be used to discover the areas of conflict of patients. Kent and Rosonoff's study of normative associates of 1000 words showed that psychiatric patients differ from normals in the word associations they generate.

The use of psychological testing for the selection of military personnel was introduced in World War I. First intelligence testing was done but later on it was realized that soldiers were also to be screened for the possibility of breakdown under the stress of combat. Robert Woodworth was assigned the task of developing a device which can be used for the screening of the candidates without making much demand on the time of the selection staff. The questionnaire which Woodworth devised was given a neutral label to conceal its purpose; it was called "Personal Data Sheet". Despite its weaknesses, the Data Sheet is the precursor of modern personality inventories.

Five years after the construction of Personal Data Sheet another important development took place. It was the introduction of the use of inkblots for psychiatric diagnosis by Herman Rorschach, a Swiss psychiatrist. The Rorschach Ink Blot Test became the most widely used tool of personality assessment. In the next decades many other projective techniques were available for the assessment of deeper aspects of personality. The Thematic Apperception Test (Murray, 1938) and the Sentence Completion Test became the parts of usual routine package of diagnostic assessment. A theoretical justification of the use of projective techniques was offered by Frank in 1939 in the form of the projective hypothesis. According to Frank (1939), a projection of private world of an individual can be elicited by giving him the opportunity to organize and interpret "plastic" fields or unstructured stimuli rather than asking him to deal with "objective" material.

While projective techniques were flourishing in the 30s, the questionnaire medium continued to be enriched by new contributions. In 1931, Vernon and Allport devised Study of Values. In late 30s there began work on an important tool. The Minnesota Multiphasic Personality Inventory (MMPI) with the purpose of aiding psychiatrists in clinical classification of patients. Hathway and McKinley (1942), who collaborated to develop the instrument, made some inbuilt provisions to deal with certain sources of response distortions. With the availability of MMPI Atlases, cookbooks, and computer programs, the inventory became one of the most popular device of personality assessment.

Contribution of Military Selection Programme

The importance of assessment programme for the selection was highlighted when the disappointing performance of German soldiers in World War I was attributed by Simoneit (1940) to (a) poor adjustment to life at the battle front, (b) lack of proper indoctrination regarding the purpose of war, and (c) insufficient utilization of manpower. Simoneit observed that the situation could be averted if soldiers were selected on the basis of psychological assessment. In preparation for the second world war, Germany established fifteen army psychological laboratories in which 84 psychologists were employed for selection of candidates. German military psychology adopted holistic framework in which the total person was to be assessed. This required collection of biographical, observational, and psychological data during "living-in". The decision about the suitability of a candidate was taken after discussing each case in the meeting of the diagnostic council.

With the beginning of World War II, the British army also modified its earlier practice of selecting officers on the consideration of the school attended, game played, and other information regarding the social background data of the candidate collected in interview. The War Office Selection Boards (WOBs) were established which adopted the procedure followed by German military psychologists for the selection. The candidates were administered a battery of tests including objective tests of abilities, self-report questionnaires, and projective tests. Observation of expressive behaviour in realistic situational tests was also a part of the assessment programme (Morris, 1949; Vernon, 1949).

The Office of Strategic Services (OSS) created by the American Congress in 1942, deserves special mention because the term assessment was introduced by the OSS (Kelly, 1967). The OSS adopted WOSB procedure of living-in assessment. Two assessment stations were established, the W centre at Washington D.C. and S (for secret) center at Virginia. A candidate found suitable by recruiting officer was directed to report to an address in Washington where he was interviewed by a representative of the branch for which he had been recruited and if still found suitable was asked to attend an "assessment school" with an assumed identity to ensure his anonymity. The three-day schedule of assessment at station 'S' included assessment of propaganda skills, sociometric assessment, stress interview, assessment of ability to evaluate, and abstract intelligence information, assigned leadership tasks, etc. The data were discussed at staff conference and attempt was made to achieve consensus. It is to be noted that in OSS assessment programme, criterion analysis and job description were not possible and the only alternative was to assess candidates with reference to a set of general qualifications considered essential to the effective performance of assignment.

Two other systematic assessment programmes that deserve attention are the work carried out at the Institute of Personality Assessment and Research (IPAR), and the Veterans Administration Selection Research Project. The IPAR was established at Berkeley campus of the university of California in the summer of 1949. Those who took initiative for the establishment of IPAR were involved in OSS assessment programme and were impressed with the potential of the OSS methods for understanding human personality. It is to be mentioned that the main purpose of work carried out at IPAR was not the selection of personnel but to develop methods to assess potential effectiveness. The IPAR staff made significant contribution by extending OSS live-in assessment system to the study of personality characteristics of mathematicians, architects, writers, research scientists, managers, air force officers and other high-level personnel. The type of work in which the IPAR was initially interested can be illustrated by referring to two principal questions in the study of air force officers:

(1) "What patterns of ability, motivation and interest are associated with outstanding effectiveness of air force officers in their military assignment"?

(2) By what psychological tests and procedures or by what combination of such techniques can distinguishing characteristics and potential promises of effective officers be identified and measured? (MacKinnon, 1958, p. 1).

The Veterans Administration Selection Research Project was concerned with the evaluation of procedures used to select clinical psychologists. E. Lowell Kelly and Donald W. Fisk who directed the programme were previously associated with the OSS. The VA assessment project was also concerned with the question of relative effectiveness of "clinical" and "statistical" strategies of selection. The VA assessment programme permitted the examination of certain assumptions of analytical approach such as: (a) ratings by assessment staff are better predictors than are test scores, and (b) staff ratings, when pooled either arithmetically or clinically as in staff conference, are better predictors than are ratings by individual judges (Wiggins, 1972).

Correlational and Factor Analytical Studies

The first personality inventory, Woodworth Personal Data Sheet, was developed following the correspondence approach (to be described in a later chapter) and the MMPI was developed following empirical approach (to be described). The beginning of the third kind of approach to the assessment of personality, the factor analytic approach, can be traced back to two Dutch workers, G. Heymans and E. Wiersma (1909) who used three dimensional system elaborated on the basis of analysis of biographical material collected from 110 historical persons. The three principles were, emotional stability, activity, and the one which is now called extraversion-introversion. Webb (1915) and Burt (1939) are among those who were first to use factor analysis in non-intellectual field. When attempts to analyze intercorrelation among the existing scales were not found to be useful, attempts were made to construct scales comprising the clusters of items identified with the help of factor analysis of intercorrelation among items. J. P. Guilford and his associates (1949), H. J. Eysenck and his collaborators (1952), R. B. Cattell and his colleagues (1950) are among those who contributed to the development of personality questionnaires with the help of actor analysis. The Guilford-Zimmerman Temperament Survey (1949) is a measure of thirteen traits which were earlier measured by three different inventories. R. B. Cattell (1957) carried out extensive studies of personality traits expressed in the three different media, L, Q, and T data and constructed the Sixteen Personality Questionnaire (16PQ) to measure sixteen "source traits" identified by him. While Guilford and Cattell were interested in measuring a large number of traits. Eysenck has been interested in typology of personality. Using factor analysis as a part of hypothetico-deductive approach, he constructed Maudsley Medical Questionnaire (Eysenck, 1952) which was later revised to become Maudsley Personality Inventory (1959a) and the Eysenck Personality Inventory (1963).

Other Multiphasic Questionnaires

Multiphasic/multidimensional scales measure different aspects of personality. We have already referred to the fact that the MMPI is the instrument which was developed for clinical diagnosis though later on it has been used for the assessment of personality characteristics of normal persons as well. An instrument that was specifically designed for multidimensional description of normal personality, the California Personality Inventory (CPI), was developed by

Gough (1957) using the empirical approach. It contains 468 self-reference items to be answered 'true' or 'false'. The items are divided into fifteen personality and three validity scales. The personality scales are: Dominance, Capacity for Status, Sociability, Responsibility, Socialization, Tolerance, Achievement via Conformity Intellectual Efficiency, Psychological Mindedness, and Feminety. For developing some of the scales, the criterion groups were obtained using directly observable behavioural index and for other scales criterion groups were formed on the basis of judges ratings. The three validity scales are known as Wellbeing Scale, Good Impression Scale, and Communality Scale. Some additional scales based on international consistency analysis have also been developed.

The Edward Personal Preference Schedule (EPPS) is a multiphasic instrument. It is a measure of "manifest needs" listed by Murray (1938). It deserves attention because it makes use of forced-choice format to eliminate the effect of social desirability on subjects' responses. Each item is made up of two statements matched in terms of social desirability. There are 210 such choices and a subject gets 28 chances to endorse a self-descriptive statement. The count of number of endorsements is taken as the index of strength of a need.

The Personality Research Form (PRF) developed by Jackson (1967) is an instrument that was developed with substantive, structural, and external considerations. The form made use of Differential Reliability Index to minimize the effect of social desirability from the responses of subjects and to maximize the content saturation by excluding irrelevant or non-substantive sources of variance. This form also measures needs. The form is described in detail in a later chapter.

Research in Personality Assessment

The purpose of research in personality assessment has been to make assessment devices more effective measures of what they measure. This purpose seems to confine the concern to the study of reliability and validity. Though no one can deny the importance of these essential qualities of an assessment device, we have to find the different sources of variance in personality scores and to minimize the sources which contribute to spurious variance. A chapter is devoted to different invalid sources of variance in personality scores. At this juncture we can mention the different sources of response distortions which are: acquiescence, social desirability, and faking. In addition to research conducted to identify different kinds of response distortions, there have attempts to improve personality questionnaire by considering item characteristics. Studies have been conducted to study the effect of endorsement percentage/popularity/communality on the measure of individual differences (Edwards, 1953; Whaler, 1965; Wiggins, 1962). Other item characteristics that have been subject of research are item ambiguity (Goldberg, 1963; Harris and Baxter, 1965), item objectivity (Butcher and Tellegen, 1960) item stability (Jones and Goldberg, 1967), item serial position (Cowen and Stiller, 1959) and a variety of item grammatical classifications (Wiggins, 1964b).

Hase and Goldberg (1967) were interested in empirical evidence as to which of the three approaches to personality assessment (rational-theoretical, empirical, factor analytic) is superior. The superiority was determined on the basis of the comparative effectiveness of rational-theoretical, empirical, and factor analytic instrument in the prediction of thirteen diverse criteria. Not much difference was found in the predictive validities of the three instruments. Hase and Goldberg (1967) concluded that the choice of a particular strategy is not as important as the test stimuli themselves. Importance of the content of items was demonstrated in the other studies as well.

A lot of research has been conducted to settle the controversy regarding the relative effectiveness of clinical and actuarial prediction. The basic question is, "How the data obtained with the help of different assessment devices are to be combined so as to have: (1) most accurate prediction of future criterion behaviour, (2) most accurate description of concurrent behaviour of a person, or, (3) classify a person correctly into a system of categories. The freedom of a clinician to combine the data the way he considers to be appropriate in a particular case and assigning different weights to the same bits of information about different individuals was compared with the rigid and fixed system of standard weights to be used in the case of every person who is assessed psychologically. The empirical evidence would be of far reaching significance for better appraisal of an individual.

Burgess (1928) was one of the early investigators who compared the efficiency of the clinical and actuarial methods of data combination. However, it was Meehl's monograph (1954) which engaged more attention and effort and stimulated more research on the controversial topic. Meehl (1954) reviewed 16 to 20 studies and tabulated their findings in the box scores under the headings 'statistical prediction better than clinical prediction, and 'clinical prediction better than statistical prediction'. Similar box scores were prepared for 27 studies available in 1957 and 51 studies available in 1965. Most of the studies furnished evidence regarding the superiority of statistical prediction. To many psychologists the evidence furnished by Meehl was not convincing because:

(1) the kind of predictions made by the clinicians were inappropriate and atypical of what the clinician does in practice (e.g., he does not predict academic success); (2) the clinicians were deprived of "uncodable information" which they gain if they have the opportunity to form impression of the client in face-to-face contact; (3) in statistical predictions cross-validated regression weights were used which gave advantage to this method. The third argument is a double-edged sword because it may put statistical prediction at disadvantage, while the clinician is free to change weights that he assigns to different bits of information in making prediction; given (fixed) regression weights are likely to shrink due to random and systematic errors.

Meehl's original monograph and his box scores are criticized on the ground that while the clinician may be involved in data collection or data combination or both, Meehl failed to make a distinction between the two phases of prediction. Sawyer (1966), therefore, suggested a joint classification of prediction methods which takes into account both method of data collection (four methods) and the two-manner of data combination, statistical and clinical. Reviewing 45 studies, Sawyer (1966) found that judgmental measurement was weakest source of data for prediction irrespective of the mode of combination.

Two offshoots of the controversy of superiority of clinical or statistical prediction are the study of components of overall judgmental accuracy, and attempt to simulate cognitive processes of a clinician when he makes an attempt to combine data for the prediction of an individual's behaviour. Cronbach (1955) drew attention to the fact that the overall judgmental accuracy can be studied in terms of the following components: Elevation, Differential Elevation, Stereotype Accuracy, and Differential Accuracy.

In an attempt to understand the cognitive processes of a clinician engaged in data combination, the clinician is often compared with a second rate IBM machine. Paramorphic representation of clinical judgement is also attempted. The term paramorphic has been borrowed by Hoffman (1960) from mineralogy where the term is used to refer to the substances which on chemical analysis are found to have the same chemical structure but optical and other kind of analysis show that the substances are different. The term was borrowed to acknowledge the fact that there can be equally good alternative mathematical representations of the judgmental processes. Goldberg (1968b) furnished empirical evidence to the effect that linear model permits the representation of reliable judgmental variance in most of the clinical judgement tasks.

Research on outcomes of prediction and their utilities for the individual and the organizations has drawn attention to the relevance of selection ratio, base rate, and veridocity of decision. Selection ratio is defined as number of people selected as compared to number of people considered. Base rate refers to the prevalence of certain category of people, e.g., mentally retarded, in a population. Taylor and Russell (1939) provided tables to indicate the expected accuracy of selection for a combination of given predictive validity, base rate, and selection ratio. The tables show that selection becomes efficient as selection ratio becomes smaller and also that a test which has relatively low predictive validity can be an effective predictor when the selection ratio is low.

Meehl and Rosen (1955) were the first to demonstrate the relation of base rate and outcomes. They made distinction among four different kinds of outcomes: valid positive (VP), valid negative (VN), false positive (FP), and false negative (FN). The sum of proportion of FN and FP, P(FN)+P(VP), constitutes base rate (BR), and sum of proportion of VP and FP, P(VP) + P(FP), constitutes the selection ratio (SR). The classification of outcomes helps us in defining discriminative efficiency of an assessment device or a battery. The extent to which an instrument or a battery helps us to identify positive and negative cases is known as discriminative efficiency. Sechrest (1963) made use of base rate in determining the quality of a good assessment device. He was interested in the question: How much a personality scale contributes to decision making? No useful purpose would be served if decision making is not improved after employing a psychological test. The extent of improvement can be found by finding the difference between the sum of proportions of valid positive and valid negative, P(VP)+P(VN), for random selection and the sum of the same proportions after the use of an assessment device. The difference in favour of the assessment device would indicate the percentage of increment in correct decision making after the use of the device.

The four kinds of outcomes mentioned above are not of the same level of adverse consequences in different situations of decision making. The outcomes may be assigned different utility values (U) to be used in the calculation of gain associated with personnel decision. Rorer, Hoffman, and Hsieh (1966) have given the following expression for the calculation of the Gain:

$$\text{Gain} = (UVP - UFN)/(UVN - UFN)$$

The problem of utility is discussed by others as well (Alf and Dorfman, 1967; Arthur, 1966; Cronbach and Gleser, 1965).

Use of Computer in Personality Assessment

With their vast memory, high speed, flexibility of data processing, objectivity, and exact execution of information computers have become indispensable equipment of psychological laboratories. The machine is not only used for doing long calculations necessary in certain kind of research but also for psychological testing and test interpretation. The post war enthusiasm for psychological testing would have vanished if the computer services were not introduced in 1950. At that point of time psychologists who were helping persons in dealing with their problems, were able to establish their credentials as therapists and counsellors but at the same time they began to look down on test administration and interpretation as a demeaning assignment. Initially computer services were introduced for doing such clerical jobs as scoring aptitude tests, profile making, and prediction of grades.

The rationale for computer based test interpretation was provided by Meehl's monograph, Clinical Versus Statistical Prediction published in 1954. In this monograph Meehl advocated the use of actuarial approach. Actuarial prediction refers to "...the empirical determination of regularities that may exist between specified psychological data and equally clearly specified socially, clinically and theoretically significant non-test characteristics of the persons tests" (Sines, 1966, p.133). The importance of computer based interpretation of MMPI was spelled out by Hathway in 1967 who referred to the limited capacity of experienced clinician to remember voluminous data on profile signs and associated clinical items. The computer with its enormous memory can store ever increasing stock of the data.

At present, the computer is no more a reliable clerical aid. The machine with its softwares can be used to do the following (Butcher, Keeler, and Bacon, 1985):

1. *Scoring.* Computer can be used not only for the scoring of limited or structured response options but also for such ideographic personality tests as the Repertory Grid (Stones, 1982).

2. *Computerized test administration.* It saves time and reduces error by eliminating intermediary data-entry step.

3. *Computerized interpretation of personality tests.* Interpretations can be descriptive, clinician modelled or actuarial.

4. *Test development.* In test development the computer technology may be helpful in the following manner:

(i) The use of more complicated scoring strategy employing configural rules.

(ii) Making use of response latency and key pressure as extravalidity checks.

(iii) Utilizing data storage capacity and flexibility for updating scoring and interpretive strategies.

(iv) Adaptive personality assessment. Developing instruments tailored to individual examinee is known as adaptive testing. In adaptive testing there can be branching from item to item according to the subject's answer to previous question. This removes the dilemma of the conventional test constructor who has to create a wideband instrument having many different quantities of a given trait. Numerous items which are to be included in a wideband conventional instrument may be relevant to some but irrelevant to some other examinees (Butcher, Keeler, and Bacon (1985, p. 809).

The MMPI has been most popular with computer based test interpretation (CBTI) system. Some important MMPI interpretive systems are: Mayo System, Albama System, Caldwell System, Lacher System, and Butcher System. CBTI systems for the 16 PF have been developed by Eber (1964) and Karson and O'Dell (1975). Computer system is available for a relatively recent assessment device, Million Clinical Multiaxical Inventory (MCMI). The MCMI can also be administered on line and scores can be used for CBTI report.

Computer Functions and Outputs

Different CBTI systems provided different kinds of outputs. The reports can be of three kinds: (a) descriptive, (b) clinician modelled, and (c) clinical-actuarial (Roid and Gorsuch, 1984). Descriptive reports are comprised of descriptive phrases or statements which may not be in narrative form. The phrases are interpretive of single scale scores. Reports tailored for individuals can be provided by using such mechanisms as gender-specific phrases. However, descriptive reports do not take configurations of scores into account.

The clinician modelled interpretations make use of expert clinicians' judgmental processes verbalized by them. The advantage of automatization of judgmental processes of experts who are known to be good predictors is that the automatized judgmental processes can be consistently applied with accuracy. The automatization do away with the variations in judgmental processes which make an expert a good predictor at some occasions but not so good a predictor at other occasions. Klientmuntz (1963) was the first to realize the possibility of simulation and automatization of judgmental processes of the best expert and the repetitive use of the 'frozen' judgmental processes in decision making.

The modelling of clinicians' judgmental processes can also be done by using mathematical models of experts' judgmental processes instead of trusting them for the delineation of their implicit processes. Such an attempt was made by Goldberg (1970) who developed mathematical models for the prediction of processes of 29 clinical psychologists attempting to differentiate psychotic MMPI profiles from neurotic MMPI profiles.

Two assumptions are involved in clinician modelled strategies: (a) the clinician's test interpretation are accurate prediction relevant to external criteria, (b) the clinician's strategy is best modelled by a linear process rather than by a configural approach.

The clinical-actuarial strategy makes use of empirical research findings for various score patterns. Only those descriptors are employed in reports which are validated as characteristics of persons with certain code type. Thus, the two assumptions required in clinical modelled strategy are not needed in the clinical-actuarial strategy.

The reports printed out by a computer may be of the nature of unconnected statements about the meaning of scales or scale elevations or they may be interpretive or integrative in nature. The interpretive reports are usually in narrative form; they describe individuals in terms of test performance. An integrated report makes use of information from various sources, including different tests, histories, demographic data, and behavioural observations.

Evaluation of CBTI Systems

Tallent (1987) pointed out that to a very large extent CBTI systems are based on psychometric theory in which predictions are made statistically. They do not conform to the triangular scheme of assessment proposed by Tallent (1983). The main limitation of the CBTI reports is that, "computer simply does its things without reference to what questions may be in the mind of the person who uses its cookbook service" (Tallent, 1987, p. 100).

Psychological evaluation is a proliferating industry. Many CBTI systems have been developed by those who are not well versed in the intricacies of personality assessment. Such authors often stray from empirical data and employ idiosyncratic scoring procedures or interpretive algorithms. The availability of CBTI reports and softwares to those who are not properly trained to make proper use of the facilities is another vexing problem.

Three kinds of studies have been conducted about the validity of CBTI systems. There have been comparisons between the reports generated by the computer and human interpreters. Most of the comparisons are anecdotal. Some rigorous studies of CBTI systems are available but it is to be pointed out that reports produced by human interpreters are poor criterion against which CBTI reports are to be judged. Giving not much importance to anecdotal comparisons and reports produced by human interpreters, Moreland (1983) preferred to review consumer satisfaction studies and external criterion studies. In consumer satisfaction studies, diverse array of clinical raters and patients are asked to rate a CBTI report in terms of clarity, accuracy, and usefulness. The major fault of such studies is that the reports were rated according to content area (e.g., psychosomatic symptoms) rather than statement-by statement or paragraph-by-paragraph (Lacher, 1974a). Moreland (1983) noted that in many customer satisfaction studies, the raters were not direct customers of the reports and many raters did not possess an expertise in evaluating the reports.

In the external criterion studies, comparisons are made between CBTI ratings based on other data, e.g., records. The most serious shortcoming of these kinds of studies is that none of the study evaluated the entire interpretive system. Moreover, the small proportion of interpretive statements in the system studies were not discovered by using the criterion instruments appropriate for covering the behavioural system covered by the system.

A list of 14 desirable characteristics for future validation studies of CBTI systems is proposed by Moreland (1983). Tallent (1987) suggested that psychologists devising a program should refrain from supplementing published correlations with private research and clinical insight. This they do to incorporate nicely crafted statements in reports to give them a life-like tinge but it is not a fair practice. Matarazzo (1983) warned the consumer of computer reports against "valid-sounding narrative statements" and the "spurious appearance of objectivity and infallibility as halo effects from the computer (p. 323). He also noted that, "To date there is no published evidence in peer-reviewed journal that one full page of the narrative description is valid" (p. 323).

Personality Assessment in India

Not much original contribution is made by Indian psychologists to the development of devices or methodology of personality assessment. For a long period they could not convince the people of India about the importance of personality assessment, though personality assessment has been an integral part of determining suitability of candidates for recruitment in armed forces. Psychological tests have been used in mental hospitals and guidance and counselling centres but there does not exist any agency which can undertake or sponsor systematic research on different aspects of assessment.

Indian psychologists began with intelligence testing and then got fascinated with projective techniques. As early as 1944 Das conducted research with Word Association Test (WAT). Studies on diagnostic utility of WAT were done by De (1956, 1957). Prasad and Asthana (1947), Sen (1949), Shanker (1956), Shanmugam (1959), Krishnan (1964) were Indian psychologists who used Rorschach Ink Blot Test. Bureau of Psychology Allahabad, Psychological Research Wing of Ministry of Defence (1954), Chowdhry (1964), Pareekh (1965), Kureshi (1971) made important contributions to the assessment of personality with the help of TAT and its derivatives.

As for personality questionnaires, Bell Adjustment Inventory became the basis of inventories constructed by Asthana (1950), De (1964), Department of Psychology, Aligarh Muslim University, Mohsin and Hussain (1969). Multiphasic inventories were adapted or developed by Krishnan (1961), Joshi and Singh (1963), Muthayya (1973), Malik (1986). Questionnaire developed by Eysenck have been translated and used by Das (1961), Jalota (1965), Dutt (1967), and Dhapola (1967). The 16 PF Questionnaire developed by Cattell and Eber (1962) is perhaps the most widely used instrument in India. Hindi translation of 16 PF was done by Kapoor (1963).

At the PGI, Chandigarh Wig and Verma (1967) developed original diagnostic scales in simple Hindi, PGI Health

Questionnaires N-1 and N-2. The Jodhpur Multiphasic Personality Inventory also included items which were collected/formulated rather than borrowed by the authors. But except for measure of Gunas (Vidhu Mohan, 1988) and measure of Gandhian (non-violent) personality (Hasan and Khan, 1983), no attempts have been made to develop measuring devices involving indigenous constructs of personality.

We can conclude this brief review of personality assessment in India by observing that:

1. Psychological tests developed in India do not measure any trait other than those listed by foreign psychologists.

2. The items of which Indian tools are constructed are borrowed from foreign instruments.

3. No evidence is furnished regarding the equivalence of the original English version and the translated/adapted version.

4. The distinction between emic and etic expressions of personality is ignored.

5. No systematic record of data collected with the help of instruments is maintained and for this reason it is impossible to develop actuarial systems of interpretations which require the existence of data bank and information exchange.

New Trends in Personality Assessment

Personality assessment has undergone the periods of depression and enthusiasm. Beginning from the second decade of the present century up to the decade of 50s the field of personality assessment was progressing with confidence. The decades of 60 and 70 witnessed the decline of personality assessment due to assault from different quarters including empirical studies furnishing evidence against the basic assumptions of consistency and stability of personality traits (Mischel, 1968, 1969). Anti-test attitudes were propagated by new theoretical viewpoints some of which considered assessment as unethical invasion of privacy, some of no use because it does not consider an individual's phenomenological state, and some emphasized immediate intervention instead of wasting time in testing. New generation of clinical psychologists were not exposed to role models of 'wizards of assessment' and they had the options to play emotionally satisfying roles instead of continuing with the role of a passive, voyeuristic and oracular tester.

The downward trend of assessment was arrested from the beginning of 70s not only because there was disenchantment with the available alternatives of assessment but because Mischel (1977), who was so uncompromising in condemnation of personality assessment, revised the earlier position and recognized the importance of assessment from different perspectives of the theorist interested in nature of individual differences, of those who are interested in behaviour modification, and the experiencing person, i.e., the subject himself. The importance of methods designed to study human as active and interpreting agent is emphasized by constructivist assessment. This kind of assessment rejects positivistic world view which believes in direct access to the external reality. The constructivist assessment believes in understanding reality through the stories' which are made by a person to give meaning to the world around him. Mair (1988) observed, "We live in through stories. We conjure world. We do not know the world other than as a story world. Stories inform life". The constructivist assessment has focus on structure as well as process of human knowing. The methods which are used for the study of structure of human knowledge are: laddering, dialectical laddering, downward arrow, and repertory grid. Process oriented methods are: self-characterization, study of stream of consciousness, and family bowties.

Changes in contemporary life have brought about changes in the practice of assessment. Dana (1984) observed that, "Environmental demand characteristics differ as a function of relative societal development, culture, and the agglomeration of personality resources presently available as a result of history of the living within each environment" (p. 49). Stress, poverty, pollution, violence, crowding, etc. are some of the new problems of contemporary life which have drawn attention to new areas of assessment. The following are some of the changes that have been taking place in assessment practice:

1. Consideration of revision in the system of personality diagnosis. The DSM III (American Psychiatric Association, 1980) has accorded special significance to personality disorders. Personality disorders are to be included in taxonomic scheme not only because they are important in their own right but also because they have a contextual role in the understanding of other pathologies. As Borderline and Narcissistic personality disorders have become common in modern individualistic societies, not only traditional tools are being tuned to assess and diagnose these new conditions but many new assessment devices such as Million Clinical Multiaxical Inventory (Million, 1983) are developed.

2. In complex societies hassles of life are sources of stress. We have to assess general stress as well as stress in specific situations called "burnout". Measures of stress have been developed by Holmes and Rahe (1967), Sarson, Johnson, and Siegal (1978); measures of burnout have been developed by Jones (1980) and Maslach and Jackson (1981). Attempts have also been made to develop instruments for the assessment of coping skills (e.g., Bell, 1977; Gilbert and Holohan, 1979; Leatherman and Dana, 1982). There is also need for the assessment of positive human characteristics which mediate between stress and good human functioning. Attempts have been made to develop devices for the assessment of such characteristics (Dana, 1981a; Carr and Dana, 1982; Kobasa, 1979). In addition to individual's coping skills we have to assess quality and number of nurturant relations which can help him to weather adverse situations of life, economic conditions, social milieu, and values and beliefs that give meaning to life.

3. Identity crisis, role conflict, and reculturation. Developing societies are witnessing transition from traditional to modern living. All sections of modernizing society are not able to keep pace with the process of modernization; even

those who are willing to change and adopt modern life style have to encounter such psychological problems as identity crisis, role conflict, and other problems concomitant to modernity. Moreover, there is much movement of people within the country and across international borders. It has become necessary to assess social skills and coping mechanisms of those who have to accommodate to a different culture. Cultural variations also call for cultural-specific measures because such measures enable us to understand the experiences and dilemmas of minority people from their perspective. While one can use moderator variables to determine the degree of suitability and applicability of norms based on majority sample, this does not preclude the need for developing culturally relevant variables and their measures.

4. Assessment of cognition and interface of personality and cognition. Mischel (1977), who led a tirade against assessment of personality traits by demonstrating specificity of behaviour, has anticipated the exploration of parallels between personality and cognitive psychology because to understand an individual's behaviour we have to pay attention to his understanding of environment and to the organisation of information by him in a meaningful and rule-guided way. Instead of observing different individual's responses to the same set of standard stimuli, there is need to study an individual's selection of situations so as to have clues about his personal qualities. According to Mischel (1977) much of the assessor's task would become easier if he helps the clients to search clear referents for their own personal constructs, instead of leading client to prepackage their problems in terms and constructs provided by the assessor. As regards the scope of assessment of person variables, Mischel mentioned the following: Construction competencies, that is, competence to generate the desired cognitions and response patterns; individual's categorization of a particular situation and differences in expected outcomes associated with a particular situation and differences in expected outcomes associated with particular

response pattern and stimulus configuration; differences in subjective values of expected outcomes; differences in self-regularity system and plans that each individual brings to the situation.

Abuses and Misuses of Assessment Devices

Two kinds of problems are found in use of personality assessment devices which if ignored create a lot of acrimony and resentment against them. These problems are: (1) inaccuracy of the usage, and (2) immorality of the usage. Before we discuss the two problems in detail, it is relevant to point out that assessment of human characteristics, howsoever, accurate it may be, is likely to draw criticism because people resent being evaluated (Amrine, 1965, p. 859). The resentment becomes more intensive when they are asked to give personal information and opinion which a person would not like to make public, particularly when he is not able to understand the relevance of imparting information to the purpose of assessment. The individual may find it painful and anxiety provoking to retrieve certain kinds of information from his memory.

Inaccuracy of Usage

Inaccuracy of usage involves improper use of a valid assessment device or the use of an invalid instrument which is "intuitively correct". Let us first consider improper use of a valid assessment device which occurs due to the following reasons:

1. *The user of device is not properly trained.* Psychological tests are to be used by well trained testers who are familiar with the existing literature on testing devices, can make right choice of assessment device and can understand the meaning of subject's responses and meaning of scores. Many people who claim to have sufficient expertise may undertake psychological testing and bring disrepute.

2. *Failure to consider base rate.* The importance of base rates in decision making is discussed in more detail. The user of assessment device who disregards base rate is likely

to indulge in unwarranted application of the instrument and valid diagnostic signs. Variations of base rate from one population to another may lead to increase of false positive and false negative cases even when the overall validity of the instruments is good.

3. *Discrimination against minority groups.* Attempts have been made to develop culture fair tests of intelligence because it is a well-established fact that the test standardized on representative samples of population contain items which are more familiar to the members of majority group. Moreover, personality assessment devices are used to eliminate unconventional and difficult persons (Lanyon and Goodstein, 1971). If one is concerned with bias against minority, one should be aware of the possibility of such inaccuracy of the usage of assessment devices.

4. *Unwarranted applications.* Even trained psychologists are found to use some assessment devices for the purpose other than for which they were devised. The use of projective techniques like Rorschach Inkblot Test and TAT for the assessment of intelligence of a subject is unwarranted use of these tests. The MMPI was originally developed for the diagnostic classification but it is now used for the assessment of personality of normal persons. Lanyon's (1968) collection of MMPI profiles of a large variety of subjects has shown that more psychopathological were the subjects, the better discrimination could be made from their profiles. The TAT was not devised for pathological classification but its unwarranted use is being made for that purpose.

Criticism Directed at the Tests

We have to pay attention to the criticism of assessment devices on the ground that certain shortcomings in the procedure of development of certain devices are disregarded at the time of using the devices. The two main problems that are to be considered are that of paying little attention to the study of criterion to be predicted by an instrument and illusory correlation. We have discussed in detail the problem of validation elsewhere. It is to be mentioned that

Holt (1958) observed that little attention is being paid to what we are trying to predict even by those who develop an instrument for selection purpose.

The presumption and belief that two events are related to each other while they are not is known as illusory correlation. Illusory correlation when perpetuated as "clinical lore" which is spurious but makes 'sense' and is 'intuitively' correct, brings a lot of disrepute to personality assessment. The term illusory correlation was introduced by Chapman (1967) who found that college students are likely to report occurrence of certain pairs of words more frequently when all the pairs are presented with equal frequency.

The empirical evidence furnished by Mischel (1968) regarding instability and inconsistency of personality traits also undermined the relevance of personality assessment in the decade of 70s though Mischel (1971) was more accommodative in his view point.

Immoral use of Assessment Device

We are now taking up the criticism of personality assessment which in the decade of 60s led to the accumulation of sentiments against psychological testing in the USA to such an extent that there were two Congressional hearings in 1965. The House Special Subcommittee on Invasion of Privacy had to take cognizance of the issue, many federal agencies were doing personality testing of government employees and job applicants and the tests contained items about their sex life, family situations, religious beliefs, personal habits, childhood, and many other intimate matters (Gallagher, 1965, p. 955).

Two aspects of invasion of privacy can be distinguished as confidentiality and inviolacy (Dahlstrom, 1969). Confidentiality has to do with individual's preference for keeping his secrets to himself as their disclosure may be used by others against him. Inviolacy has to do with a Pearson's unwillingness to have another person impose and intrude upon him and upon his private style of life.

In the context of invasion of privacy, a distinction is to be made between client functions of personality assessment and personnel functions. When a client seeks professional help, there is no conflict between the interest of client and the assessor. But when assessment leads to a decision which is in the interest of an institution of society, the question of invasion of privacy becomes a major issue. Whatever the purpose of testing, the protection of privacy involves two key concepts; relevance and informed consent. The information which an assessment device obtains from an individual is to be relevant to the stated purpose of testing. It is preferable to obtain informed consent of the subjects before they are asked to participate in an assessment programme. For this purpose they are to given information about the purpose of testing, kind of data sought, and the use of the data. The problem arises when informing the subject regarding the purpose of assessment is likely to make the subject defensive.

The American psychological Association has formulated certain principles which are expected to be followed by psychologist while imparting knowledge, conducting research and giving services. Like others, psychologists are expected to adhere to common moral and legal standards and not to indulge in or condone inhuman, illegal, exploitative, or unjustifiable practices. They have to ensure that there services are properly used and there is no misuse of the assessment data by any agency. For this, confidentiality of storage and disposal of record is to be maintained so that the assessment data is not made available to any one without the consent of the client. When a psychologist has to undertake assessment on the request of others like family members, friends, or an employment agency, there should be clear understanding among all concerned in regard to nature of assessment, disclosure of information, and decision making.

Psychologist are trained to put aside their personal preferences, wishes and desires while discharging their professional responsibilities and giving services. They should not exploit client's dependency and have not to have dual relationship such as sexual intimacy. Recognition to limitation of ones competence and that of their techniques and not creating an impression that the assessment is 'final' or 'infallible' are principles to be followed so avoid a indeliable negative impression that would curtail the freedom of the client. It has been observed that the selection programmes that were developed in past perpeture the myth that the kind of personnel that were most suited in the past time will be optimal in the future as well. This myth leads to the problem of "prevention of progress by encouraging the mundane and prosaic" (Guion, 1965, p. 372). It has been noted that putting a person in a certain diagnostic category make him to behave according to expectations of others. This can be prevented by deemphasizing the use of personality data for assigning psychiatric labels.

3

Rational-theoretical Approach

Like other psychological tests, the purpose of personality measure is to obtain sample of behaviour which a person usually displays in his life. So as to get the same sample of behaviour for all the persons who are to be assessed and compared with respect to the same set of personality characteristics, it is important that the same set of items be used in the instrument and responses to the items be evaluated in the same way so as to have quantitative description of those who are assessed. The approaches that have been discussed in this and following two chapters have to do with the procedure of selection of items, evolving a scoring system, and evaluating the goodness of the instrument. It is to be mentioned that the strategy adopted for the construction of an instrument cannot be independent of the purpose of assessment.

The three strategies of the construction of personality questionnaires are rational-theoretical, empirical, and factor analytic. One can treat the substantive approach as a separate strategy or as a refined version of the first approach. Moreover, there is no restriction on the combining the three strategies for developing an instrument.

In rational-theoretical approach, common sense or a theory of personality becomes the basis of decision of what is to be assessed, what items are to be initially included in the pool of items to be considered for inclusion in the instrument, what responses are to be considered as the evidence of presence/absence of a trait. When a psychologist proceeds to develop an instrument for measuring personality characteristics which he himself conceptualized on his own thinking about what items should be used for eliciting individuals' responses and which response, 'True' or 'False', be considered an indicative of presence of the trait, this procedure is known as rational approach. But when the decision regarding the trait to be assessed, items to be used for the assessment of the trait, the evaluation of responses, and other phases of the construction of an instrument are governed by a theoretical system, we have theoretical approach. However, most of the instruments cannot be placed in the dichotomy and we have to regard rational and theoretical as two poles of a single continuum.

A number of instances of the use of rational approach in devising scoring system of even projective tests can be furnished to bring out the nature of this approach. Murray's TAT (1943) is based on the following rational assumptions:

1. Attributes of the hero or the main character in the story reflect the respondent's own tendencies.

2. The characteristics of the hero's environment represent significant aspects of respondent's own environment.

Rational considerations are evident in the following inference in Machover's Draw-A-Person Test: "The width and massiveness of shoulders are considered the most common graphic expression of physical power and perfection of physique".

Wiggins (1973) calls rational-theoretical approach the correspondence approach because it rests on the assumption of existence of one-to-one correspondence of verbal response and the hypothetical internal state. The adequacy of verbal report to communicate the internal mental state is an assumption which is not unique to this approach. It is a well-known fact that Structurists and Gestalt psychologists made use of verbal reports in their studies. Behaviourism was the first school of psychology which began a tirade against the assumption of correspondence between verbal report and behaviour.

As pointed out earlier, Woodworth was the first psychologist who used responses to self-descriptive statements as a substitute of psychiatric interview. During World War I, while group tests of intelligence were being used for recruiting personnel of armed forces in U.S.A., it was discovered that applicants were also to be screened so as to minimize the cases of neurotic breakdown. It is said that request for psychiatric screening of candidates came through a cable of General Pershing, Commander-in-Chief of the United States expeditionary forces. As there were not many psychiatric interviewers for screening out the 'mentally unfit' before sending the troops overseas, R. S. Woodworth and A. T. Poffenberger hit upon the idea of interviewing the candidates through printed questions. The questions were common symptoms associated with mental disorders. It was presumed that if an individual says that he has some symptoms, his statement is to be regarded as factual. Counting number of responses indicating the presence of symptoms, a score was obtained which indicated overall assessment of individual's psychiatric status. The Woodworth Personal Data Sheet contains 116 questions.

Steps in Developing Rational-theoretical Instruments

Unlike Woodworth Personal Data Sheet, rational-theoretical instruments developed later on are not merely the lists of psychiatric symptoms. A number of steps are involved in the construction of such instruments some of which are the same as involved in other strategies as well. The steps are as below:

Defining the Construct

In order to develop rational-theoretical instrument we have to begin with the definition of the trait to be measured. This definition is to be formulated by the psychologist who is developing the instrument if he makes use of common sense and rational thinking in deciding what he has to measure. If the psychologist is depending upon some theoretical formulation in deciding what he has to measure, he can borrow the definition from the theoretical system. The purpose of defining the concept is to determine the domain of the content of items to be used in the instruments. An unambiguous definition encompassing behavioural connotations of the construct helps the test constructor in the formulation and collection of items from different sources. If the trait is clearly defined and the test constructor can think of one person who can be personification of one end of the trait continuum and another person who can be personification of other end, their behaviour would be of much help in generating the initial pool of items.

Editing and Improving Language of Items

Since one of the fundamental assumption of rational-theoretical approach is that responses given by a subject are the verbal representation of his mental interior, the items in the instrument should convey the same meaning to all the subjects so as to have a sample of their same kind of mental interior. To ensure that all the subjects get the same meaning of statements, the statements should be easy to understand and not open to more than one interpretation. Some informal criteria for the editing of attitude statements given by Edwards (1969) can be used for the selection of items. The criteria are:

- Avoid statements which can be interpreted in more than one way.
- Avoid statements which are likely to be endorsed by every one or almost by no one.
- Select statements that cover the entire range of variation along the continuum.
- Keep language of statement simple, clear and direct.
- Statements should be short; rarely exceeding twenty words.
- Each statement should contain one complete reference of feeling or behaviour.
- Statements should avoid universals such as 'always', 'all', 'none', 'never', etc. because universals introduce ambiguity.
- Words such as 'only', 'just', 'merely', and others of similar nature should be used with care and mod-

eration in writing statements.

- As far as possible statements should be in the form of simple rather than complex sentences.
- Avoid words that are not understood by those who have to give responses.
- Avoid use of double negatives.

Language used in the instrument should not only take care of problems of ambiguity and equivalence of meaning for all respondents, it should also take care of certain kinds of biases which undermine the validity of the measuring device. The biases are:

Context sex bias. Context sex bias is introduced when the content of items is such as that it can provide appraisal of the characteristic to be measured for only one gender, male or female, but not for both kinds of subjects. This kind of bias is exemplified by Geer's Fear Survey (1965) which is a measure of situation that provoke anxiety. The consistent finding of sex differences (women reporting more fear than men) led Hersen (1973) to observe that, "items comprising the inventory are biased in the direction eliciting endorsement from female subjects" (p. 244). The evidence of context sex bias in a measure of personality makes it necessary to either revise the instrument to make it free from content sex bias or specify the sex of in the label of the instrument if it is not possible to remove sex bias from the content of items. We can have Fear Stimulus Survey for Men and Fear Stimulus Survey for Women.

Grammatical sex bias. This kind of bias is evident when sex bias is not explicitly elicited by the content but respondents interpret non-sex specific nouns or pronouns as having particular sex reference. An example of this kind of bias is the transformation of 'healthy adult' into 'healthy male', rather referring to both disregarding gender.

Determining Item Homogeneity

A rational-theoretical instrument is developed to assess individual differences in respect to the trait to be assessed. The total score obtained by adding the scores assigned to individual items should have the contribution of only one source but this is possible only when all the items comprising the scale are internally consistent due to their being the measure of the same characteristic. Kuder-Richodson formula 20 (K-S 20) can be used for finding the coefficient of internal consistency of items included in a scale:

$$r_{kk} = \left(\frac{k}{k-1}\right) \frac{S^2x - \Sigma\, p_i q_i}{S^2x}$$

Where k = number of items in the scale; Sx = standard deviation of total scores on the scale; and $\Sigma p_i q_i$ = sum of the product of proportion of 'keyed' and 'non-keyed' responses to each item.

The low value of r_{kk} is an indication of relative independence of responses to items in a scale; high value of r_{kk} is an indication of internal consistency or homogeneity of items in the scale. It is to be noted that the value of r_{kk} depends on average inter item correlation r_{ij} as well as on number of items in the scale, k.

$$r_{kk} = \frac{k^2 \bar{r}_{ij}}{\sqrt{k + k\,(k-1)\,\bar{r}_{ij}}}$$

It is evident by the formula that the value of r_{kk} can be increased in spite of low $\bar{r}_{ij}$ by increasing the number of items in the scale.

Procedure for the Selection of Internally Consistent Items

The following is the procedure to be followed for the selection of internally consistent items:

1. The edited initial pool of items is administered to a large representative sample of the population for which the instrument is being developed.

2. The responses of subjects are scored using the scoring key already devised according to rational or theoretical considerations.

3. An item analysis chart is prepared showing the responses of the subjects to each item. This chart is used for the calculation of pi and qi products for the items.

4. Total score of each person is also found by adding his scores for all the items. The S.D. of total scores is calculated and the value of r_{kk} is obtained using formula K-R 20.

5. To eliminate the items which do not covary with the total score, item-total correlation is calculated using one of the following methods biserial, point biserial, tetrachoric, phi. The selection of appropriate method depends upon the fact whether the responses are dichotomous or form a continuum.

6. Items which have relatively low correlation with the total are to be eliminated.

7. If sufficient number of items are left after the elimination of non-covarying items, the value of r_{kk} is determined again. At this stage a decision is to be taken to add more items in the scale if the value of r_{kk} is low and number of retained items is also not sufficient. If new items are added, steps 2 to 5 are repeated.

It is to be noted that step 4 may come after step 5 but the proposed order is helpful in finding the improvement in the consistency of items after eliminating less covarying items. However, interitem correlation is not likely to reach the value of 1 because the proportion of keyed responses to all the items are not likely to be equal. But from the point of view of making discrimination between individuals and ensuring higher dispersion of scores, the difference in the proportion of keyed responses is not unwarranted. When the proportions of keyed responses are equal, total scores on the scale shall assume only two values, 0 or highest possible score.

As pointed out earlier, value of r_{kk} can be increased by increasing the number of items in the scale even when the average interitem correlation is low. One can obtain r_{kk} value as high as .9 by using 891 items which are as heterogeneous as having as low item-total correlation as .01. Edwards (1970, p. 34) observed that if a rational scale with reasonably high r_{kk} value cannot be constructed with fifty or fewer items, then this indicates that the trait is not well defined or items used in the scale are not relevant to the trait being measured. If r_{kk} value is reasonably high, say .8, for a set of fifty items, we can examine the mean and range of scores on the scale. Edwards (1970) suggested that the mean should be one-half of number of items and the range should fall within Mean ± 2 SD.

Determining Reliability and Validity

Coefficient of Internal Consistency obtained with the help of K-R 20 can be regarded as the reliability of the instrument determined by the method of Parallel Form. According to Edwards (1970) r_{kk} is the coefficient of correlation between two scales which comprise k randomly selected items from the same domain or population of items. The r_{kk} value may also be regarded as average split halves reliabilities by breaking the instrument in as many parts as there are items. As far as test-retest reliability is concerned, Edwards (1970) has shown that

$$r_{12} = \frac{k\bar{r}_{ii} + k\,(k-1)\bar{r}_{ij}}{k + (k-1)\,\bar{r}_{ij}}$$

Where r_{12} = test-retest correlation coefficient
$\bar{r}_{ii}$ = average of coefficients of correlations between responses to the same items after the two administration of the scale,
$\bar{r}_{ij}$ = average inter item correlation.

If r_{kk} is high, r_{12} also tends to be high and r_{kk} provides lower-bound estimate of r_{12}. But when r_{kk} is high and r_{12} is low, this is an indication of the fact that trait measured by the scale is not stable over time interval between two testings. It is to be noted that the value of r_{12} can be high even when the value of r_{kk} is low. This happens when individuals give fairly consistent responses to a set of items which are measuring not one common trait but many different characteristics. It is, therefore, evident that for ascertaining the reliability of a scale developed by the rational-theoretical approach we have to obtain both coefficient of internal consistency and test-retest coefficient.

The validation of rational-theoretical instrument is not as direct and simple as that of an instrument developed to predict a definite criterion. According to Edwards (1970) since rational-theoretical instrument measures a trait which is defined by a set of internally consistent items, nothing external to the scale can be a good criterion of the trait measured by the instrument. However, it is not being asserted that because a set of internally consistent items measure something, there is no need to determine the validity of rational-theoretical instrument. Validation studies are to be conducted to discover the nature of 'something' measured by the scale so as to verify the effectiveness of assessor's attempt to assemble the pool of indicators of the trait constructed by him. It is reasonable to expect that test developer must have given thought to the relationship of the trait which he conceptualized and formulated a number of hypotheses regarding the situations in which the trait would be involved. It is also expected that the interlocking of the trait in the nomological network has also been laid down. Confidence in interpreting scores obtained with the help of rational-theoretical instrument can be enhanced with the accumulation of evidence regarding the veridocity of the hypotheses involving the trait.

The above mentioned theoretical underpinnings of test scores has to do with construct validity. Construct validation was suggested by a joint committee of educators and psychologists setup in 1954 by American Psychological Association (APA). According to Cronbach and Meehl (1955) a construct is "some postulated attribute of people, assumed to reflect in test performance (p. 283). Thus, construct validity of an instrument is a numerical statement of proportion of test score that is attributed to the construct. The procedure of determining construct validity is the same as general scientific procedure of developing and confirming theories (Cronbach and Meehl, 1955, p. 300)."

Although rational-theoretical scales are seldom developed for the purpose of a definite criterion, they can be used for improvement of accuracy in prediction. When, for example, individual differences in the performance of a task cannot be accurately predicted with the help of an ability or aptitude test, we have to search the personality characteristics which would help in improving the accuracy of prediction and then to use rationally constructed scale(s) of the trait(s) which are found to be helpful in improvement of prediction.

Evaluation of Rational-Theoretical Approach

An instrument developed by rational-theoretical approach cannot be expected to provide accurate description of personality unless the following assumptions hold good:

1. The meaning of every item contained in a rational-theoretical instrument is the same for all the subjects and the assessor. "Do you avoid social situations?" In this item the meaning of 'avoidance' and 'social situations' should be same for all the subjects and there should be no variation in the meaning understood by the subjects and assessor's meaning of the two words if we have to have access to 'mental interior' of the subjects through their self-description. In spite of all the precautions to be taken in the selection of items, it cannot be ensured that the meaning of items is the same for all the respondents and the assessor.

2. All subjects are equally good in their awareness of their mental states. However, this assumption would not be valid if some subjects were more attentive to their reactions to external stimuli and have better memory of how they usually behave in the presence of certain stimuli.

3. All the subjects are equally willing to describe themselves honestly without fear of the consequences of negative evaluation. However, people may be motivated to fake good or fake bad depending on the anticipated consequences of assessment.

4. The content of items is suitable for eliciting the responses indicative of the trait to be assessed. As pointed out earlier, the relevance of the content of items is the main consideration in the selection of items to be included in a scale. However, many would agree with Meehl (1945) that, "We do not have the confidence of traditional personality test makers that the relationship between behaviour dynamics of a subject and tendency to response verbally in a

certain way must be obvious." To the extent the relationship between content of items with trait to be measured is obscure, one may not be successful in collecting a pool of items capable of providing quantitative scores representing the contribution of only one source of variance, i.e., the trait to be measured. Studies conducted by Norman (1963a, 1963b), Duff (1965), and Goldberg and Slovic (1967) have shown that rational selection of content of test items is a necessary but not sufficient condition of validity of an instrument.

5. If an instrument is to be based on a theory, there should exist a well developed theory comprising the definitions of the terms, a nomological network of the constructs some of which are directly linked with observable behaviour. The fact of the matter is that there are few molor approaches to personality which qualify to be theories. Microtheories that have been developed to explain limited segment of behaviour are not of much use in encompassing the sphere of personality. Pervin (1971) noted that psychometricians have been more interested in refinement of techniques of test construction than in theoretical anchorage of the instrument.

6. As pointed out earlier, internal consistency of items determined with the help of K-R 20 and item-total correlation are the main considerations in the selection of items for a rational-theoretical approach. What internal consistency ensures is that all the items have the same source of variance but internal consistency is likely to remain undisturbed if all the items have more than one source of variance common to all items. In such an eventuality the scale would not be a measure of a single trait but a number of traits whose individual contribution to the total score remains unknown.

While Edwards (1970, pp. 29-37) has equated rational approach with construct point of view, Wiggins (1973, p. 401) insists that rational scales may be thought of as "pretheoretical" or "preconstructural". The basis of distinction is the fact that to Wiggins those who construct rational scales have some sort of construct in mind but the construct is not so clearly formulated as to be evaluated by the procedures of construct validation suggested by Cronbach and Meehl (1955) and Loevinger (1957). Keeping in view the distinction between rational and construct point of views as delineated by Wiggins, we shall present an account of substantive approach following Loevinger's "naively realistic" view of constructs. Before we do that we have to take up the description of some of the rational-theoretical instruments developed in India and in foreign countries.

Rational-Theoretical Scales

In this section we propose to describe some scales that have been developed following rational-theoretical strategy. It would not be possible to give as much information about the scales as is available in their respective manuals. Some important instruments developed following the approach are Study of Values, Fascism (F) Scale (Adorno et al., 1950). Dogmatism Scale (Rokeach, 1960), Edwards Personal Preference Schedule (EPPS), Jodhpur Multiphasic Personality Inventory (JMPI), and the Guna Scale. Some of these instruments are described below.

Study of Values

This instrument is based on the theory of personality proposed by Spranger (1928). According to this theory, people can be described in terms of relative prominence of any one of the following six motives:

Theoretical. This value refers to the dominant interest in the discovery of truth and empirical, critical, rational, and "intellectual" approach.

Economic. This value is defined as concern with what is useful and profitable. The person who has predominance of this value is similar to prevailing stereotype of the "average American businessman".

Aesthetic. One who prefers this value is interested in form and harmony; he is more concern with beauty rather than truth or utility.

Social. In altruistic and philanthropic sense love of people is the main motive of this kind of man.

Political. This refers to an interest in having control over others, influence, and renown. Political value is not necessarily limited to the field of politics.

Religious. Seeking to comprehend the cosmos as a whole, and need for establishing transcendental understanding or the universe in personal way, is the main motive of religious person.

The Study of Value was originally devised by Vernon and Allport (1931). It was revised in its present form in 1951. The items were formulated to refer to each one of the six values. The criterion for final selection of items was internal consistency within each of the six areas. The format of the test is ipsative as subjects are required to give preferential ratings of either two (in part I) or four (in part II) alternatives.

Although the normative data are provided, the authors of the test do not recommend the use of percentile or other types of scores. The raw scores are to be plotted in a profile for the relative standing of a person with respect to six values.

The split-half reliabilities of the six scores range from .84 to .95. Test-retest reliability after intervals of one month and two months between test and retest was found to be .77 and .93 respectively. Evidence of validity of the instrument is in the form of comparison between contrast groups, self-ratings, associates' ratings, overt behaviour indices, description of one's ideal person. However, it is doubtful that the value scores are undimensional.

Edwards Personal Preference Schedule (EPPS)

The theory on which the EPPS is based is the need system proposed by Murray et.al. (1938) who defined personality as the organization of needs. The instrument was developed to provide, quick convenient measures of a number of relatively independent personality variables (Edwards, 1959, p. 5). The main features of EPPS are: (a) attempt to minimize the effect of social desirability on responses of the subjects, (b) making use of the variables which do not have maladaptive or clinical connotations, provision for obtaining a measure of subject's response consistency and a measure of profile stability. The 15 manifest needs which were selected by Edwards for assessment with the help of the EPPS are described below:

Achievement (ach). To do one's best, to accomplish, to manipulate or organize physical objects, human beings, or ideas. To overcome difficulties, to do better than others.

Deference (def). To admire and support the superior, to get suggestions from others, to follow instructions, to praise others, to conform to customs and avoid unconventional, to let others make decisions.

Order (ord). Order refers to put things in order. To achieve cleanliness, arrangement, organization, balance, neatness, tidiness and precision.

Exhibition (exh). To make impression. To be seen and heard. To excite, fascinate, entertain, shock, amuse, entice.

Autonomy (aut). To get free, shake off restrain, break out confinement. To resist coercion and restriction. To be unattached.

Affiliation (aff). To draw near and enjoy co-operativeness or reciprocate with an allied person. To please and win affection of cathected person. To remain loyal to a friend.

Intraception (int). To look within, to analyze thoughts and feelings of oneself and others.

Succorance (suc). To have one's needs gratified by sympathetic aid of an allied person. To be nursed, supported, sustained, protected, loved, advised, guided, forgiven, consoled.

Dominance (dom). To control one's human environment. To influence and direct the behaviour of other persons. To restrain, dissuade, prohibit. To convince others of the 'rightness' of one's opinion.

Abasement (aba). To submit passively to external force. To accept injury, blame, criticism, punishment. To admit inferiority, error, wrong-doing or defeat. To seek and enjoy pain, punishment, illness and misfortune.

Nurturance (nur). To give sympathy and gratify needs of a helpless person. To feed, help, support, console, protect, nurse, heel.

Change (chg). To move and wonder, to have no fixed habituation, to seek new friends, to adopt new fashions, to change one's interest and vocation. To be inconsistent and unstable.

Endurance (end). To endure, persist, to have cognitive perseveration.

Heterosexuality (het). To form and further heterosexual relationship. To have sexual intercourse.

Aggression (agg). To overcome opposition forcefully. To fight, take revenge, injure. To attack or kill another person. To oppose forcefully or punish an individual.

Beginning with the items whose content fit the above description of different needs, Edwards collected 210 pairs of statements in which items from each of the 15 scales are paired with items from other 14 scales. The subjects are instructed to select one of the two alternatives of the pair which is more characteristic of himself. The items are matched in respect of their social desirability scale values (SDSVs). The EPPS has introduced an index of respondent consistency. For this 15 pairs of statements are repeated. The number of identical choices provides the index of consistency. Another check, profile stability score, is the correlation between the individual's odd and even items in the 15 scales. When no choice is given by the subject for certain pairs of items, the responses are provided by tossing a coin. If the coin turns up 'head' alternative A is provided; if the coin turns up 'tail' B alternative is entered in the response sheet.

Percentile norms are provided for the interpretation of 15 need scores obtained from the EPPS. Norms for college students are based on 760 men and 749 women tested in 29 colleges scattered over the USA. Norms for adult population are based on a sample including 4,031 men and 4932 women drawn from urban and rural areas of 48 states.

However, before interpretation of scores is undertaken, it is preferable to consider the consistency score of the subject. If his consistency score is less than 9, his score on 15 personality variables may be questioned. One should also keep in mind the fact that average Profile Stability Coefficient is .74 and that the coefficient of .44 is significant at 5 per cent level.

The evidence regarding the validity of EPPS scales is in the form of agreement between self-ratings and scores obtained with the help of the schedule. The subjects were provided definitions of the fifteen EPPS variables and they were asked to rank themselves in on the fifteen personality variables while they were not informed about their scores on the EPPS scales. The self-rankings of the subjects agreed perfectly with their rankings based on the EPPS (Edwards, 1959, p. 21). In another study Q sorts of the subjects using statements appearing in the EPPS were compared with their EPPS scores. The results were comparable to the results reported above but for a small group of subjects a tendency to regard the highly desirable statements as being characteristic of themselves was observed. Evidence regarding the validity is also in the form of correlation between EPPS scores and Taylor Manifest Anxiety Scale and Cooperation. Agreeableness, and Objectivity scales of the Guilford-Martin Personnel Inventory. The correlations are in the expected direction but one can interpret them in terms of common factor of social desirability. Except the correlation between the aggressiveness scores obtained with the help of EPPS and the Guilford-Martin Personnel Inventory, no value of r is as much as .5.

Jodhpur Multiphasic Personality Inventory (JMPI)

The inventory is one of the few instruments developed in India which made use of original pool of items. The inventory provides scores for four broad categories: psychoneurosis, psychosis, psychosomatic disorders, and validity indices. The scales are listed below:

Psychoneurosis Scales. Scales included in this category

are measures of anxiety, phobia, obsessive compulsive reactions, conversion reactions, hysteric-dissociation, neurotic depression, and neurasthenia. Besides these clinical scales, this part also includes a measure of social introversion.

Psychosis Scales. The scales falling into this category are schizophrenia simple, hberphrenia, schizophrenia-paranoid, paranoia, manic depression, psychotic depression.

Psychosomatic Scales. The JMPI has five scales for assessing psychosomatic problems. The scales are for the diagnosis of peptic ulcer, ulcerative colitis, hypertension, bronchial asthma, and anorexia nervosa.

Validity Scales. The three validity scales are L, F and K. The validity scales are similar to MMPI validity scales to be described later on.

The experimental form of JMPI included 213 items for the psychoneurosis scales, 273, items for the psychosis scales, and 193 items for the psychosomatic scales. The items were constructed in Hindi after a survey of 41 books and journals dealing with different aspects of psychopathology. The JMPI appears to be a counter part of MMPI but it is rational-theoretical instrument instead of empirical instrument because the scoring system is a priori and the selection of items from the original pool was based on item-total relation.

Tryout and Item Analysis

The tryout sample included 280 male and 120 female students of Jodhpur University in age range of 17 to 20. Responses were obtained under five categories: Always, Most of the time, Generally, Seldom, Never. In scoring the responses are assigned 4, 3, 2, 1, and 0 scores, respectively.

The internal consistency and discriminative power (D.P.) were the two consideration for the selection of items. But the later was considered to be a must for the inclusion of item in a scale. As the score for response to an item can vary from 0 to 4, Pearson Product Moment Correlation was used for finding item-total correlation. The value of r which is significant for the sample size (N=400), is .08 at .05 level, was taken as minimum requirement for the item selection. For finding D.P., the subjects were divided into two groups high and low on the basis of the criterion mean + 1 to -1 PE or mean +.834 to –.834 S.D. While the items which were found to be good on both the considerations, r and D.P. were to be definitely selected, items which had only satisfactory D.P. value were also to be selected because it is argued that in diagnostic testing discrimination power is of utmost importance because the syndromes are not consistently organized. It is to be noted that the D.P. values of items are not obtained for certain external criterion.

A large number of items which could not have satisfactory item-total r and D.P. value were tried out again on a group of 377 psychiatric patients due to two reasons: (1) psychiatric patients might have undergone the experience described in the statement while normal university students might have not, (2) so that adequate number of items are available for the scales. The items which were found to have satisfactory IC and D.P. after tryout on the psychiatric patients were included in the scale to which they belong. It is to be pointed out that there is much variation in the number of items selected for different scales.

Scoring. Scoring keys are provided for each of the scales. There are two kinds of items. One, where scoring weights vary from 1 to 4 or 4 to 1 and two, where scoring weights vary from 0 to 4 or 4 to 0.

Reliability. Evidence regarding the reliability of the scales include Index of True Variance determined by Flangan formula, Standard Error of Measurement, Coefficient of Determination, Coefficient of Stability (test-retest), and Coefficient of Homogeneity (Split-half). Two weeks and twelve weeks were the intervals which lapsed between testing and retesting. For Psychoneurotic Scales, Coefficient of Stability were found to range from .63 to .95 when the gap was 2 weeks, and from .72 to .89 after a gap of 12 weeks. Coefficient of Stability were in range of .63 to .95 after a gap of 2 weeks, and .72 to .89 after a gap of 12 weeks. The range of Coefficient of Stability for the Validity Scales were .73 to .80

and .69 to .81 after the gaps of 2 and 12 weeks respectively.

Validity. Criterion related, construct related, and content validities are reported for each scale of JMPI. Evidence about criterion related validity include intra-psychopathology comparisons, inter-psychopathology comparisons, contrasted group comparison, concurrent measures obtained with the help of MMPI. In intra-psychopathology, comparisons groups of patients diagnosed to have different kinds of pathologies were administered the JMPI scales and taking each pathological group at a time, mean scores on different JMPI scales were compared with the mean on the scale which meant for the assessment of the syndrome corresponding to particular diagnostic group. The evidence of validity would has been furnished if, for example, the group of subjects diagnosed to suffer from paranoia get significantly high mean on JMPI Paranoia Scale than any other scale. Intra-psychopathology comparisons provided evidence in favour of all psychosis and psychosomatic scales but in the case of psychoneurotic scales evidence was only for the validity of Neurasthenia, Depression, Obsessive-Compulsive, Hysteria Dissociate, and Conversion Reactions.

Inter-pathology comparison involved comparison of scores of a particular group on the measure of that kind of pathology which the group diagnosed to suffer from, with the mean scores of the group on other two scales. The evidence of validity was taken to be significantly higher of the group on the relevant scale than on other two scales. Inter-pathology comparisons are reported to furnish evidence of validity of all scales.

Evidence of validity from contrast groups comparisons involved comparison of means of normal subjects with diagnosed psychiatric patients. All the contrast group comparisons are reported to provide positive evidence of validity of the JMPI scales. Correlations of scores of normal subjects on the following clinical scales and three validity scales with the corresponding MMPI scales furnished evidence of concurrent validity: Depression, Hysteria Dissociate, Neurasthenia, Schizophrenia (simple), Paranoia, and Manic Depression.

Lack of overlapping between the scores of normal subjects and psychiatric patients was another kind of criterion-related validity reported for JMPI scales. For each scale frequency distributions of normal subjects and patients were prepared using the same class intervals. Taking each class interval as an element in the distribution of variable, indices of correlation were obtained using McNemar (1962) formula. It is reported that Obsession-Compulsion, Schizophrenia (simple), Paranoia, Schizophrenia-Paranoid, and Heberphrenia there is no overlapping in scores; for Psychotic Depression, Hysteria Dissociate, Hyper Tension, and Phobia Scales there is slight overlapping. A great deal of overlapping is found in the case of Neurasthenia Scale; in the case of remaining scales, the overlapping is moderate.

Evidence of construct validity of JMPI scales include correlation with the measures obtained with the help of other instruments and factor analysis. Details about the correlation of JMPI with 16 PF are given by Malik (1986). Using a sample of 100 young adults, three factor analyses were carried out to find the factor structure of the three parts of the inventory. Factors extracted from the matrix of correlation among Psychoneurosis Scales and three validity scales are labelled as: General Maladjustment, Treatment Dissatisfaction, Social Ease with Inner Timidity, and Personal Insecurity. The four factors emerging from the matrix of correlation among Psychiatric Scales and validity scales were identified as: General factor of Psychoticism, Psychotic Distortion, Affective Ambivalence, and Low Morale. The three Psychosomatic factors are: General psychosomatic Disturbance, Dependence-Experience, and Social Conformity.

Opinion of 15 practicing psychiatrists and clinical psychologists regarding the items and internal consistency of items are reported as evidence of content validity of the scales.

Norms

Norms are in the form of normalized T-scores equivalent of raw scores. Separate norms for male and female are provided where sex differences were found in item analysis data. The normative sample had 5005 subjects out of which 200 subjects were rejected for high L and F scores. The age rage of the subjects was 15 to 25 and the subjects were normal males and females drawn from all socio-economic classes. Not all subjects were used for preparing the norms of the three sets of scales. Norms for Psychoneurosis Scales are based on 874 males and 902 females; norms for Psychosis Scales are based on 743 males and 902 females; norms for Psychosomatic Scales are based on 808 males and 805 females. No K correction in the scores are recommended because research on K Scale as catalytic measure in diagnosis of certain disorders is yet to be completed (Malik, 1986, p. 188).

Evaluation of JMPI

The JMPI is the first multiphasic instrument developed in India which contains items selected from a painstaking collection of a pool of items after a thorough study of literature on psychopathology. However, the selection of items based on power of an item to discriminate between high and low groups formed on the basis of scores obtained with the help of a set of items, excluding the item itself from the set, creates doubt regarding the utility of the JMPI as a diagnostic tool. If items were selected following the same strategy as that of MMPI in which contrast groups were normal subjects and matched psychiatric patients, the JMPI would have been a better instrument. Further, the JMPI cannot be a measure of unitary personality traits because the scales are not made up of homogeneous items.

Tri-Guna Personality Inventory (TGPI)

The TGPI developed by Vidhu Mohan and Sandhu (1986) is a theoretical instrument based on the three dimensional theory of personality derived from Sankyan School of Indian Philosophy. According to this school of thought, man is manifestation of *Prakirti* or nature. This Prakirti has three *Gunas* which are like three strands of a rope. The three

Gunas are *Sattva, Rajas*, and *Tamas*. The effect of relative dominance of the Gunas is described in the verse 10 chapter 14 of Bhagvat Gita, "When Sattva increases, then coming to its own, it provides its effect — knowledge, happiness, etc. Similarly, when the quantity of Rajas increases by overpowering both Satva and Tamas, then it produces its own effects — activity and hankering. When the quality called Tamas increases by similarly dominating over Sattva and Rajas, it then provides its own effects — obscuring of knowledge, etc". (Gambhiranand, 1984).

The TGPI is made of 40 items depicting different aspects of life such as metaphysical, spiritual, intellectual, social, emotional, food habits, housing, clothing, music, literature, etc. The subject is required to select one of the alternatives. Whichever alternative is preferred by the subject, a score of 1 is given in respect of the Guna reflected by the alternative.

The effect of social desirability was clearly observed in the response preference of the subjects. The order of preference was observed to be Sattva, Rajas and Tamas. This preference required modification in the wordings of the statements: change from third person to first person, substitution of word "should" by mostly. Attempts have been made to find relationship between Eysenck's dimensions of personality and the three Gunas. It is to reported that Sattva is negatively related to extraversion-introversion and neuroticism; Rajas is positively related to extraversion-introversion and neuroticism; Tamas and Psychoticism are slightly related.

Cope

The Cope is a rational-theoretical instrument developed by Craver, Scheier, and Weintraub (1989) for measuring copying styles and strategies adopted by individuals so as to deal with stressful situations. The instruments was developed by using two theoretical modelled as guidelines: the Lazarus model (Lazarus, 1966; Lazarus and Folkman, 1984), and a model of behavioural self-regulation which guided researches of Craver and Scheir (1981, 1983, 1985, 1989).

The Cope incorporates 13 conceptually distinct scales assessing both problem focused strategies and emotional focused coping. The scales are described below:

1. *Active Coping.* "Taking action, exerting efforts, to remove or circumvent the stressor".

2. *Planning.* "Thinking about how to confront the stressor, planning one's active coping efforts".

3. *Seeking Instrumental Social Support.* "Seeking assistance, information, or advice about what to do".

4. *Seeking Emotional Support.* "Getting sympathy or emotional support from someone.

5. *Suppression of Competing Activities.* "Suppressing one's attention to other activities in which one might engage, in order to concentrate more completely on dealing with the stressor".

6. *Religion.* "Increased engagement in religious activities".

7. *Positive Reinterpretation and Growth.* "Making best of the situation by growing from it, or viewing it in a more favourable light".

8. *Restraint Coping.* "Coping passively by holding back one's coping attempt until they can be of use".

9. *Acceptance.* "Accepting the fact that stressful event has occurred and is real".

10. *Focus on Venting of Emotions.* "An increased awareness of one's emotional distress, and a concomitant tendency to ventilate those feelings".

11. *Denial.* "An attempt to reject the reality of stressful event."

12. *Mental Disengagement.* "Psychological disengagement from the goal with which the stressor is interfering, through daydreaming, sleep, or self-distraction".

13. *Behavioural Disengagement.* "Giving up, or withdrawing effort from, the attempt to attain the goal with which the stressor is interfering".

Later on two more scales were added to the Cope scale:

14. *Alcoholic/Drug Use.* "Turning to the use of alcohol or other drugs as a way of disengaging from the stressor".

15. *Humour.* "Making jokes about the stressor".

The Cope can be used as a measure of disposition as well as a measure of specific coping responses that had been used or being used in stressful situations encountered or being encountered by a person. The instrument can be converted from disposition form to "state" or situational form by rephrasing each item and response choice in present tense progressive ("I am..."), or present perfect tense ("I have been..."). To assess the use of coping strategies in the past stressful situations we can specify the period and ask the subject to report the coping strategies adopted by him to deal with stress experienced by him during that particular period.

The Cope is different from other measures of coping styles in many respects. Most of the earlier measures were developed empirically though factor analysis of empirically selected items done to identify dimensions that might underlie them. The approach was not suitable for theoretical link between theoretical principles and the measuring instrument. Carver, Scheier and Weintraub (1989) collected items on the basis of theoretical consideration and determined their internal consistency with the help of factor analysis and Cronbach's Alpha Reliability Coefficient. It is to be pointed out that the inventory went through several revisions. During the course of revisions the items were administered to several hundred persons, items with weak factor loadings were modified or discarded, new items written, and inventory readministered. The process of revision also included attempts to measure different distinct tendencies. The final set of items was completed by 978 undergraduates at the University of Miami. Three different studies were conducted with the help of collected data. We are giving the instructions used in the first study for the purpose of illustration of the response categories and scoring system:

"We are interested in how people respond when they confront difficult or stress events in their lives. There are lots of ways to try deal with stress. This questionnaire asks you to indicate what you generally do and feel, when you experience stressful events. Obviously, different events bring out somewhat different responses, but think what usually you do when you are under a lot of stress".

The response choice were "I usually don't do this at all", "I usually do this a little bit", "I usually do this a medium amount", and "I usually do this a lot" (scored from 1 to 4).

The factor analysis of responses 12 yielded factors with Eigen values greater than 10 out of which 11 were fully in accord with a priori assignment of items. However, all of the social support items loaded on a single factor. Moreover, Planning and Active Coping loaded on a single factor. The last two scales, Alcohol/Drug Use and Humour, were not included in factor analysis as these scales were added later on. The Alpha and test-retest reliability coefficients reported in respect of each scale are acceptably high. Means and S.Ds. of the scores of 978 students on each of the Cope scales are reported. Correlations of the Cope scales with measures of Optimism, Control, Self-esteem, Internality, Hardiness, Type A, Monitoring, Blunting, Anxiety and Social desirability are reported. These correlations and other relevant data reported by the authors may be regarded as the evidence of validity of the scales.

Substantive Approach

This approach is based on Loevinger's (1957) departure from the view-point of Cronbach and Meehl (1955). Loevinger is interested in substance, the real nature or essential part rather than in constructs which exist in the mind of an assessor and journals of psychology. Loevinger's point of view is clearly brought out in the following statements, "...It is true that psychologists never know traits directly but only through the glass of their constructs, not manifestations of construct. Cronbach and Meehl and their colleagues on the APA appear reluctant to assign reality status to constructs of traits" (p. 642). Assigning reality status to constructs and traits, Loevinger (1957) emphasized three considerations that are to be taken into account in test construction and establishing construct validity of a test scores:

1. *Substantive domain of items.* Substantive domain demands careful selection of items to be included in an instrument. It is critical of the tradition of collection of item pool from the items available in already existing inventories. It demands that implicit theory should be substituted by explicit theory so that the content of universe be specified and items be randomly sampled from a well-defined universe of substance. If an attempt is being made to assess a general construct which can be broken into subareas of behaviour, sampling of items should be done after identification of subareas because items are to be selected to represent each area. Loevinger also recommends the inclusion of those items in the pool which on theoretical ground are not expected to be related to the external criterion. This enables us to test the theory on item level. The theory or the method of measurement is to be reviewed if the items which are theoretically expected to be related to the criterion are found to unrelated to and the items which are not expected to be related to the criterion are found to be related to it.

The substance is to be presented to respondents in different formats so as to find the contribution of trait and method variance. If greater part of variance in the unit represents trait variance rather than method variance, there is evidence of construct validity of the trait-method unit. One can make use of multitrait-multimethod matrix for this purpose. The multitrait-multimethod design was introduced by Campbell and Fisk (1959) for determining convergent and discriminant validity of a measure. Evidence of convergent validity is furnished when a scale is found to related to independent measures of the same trait. The evidence of discriminant validity comes when a scale is not found to be related to measures with which it is not expected to be related. The details about the method are given in another chapter.

2. *Structural considerations.* While discussing rational theoretical approach we have discussed the importance of internal consistency of items. Structural consideration "refers to the extent to which structural relations between test

items parallel the structural relations of other manifestations of the trait being measured" (Loevinger, 1957, p. 661). Thus we should not require higher level of internal consistency of items than the degree of relationship that prevails among different manifestations of the trait. Structural considerations include what Loevinger call "inter-item structure" and "structural fidelity". The first notion has to do with the interitem consistency; the second notion, structural fidelity refers to how well the particular measurement model selected corresponds to the substantive domain under study. Two kinds of correspondence is needed, correspondence of internal consistency of items with the "characteristic correlation, and corresponding of combining of items in the scale and the combination of different manifestations of traits specified in the model. To understand the meaning of characteristic correlation, let us make a distinction between test behaviour, non-test behaviour (external criterion) and the relation of both with the trait and each other. As it is not possible to know the relationship between a trait (i.e. the unobservable construct) and the criterion behaviour, we have to assume that relationship among non-test manifestation of a trait are highly representative of the relationship between the trait and the non-test (criteria) behaviour. Further, assuming that interrelationship among non-test behaviour shall vary from trait to trait, we can set the upper limit of the degree of structure for a particular trait equal to the relationship observed among the measure of the criteria. The degree of internal structure that exists for a given domain is called "characteristic correlation" for the trait. In principal, the correlation among items to be included in a scale should not exceed the upper limit set by the characteristic correlation.

Having selected the set of items with internal consistency corresponding to the characteristic correlation, we have to obtain total score by combining responses to individual items. For the combination of item responses we have to make use of the three measurement models suggested by Loevinger:

Cumulative Model. This is the well-known procedure of adding keyed responses to each item to get total score.

Class Model. In this model presence or absence of a particular trait is inferred from presence or absence of a number of manifestations.

Dynamic Model. In this model two or more "contradictory" behaviours are believed to be the manifestations of underlying trait (for example over concern for the welfare of others and hostility as two manifestations of aggressiveness).

3. *External considerations.* The substantive approach does not consider it sufficient that items containing a common substance be internally consistent to the extent of characteristic correlation; it also requires that items should be correlated to external criterion and should have convergent and discriminant validity. The multitrait-multimethod matrix used in the study of item characteristics can also be used for the study of items from the point of view of external considerations. For this we have to obtain correlations not only among the items measuring the same and different substance in different formats but also among the items to be included in the scale and the external real life manifestations of the trait to be assessed by an instrument.

Personality Research Form (PRF)

To give an example of the use of substantive approach we are describing the PRF developed by Jackson (1967). This scale measures 20 need variables listed by Murray (1938). Jackson began with a thorough review of available research and theoretical literature on the 20 personality variables so as to have mutually exclusive substantive definitions of the 20 variables. A heterogeneous team of item writers formulated items representing the positive and negative poles of each trait in conformity to the definitions provided to them. The procedure of selection of items for the measure of 20 personality variables was designed to ensure that items included in each scale have maximal convergent and discriminant content saturation. First of all responses to items obtained from groups of subjects were used to determine the internal consistency of items formulated to reflect the variables. For this K-R 20 was used and it was found that indices of homogeneity ranged from .80 to .94.

In the next step of construction of PRF each item was correlated with each of the 20 provisional content scales to determine discriminant and convergent validities of the items. Items which were found to have highest correlation with their appropriate content scale were retained on the ground of having convergent validity and the items which correlated higher with content scales other than the one for which they were formulated were discarded on the ground of lacking discriminant validity.

Jackson made an other attempt to remove the source of variance which decreases content saturation on the scales. To minimize the effect social desirability on subjects' responses and hence on the total scores, Jackson obtained Differential Reliability Index of each item. This was done by finding the correlation of each item with a measure of social desirability (r_{id}) in addition to an item's correlation with its provisional content scale (r_{is}). Using under root of the squares of the two values of rs, the Differential Reliability Index of an item was obtained:

$$D_{ri} = \sqrt{r^2_{is} - r^2_{id}}$$

Jackson did nothing to determine the structural fidelity of items except finding intercorrelation among the items which were assumed to reflect the interrelation among nontest manifestations of the trait. For combining items to obtain total scores, cumulative model was followed because according to Jackson (1972) this model represents the "method of choice" in personality scale construction as the evidence of success of other models is not impressive. A variety of innovative procedures were employed for the purpose of achieving homogeneity due to content saturation rather than due to substantively irrelevant response style. Correlation of the PRF scales with the external criteria are also reported.

The PRF is available in two parallel short forms and two

parallel long forms. In addition to provide twenty trait scores, PRF has two validity scale to guard against response distortions. The Infrequency Scale is measure of number of highly unlikely responses indicating carelessness, lack of understanding of instructions and similar other reasons of trivial responding which cannot be used to place the subject on the trait scales. The Desirability Scale is a measure of deliberate attempt to create impression but besides being a measure of response distortion, it is also a measure of conventional socialization versus low self-regard.

Normalized T score norms, based on data collected from 1000 males and 1000 females of north American colleges and Universities, are provided. The different kinds of reliabilities - Odd-even, Kuder-Richardson, and test-retest reported for the scales cluster around .80 for the longer from and fall in .50s for the shorter version. The construct validity is taken care of in the development and selection of items for each scale.

Factor analysis also corroborated the grouping of items in to the 20 scales. Moreover, the correlations of the PRF scales with comparable scale in California Psychological Inventory and Guilford-Zimmerman Temperament Survey confirmed the identification of traits. However, is to be pointed out, that the needs measured by the PRF and instruments like T.A.T. and EPPS are not equivalent.

The PRF is an example of technical advances in test construction including methods of item-selection, made possible with the availability of high speed computers. It is also an example of combining different approaches to development of instruments. Such an amalgamation has the advantages of different approaches.

4

Empirical Strategy of Construction of Personality Questionnaire

The empirical approach to the construction of an assessment device is the most suitable approach when the devised instrument is to be used for the prediction of some external criterion such as success in a job, membership in a diagnostic category, and identification of those who are likely to be benefited by certain kinds of psychotherapy. The empirical approach is theoretically a blind approach because it does not lead to the assessment of some known trait and is indifferent to the question as to what should be the content of the items to be used in the instrument. This approach makes no assumption regarding the correspondence between response to a self descriptive item and feeling, thinking, and behaviour of the respondent. From the point of view of empirical approach an item like "I am feeling hungry" and "True" or "Yes" response given to it are no more than stimulus and response as it is irrelevant for the assessor to know whether it is a veridical description of hunger. If "Yes" response to this item can indicate, for example, a state of depression, the item may be included in a measure of depression irrespective of lack of knowledge about the relationship of feeling of hunger and depression and the fact that there is or there is no any correspondence between nonavailability of food to the respondents for a number of hours and "Yes" response to the item. In the absence of the assumption regarding the correspondence of verbal response and mental interior, the scoring system is to be devised by comparing the responses given by individuals belonging to the criterion groups. The fact of the matter is that the empirical approach is not aversive to admitting that it does not bother about the question as to what trait is involved in giving rise to the difference in the behaviour used as the criterion of categorization of people in the extreme groups. The empirical approach finds it unnecessary to infer some trait from responses given to a set of items and then making this inference as the basis for the prediction of real life behaviour, because personality trait is not believed to be an essential link between test response and prediction.

It is to be stressed that the followers of empirical approach do not share the confidence of rational-theoretical approach regarding the understanding of relationship between verbal responses and personality dynamics. For them a response to an item of personality inventory is "an intrinsically interesting and significant bit of verbal behaviour, the nontest correlates of which must be discovered by empirical means" (Meehl, 1945). Buchwald's (1961) following observation is also helpful in explaining the empirical point of view, "the psychologist who operates from instrumental viewpoint has his attention focused on what he can conclude about the subject on the basis of the subject's verbal utterances rather than on what the subject can tell him" (p. 464).

How in the absence of apparent link between content of the items and the trait of the personality to be assessed, a set items is able to predict criterion? Answer to this question comes from the deviation hypothesis proposed by Berg (1955). This hypothesis makes a distinction between critical and non-critical areas of behaviour and asserts that deviation in non-critical area can be used for assessing deviation in some critical area. Critical behaviour is the behaviour which a society considers as critical for its well being such as interpersonal relationship which are of great significance for the members of the society. Non-critical behaviour is not related to society's welfare and for this reason society is not concerned with this kind of behaviour. While the criterion to be predicted by a psychological test is likely to be critical behaviour, (for no one would pay for the prediction of non-critical behaviour), the response given by a subject to a set of item included in a psychological test are non-critical for the society at large. The distinction between critical and non-critical behaviour is very well brought out by Berg (1967, p. 152), "...a patient may be legally committed to a mental hospital because of significant deviant responses like delusion, but never solely on the basis of deviant responses to inkblot, design and such. But non-critical behaviour can be used for the prediction of deviation in critical behaviour because of generality of deviant behaviour: "deviant response pattern tend to be general; hence those deviant behaviour patterns which are significant for abnormality and thus regarded as symptoms are associated with other deviant response patterns which are in non-critical areas of behaviour and which are not regarded as symptoms of personality aberration" (Berg, 1955, p. 62).

It is important to make a distinction between 'absolute' and 'relative' deviation. Absolute response deviation has to do with the departure from statistically expected distribution. An example of such distribution is the tendency of 80 per cent of subjects to call 'head' on the first toss of a coin while the probability of 'head' and 'tail' on the first toss is 50 per cent. Another example of absolute deviation is the tendency of the three out of four person to turn to right rather than left when both the paths arrive at the same point (Robinson, 1933). Relative response deviation is of interest for empirical approach to personality, because it is the deviation shown by a specific group. If, for example, 90 per cent of schizophrenics give 'True' response to an item and only 50 per cent of normals give this response to the item, this information is sufficient to distinguish between the two groups and there is no need to consider the relation of content of the item and response to schizophrenia. Berg (1957, p. 160) observed that "stimulus patterns of any sense modality may be used to elicit deviant response patterns; thus particularly stimulus content is unimportant for measuring behaviour in terms of the deviation hypothesis". Apparent movement of light, spiral after-effect, musical excerpts, geometrical designs, are the examples of the materials which have been used for the construction of content — free tests for distinguishing between different criterion groups. Little importance of item content in the construction of group-discriminative tests is explicit in Berg's statement that it is possible to construct MMPI Scales from Strong Interest Blank.

Procedure for Developing Empirical Scales

The most important step towards the construction of empirical instrument is the identification of criterion for the formulation of the two extreme groups whose responses to a set of items are to be compared. Because the main purpose of empirical approach is to devise an instrument to differentiate subjects in the categories formed in accordance with their position on the criterion variable, a reliable and critical criterion is the most important aspects of construction of an empirical device. Wiggins (1973) suggested that it is preferable to concentrate on the standard of performance rather than the psychological criterion. According to Stern, Stein and Bloom (1956) "standard of performance" is an abstract concept which exists in the mind of significant others. An example of concretization of standard of performance is representation of standard of "intellectual competence" through grade-point average.

The second step in devising an empirical instrument is to collect an initial pool of items which are expected to differentiate the levels or categories formed according to the criterion. We have already pointed out that empirical approach is theoretically blind and one can use any kind of items irrespective of the relevance of content to what is to be assessed but the constructor of the instrument cannot be prevented from his natural inclination to think in terms of the abstract standard of performance and let his hunches influence the collection of items. However, empirical approach does not consider responses as surrogate of behaviour, and for this reason it has not to pay attention to the problem of conveying the same meaning to all the subjects. Such sources of ambiguity are of little concern for empirical approach as words like "often" occurring in items (e.g., "I have often headache") as long as they are helpful in making discrimination between the criterion groups.

The third step in the construction of an empirical instrument is to administer an initial pool of items on contrast groups representing the two ends of trait under consideration if the purpose is to differentiate between the extreme positions of a continuum or two categories (like normal and depressive) if the instruments is to be used for identification of category membership. Responses of the subjects to the items are tabulated for the two groups separately and suitable statistics is used for determining whether a item can significantly differentiate between the two groups. Depending upon the format of items, response categories, and assumption about the nature of the trait and the nature of criterion variable, one can use one of the following statistics for finding the item discriminability: biserial correlation, point biserial correlation, tetrachoric correlation, and Phi coefficient, critical ratio for the difference in proportions. In addition to item discrimination index determined by one of the above methods, the criteria for the selection of items may include: (a) removing overlapping in different scales of a multiphasic instrument by selection of an item for only one scale if it is found to discriminate between more than one criterion groups (b) eliminations of items which are endorsed by a high percentage of the contrast groups, and (c) the inclusion of equal number of items keyed in agree/true and disagree/false direction to indicate an individual's position vis-a-vis the criterion. Presence of equal number of items keyed in opposite direction minimizes the effect of acquiescences on the score obtained by a person. It is to be pointed out that key for the scoring of items for obtaining total score on the scale is not prepared on a priori ground but on the basis of the study of direction of responses given by the criterion groups.

There remains the possibility that items could discriminate between the original criterion groups just due to chance. It is, therefore, necessary to carry out cross validation of items drawing new criterion groups. In the phase of cross validation the most important decision is the selection of new criterion groups. If the new criterion is different from the original criterion, item selected earlier would not be found to be able to discriminate.

The procedure of item selection mentioned above does not lead to the selection of a set of homogeneous items. Thus, the empirical approach differs from rational theoretical approach in making use heterogeneous rather than homogeneous items. Because the main purpose of empirical approach is to predict certain criterion and the subjects belonging to the contrast criterion groups may differ in respect of more than one characteristics, the items comprising and empirical instrument should be heterogeneous so as to cover different aspects of the criterion. Edwards, (1970, p. 42) has shown that the correlation between criterion measure (c) and scores on an empirical instrument (x) is given by:

$$r_{cx} = \frac{k\bar{r}_{ck}}{\sqrt{k + k\,(k - 1)\,\bar{r}_{ij}}}$$

Where k refers to number of items in the scale, r_{ck} is average of correlations of different items with the criterion, and r_{ij} is average value of intercorrelations among the items. According to the expression given above, it is evident that for the increment of correlation between scores obtained with the help of instrument and the criterion measures, the correlation among items should decrease and correlation between each item and the criterion should increase. The ideal situation for the prediction of criterion would be one in which average inter-item correlation is zero. In that situation the variance of the predictor score would be equal to k. An instrument with zero or low intercorrelations among the items would not be a measure of single trait and as such there is no basis for interpreting scores representing individual differences as contributed by single trait.

Reliability and Validity of Empirical Instrument

Like any other instrument, empirical measure is to be reliable. Because empirical instrument is made of heterogeneous items, it is of no use to determine the reliability of this kind of instrument with thc help of any method which is based on internal consistency of items. We can make use of parallel form of reliability but this depends on the availability of parallel form of the instrument. Thus, test-retest reliability seems to be particularly most suitable for an empirical instrument because the instrument is to be used for the prediction of criterion measure which would be available in future.

An empirical instrument is not a measure of a theoretical construct or unitary trait, and for this reason no attempt is to be made to determine construct validity of an empirical tool. Concurrent and predictive validities are more suitable for this kind of instrument. It is to be noted that predictive validity is of great social importance. If it is possible to know in advance who would become criminal or alcoholic, successful entrepreneur, etc., we can take remedial and/or supportive steps.

Evaluation of the Empirical Approach

The greatest advantage of empirical instrument is lack of substantial consideration in the selection of items. Because empirical approaches have no consideration of relevance of item content to what is to be measured, it welcomes item ambiguity if item can discriminate between the members of criterion group. The lack of correspondence between response and item content makes it possible to have subtle items in the scale. Item subtlety is concerned with the respondents' ability to relate an item to its, keyed scale (Holden and Jackson, 1979). It is to be pointed out that the word 'ability' appearing in the previous sentence is not used to refer to respondents' characteristics, such as low level of intelligence, or verbal comprehension but to the content of the item which makes it difficult, rather impossible, to establish some kind of relation between response to an item and what is to be measured by the item. Seemen (1952) pointed out that, "... subtlety refers to the degree to which meaning can or cannot be assigned in a priori fashion (to an item)" (p. 278). Distinction between obvious and subtle items can be explained by considering the following examples:

Example of obvious item: "I would enjoy the occupation of butcher". It is not difficult to understand the relationship of 'Yes' response to this item and sadism if a common man is told the meaning of sadism.

Example of subtle item: "I have been quite independent and free from family rule and restrain". Perhaps it would not be possible for a person to associate 'False' response to this item with the presence of psychopathic tendencies if he is informed that psychopathics violate social norms and indulge in anti-social behaviour. Similarly, no logical link can possibly be found between 'False' response to the items given below and the scales in which they appear:

"I tend to be on guard with the people who are somewhat more friendly than I had expected". (MMPI Paranoia Scale)

"I do not have great fear of snakes". (MMPI Prejudice Scale)

Presence of subtle items in an instrument prevent faking good or bad. Faking refers to an attempt to appear abnormal when one is really normal or appearing normal when one has certain behavioural problems.

Having discussed the nature of item subtlety and importance of subtle items in preventing faking, we can move to examine other aspects of empirical scales. One of the main criticisms against the empirical approach is that it does not provide scores which can be interpreted in terms of unitary theoretical construct. The theoretical blindness of an empirical instrument makes it of little use for research in which certain hypotheses are to be tested and theoretical questions are to be answered. Even when the criterion used for the selection of items is of theoretical relevance, one cannot do more than speculating about the nature of trait(s) assessed by the scale because it is a tedious job to break the total variance into components and to determine the amount of variance which can be attributed to personality traits expressed through the criterion behaviour.

Lack of understanding of what is measured by an empirical instrument makes it only a provisional scale which is to be revised with slight modification of criterion or change in the situation in which the criterion behaviour occurs. Regarding limited generality of empirical approach, Wiggins (1973) observed, "Minor variations in the population studied, the criterion employed, or the conditions under which the test is administered may result in reduced validity coefficient" (p. 394). Since in the case of empirical instrument the meaning of scale score is tied with the unknown characteristics of the original criterion groups, we have to repeat the entire procedure of item selection of items whenever we have to use the empirical instrument for categorizing member of different populations. It may, however, be pointed out that MMPI is an empirically developed instrument which is being used for more than fifty years for clinical diagnosis and personality description. But this could happen because empirical correlates of scores on its clinical and validity scales have been discovered for subjects drawn from populations which were not necessarily similar to the original population.

While according to Wiggins (1973) empirically developed scale is most economical with minimum guarantee of success in 'one shot' assessment programmes, analytical approach is to be preferred when an instrument is to be used time and gain for the prediction of similar criterion. In the analytical approach there is heavy reliance on personality theory in defining the criterion.

The disregard of relationship between the content of items and the criterion to be predicted, which is fundamental feature of empirical approach, generated a number of studies with the objective of comparing the effectiveness of tools comprising different kinds of items. Norman (1963) conducted a study in which the criteria to be predicted were peer ratings. Three kinds of stimuli were used for the prediction of the criteria: personality descriptive adjectives, occupational titles, and abstract figures. The discriminative effectiveness of items showed the relevance of item content as the content relevant material was found to be better predictor of the criteria.

Goldberg and Slovic (1967) provided additional evidence in favour of importance of content for the prediction. The criteria to be predicted were two measures of academic achievement and four measures of social affiliation. Four kinds of items were employed for the derivation of predictive scales: 60 geometrical forms, 60 self-report statements related to achievement, 60 self-report statements selected at random and irrelevant to both achievement and affiliation. Groups of undergraduate students rated the relevance of 180 statements for each of the six criteria. The scales constructed with the help of a contrast group strategy for the prediction of each of the criterion were found to have substantial and significant validities irrespective of the fact whether they were made up of items falling in any of the three categories of relevance. But in new cross-validation samples, the validity of all non-verbal scales went down to zero and scales made up of items of high relevance were found to have significant validity coefficients. It was concluded that: (1) Verbal items are better predictors of intellective and social criteria than non-verbal items, and (2) criterion-relevance ratings of items are correlated with predictive validity of the items.

The empirical approach discussed above is a convenient approach when a large number of candidates are to be processed and the criterion situation is not understood beyond the classification of subjects in predetermined categories. The purpose of prediction of a criterion is better served when attempt is made to understand the psychological nature of the criterion besides the collection of items effective in prediction of the criterion. The analytic and synthetic approaches are preferable when the interest is to include an understanding of psychological nature of what is to be assessed. In analytical approach a better understanding of criterion is obtained by locating significant others and eliciting their opinion regarding what constitutes good and poor performance. This helps in arriving at explicit and implicit criteria. The nature of implicit criterion can be discovered by finding that successful and unsuccessful personnel identified by significant others do not differ in the characteristics which are mentioned by significant others to be important but in some other characteristics which significant others could not mention. An example of this situation is two secretaries who are equally proficient in their job but one is not as good looking as the other. The views obtained from significant others are used by psychologists to state job requirements in psychological terms.

The synthetic approach is an alternative to the analytic approach. When due to certain reasons including familiarity of the criterion to the assessor, analytic approach is not considered, the assessor may intuit the psychological requirement of the criterion. Though this global situational analysis cannot be a substitute of analytic approach, it is better than making no attempt to understand the nature of the criterion.

Empirical Scales

We propose to devote this section to the description of some empirical instrument for the purpose of giving example of the application of the approach in the development of measuring devices. The most important instrument developed by using this approach is the Minnesota Multiphasic Personality Inventory (MMPI). The PGI health Questionnaire No. 2 (PGI 2) is another instrument which deserves attention because it is an instrument developed in India making use of the pool of items collected from psychiatric patients visiting PGI Chandigarh.

Minnesota Multiphasic Personality Inventory (MMPI)

The MMPI is an instrument which is widely used in routine examination of psychiatric patients along with WAIS,

TAT, and Rorschach Ink Blot Test. The instrument was developed by Strake R. Hathway, a clinical psychologist, and J.C. McKinley, a neuropsychiatrist, who from 1937 began their collaboration for the purpose of developing this instrument. An elaborate statement of the purpose of the construction of the instrument is given by Hathway (1964, p. 463) who stated that he and McKinley set out to construct an effective and practical instrument "as an objective aid in the routine psychiatric case work-up of adult patients and as a method of determining the severity of the conditions. As a corollary to this, the inventory was expected to provide an objective estimate of psychotherapeutic effect and other changes in the severity of their condition over time". However, it is to be emphasized that although the clinical scales of MMPI are named according to the abnormal manifestations of symptomatic complex, they have shown to have meaning within the normal range (Hathway and McKinley, 1951). Hathway (1964) observed that the MMPI can be used for the screening of normal persons (for example, high school students, job applicants) in the same way as chest X-ray is used in preventive health measures. The three main features of the MMPI which make it distinct from other inventories are:

1. It is multiphasic inventory designed to provide, in a single test, scores on all important phases of personality.

2. It is an instrument developed with the help of empirical approach in which selection of items for a scale is not based on the consideration of relation of content of items to what is to be assessed by the scale.

3. It has four validity scales which tell us whether a test protocol contains genuine information about the subject.

In addition to the three features mentioned above, we can also refer to the fact that the MMPI is the instrument containing such a large pool of different kinds of items that its item pool has been used as the source of items for hundred of new instruments. Moreover, simply for the reason that huge literature regarding the use of the MMPI for different purposes has been accumulated, one should not be deprived of the information by discontinuing the use of the instrument despite its many shortcomings to be discussed later. But first of all let us have a description of the MMPI scales. Since scrutiny of protocol precedes attempt of interpretation, we are first undertaking the description of the validity scales. The term validity as we are using in the context of MMPI validity scales has a meaning different from the common meaning of the term. The common meaning of the term validity refers to the overall quality of a test but in reference to validity scales of MMPI, it assumes the meaning of "adequacy and suitability" of an individual's test data for making decisions about him. The four validity scales are described below:

The Question or Cannot Say Scale (?)

This scale has no items of its own. The question score is obtained by counting the number of items which were left unresponded or which were given both 'True' and 'False' responses by the subject indicating his inability to decide in favour of this or that alternative. It is to be noted that Cannot Say scores do not form a hypothetical continuum of evasiveness because the total is not contributed by the same set of items. However, the T scores conversion of raw Cannot Say scores are provided with the consideration of the extent of adverse effect of omission on other scales of the test. The raw scores below 30 are entered on the profile as equal to a T score of 50, or simply 'OK'. The omission of a large number of items contributing to the increase of the total score may be due to different reasons: subject's inability to understand the items, his unwillingness to cooperate with the tester but still going through the motion of compliance, defensive omission of a number of items so as not to reveal certain information about himself. As high Cannot Say score has adverse effect on profile elevation, many suggestions are given to make allowance for the omitted responses. However, the suggested correction involves the risk of vitiating the norms and scales of MMPI derived on data from traditional mode of administration.

The Lie Scale (L)

The Lie scale has fifteen items similar to items devised by Hartshorne and May (1928) from their studies of deceit among school-going children. The L scale is an indicator of deliberate and intentional attempt to conceal faults and foibles by denial of their presence in oneself. The content refers to aggression, bad thought, weakness of character or resolve, poor self-control, prejudices, and even minor dishonesties. The personal faults referred to in the L scale items are of the nature which an ordinary person cannot avoid. He is, therefore, expected to give 'True' response if he is frank and honest and 'False' response if he wants to look better. The L scale was devised with the assumption that the test-taking attitude manifested through the responses to the L scale items shall be carried over to responses to items of other basic scales. This assumption is supported by the fact that the number of profiles with primed scales in it drop appreciately at and beyond a raw score value of 9 or T score value of 66 of the L score (Mark and Seeman, 1963).

The Frequency Scale (F)

This scale is devised to detect unusual responding due to different reasons. There are 64 items in the scale which are selected on the basis of skewed distribution of their endorsement by men and women in the normative samples. The specific criterion for the selection of items was: not more than 10 per cent of responses to an item falling in one response category, 'True' or 'False'. The items of the F scale are keyed in deviant minority (infrequent) direction. A subjects is likely to obtain high F score due to one or more of the following reasons (Dahlstorm, Welsh, and Delhstorm, 1972):

1. Limitations of visual acuity or physical conditions of testing which make the reading of items difficult.

2. Marginal reading proficiency, border line or mentally deficient intellectual range.

3. The subject does not share the common cultural framework of the derivational sample employed by the au-

thor of the inventory.

4. Pervasive personality disorganization which makes the person out of contact with his surroundings during the acute phase. In the acute phase, a person may not be able to follow instructions, may not understand the meanings of items, or may not able to record his responses on the answer sheet at the proper place.

5. Special test-taking attitude of the subject who may use the opportunity to give responses for the purpose of dramatizing his condition rather than as an opportunity for careful self-description. However, in some cases the deviant responses may bear upon some special aspects of person's life. Twenty of F scale items are in Grayson's Critical Items list which is a collection of 38 statements which may have the some special pathological meaning in a person's life circumstances.

Suppression Scale (K)

The purpose of K scale is to sharpen the discriminatory power of the corrected scores by minimizing the two kinds of test misses, false positive and false negative. False positive are those normal subjects who have abnormal MMPI profile and false negative are those abnormal subjects who have normal MMPI profile. It is to be noted that in the derivation of the K scale hits and misses were identified in terms of the whole clinical profile rather than particular diagnostic groups identified by separate scales. The K is a suppressor variable (Meehl and Hathway, 1946) because it suppress the irrelevant variance for the purpose of the improvement of the discriminatory power of the clinical scales which it corrects.

The K scale includes 30 items, 22 included in the L 6 scale and 8 items which were found to discriminate between normals and psychiatric patients. The L 6 (Meehl and Hathway, 1946) is considered to be a measure of defensiveness. It contains 22 items which were found to discriminate the normal and patient groups in their endorsement by at least 30 per cent. As it was found that some psychiatric patients obtained low scores on the L 6 scale, it became necessary to add items which could discriminate between normals and psychiatric patients. Eight items from the subset of items on which normal subjects could not simulate the responses of psychiatric patients when instructed to do so, were added to 22 items of L6 scale to have a set of 30 items for the K scale.

Though the K scale was devised for giving warning to be careful against the possibility of the invalidity of the test protocol, it was later used for the correction of some of the clinical scales. The routine procedure of adding some portion of the K scale to the scores on certain clinical scales was introduced by McKinley, Hathway, and Meehl (1948) for improving the discrimination of normal profiles from abnormal profiles. The weights to be added were determined empirically by gradually adding one-tenth of K raw score to the original raw scores of the subjects and then finding the weight which would sharpen the discrimination of normals from psychiatric patients.

Clinical Scales

The MMPI has the following basic scales:

1. *Scale 1.* Hypochondriasis (Hs). This scale was developed by using a group of patients who showed exaggerated concern about their physical health, made complaints about physical problems which had a psychological basis.

2. *Scale 2.* Depression (D). Persons suffering from intense unhappiness, poor morale, lack of hope about the future, and having other symptoms of pure depression were employed for developing this scale.

3. *Scale 3.* Hysteria (Hs). Patient diagnosed as case of "psychoneurosis-hysteria" having physical symptoms coupled with la belle indifference or bland unconcern about their condition were employed for the derivation of this scale.

4. *Psychopathic Deviate (Pd).* Those who showed difficulties in social adjustment, and had histories of delinquency and other anti-social behaviour were compared with the

normal control group for the construction of this scale.

5. *Masculinity-Femininity (MF).* The items for this scale were selected by comparing the responses of a group of male homosexual, all of whom were free of other psychopathology, with the responses of normal subjects.

6. *Paranoia (Pa).* The group of patients used for the construction of this scale were rarely diagnosed to be paranoid, they showed such symptoms as ideas of reference, suspiciousness, interpersonal sensitivity, feeling of persecution, and delusion of grandeur.

7. *Psychasthenia (Pt).* Those who showed unreasonable fear, high anxiety, feelings of guilt, and excessive doubts were the subjects for the derivation of this scale.

8. *Schizophrenia (Sc).* Patients diagnosed as suffering from various forms of schizophrenia formed the criterion group for the development of this scale.

9. *Hypomania (Ma).* The criterion group contained the patients who showed the milder degree of manic excitement typically occurring in manic-depressive psychosis. They were characterized by excessive activity, easy distractibility, elevated mood, and a rapid but disjointed flow of speech.

10. *Introversion-extroversion (Si).* This scale is not a clinical scale but it is valuable for use with normal subjects coming for guidance and counselling. There are 70 items in the scale selected on the basis of their ability to discriminate between contrasting groups of subjects formed on the basis of cuttings points of 65th percentile and 35th percentile of scores on subscale for social introversion in the Minnesota T-S-E Inventory.

Derivation of the Clinical Scales

Over 1000 items were collected from different sources: scales of social and personal attitudes, clinical reports, case resume, psychiatric interview manual, forms, guides, etc. Eliminating duplicates, evaluating readability of items restating items in personal declarative form, considering excessive correspondence between answering "True" and acceptance of pathological or socially stigmatized characteristics, a set of 504 items were retained for the derivation of the clinical scales. The items can be divided into 26 content categories. The MMPI scales were developed with the help of empirical approach. For the selection of items to be included in different clinical scales, over 800 clinical cases and 724 normals were used as the contrast groups. Clinical cases were drawn from the neuropsychiatric division of Minnesota University Hospital. Normal subjects were friends and relatives of patients who were visiting them and were willing to complete the inventory while sitting in the waiting room. The sample included both men and women and it was representative of the adult population of Minnesota. While the responses of all the 724 normal subjects were used for the derivation of every scale, 800 clinical cases were divided into diagnostic categories on the basis of case history material, psychiatric observations and other considerations. There were at least 50 patients in each criterion group. The responses of subjects were tabulated for each item and frequency of the two kinds of responses for criterion groups were compared with normal control (N.C) as shown below for three items and the criterion group (C.G) of schizopherenia (Wiggins, 1973):

Items	*Control Group*		*Criterion Group*		*Difference in %*		*Scoring weights*	
	T	*F*	*T*	*F*	*T*	*F*	*T*	*F*
I like mechanics magazines.	50	50	51	49	1	-1	0	0
I hear strange things when I am alone	5	95	35	65	30	-30	1	0
I get all sympathy I should	80	20	50	50	-30	30	0	1

The above table shows that the difference in the percentage of True and False responses of normal and control groups is negligible in the case of the first item but it is as much as 30 per cent in the case of remaining two items. While the first item shall not be included in the Sc Scale, the second and third items are to be included in the scale and weight of 1 is given for True response in the case of second item and False response in the case of third item. It is to be noted that both selection of item and the weight of response depend on the existence of reliable difference in the percentage and the direction of difference. If the difference is positive for True response, score 1 is given for this alternative; if difference is positive for the False response, choice of False response is scored as 1.

Reliability and Validity

Hathway and McKinley have drawn attention towards the fact that reliability coefficient should not be the same for normal and psychiatric samples. Moreover, test-retest reliability also depends upon the stability of what is measured by the test. For example, one should not expect that test-retest reliability of the Depression scale would be as high as that of Mf scale because variation of mood and stability of interest and attitudes.

The manual of MMPI (Hathway and McKinley, 1951) has reported three sets of test-retest reliability coefficient. The first set is based on their own studies in which individual Form was administered on samples of unselected subjects with intervals ranging from three days to one year. The reliability coefficient are as follows:

Hs = .80, D = .77, Hy = .57, Pd = .71, Pt = .74, Ma = .83.

The second set of test-retest reliability coefficients were determined by Cottle who used Individual Form alternatively with group forms for test and retest within one week, the data were collected forms normal subjects. The coefficients are:

L = .46, F = .76, Hs = .81, D = .66, Hy = .72, Pd = .80, Pd = .71, Mf = .91, Pa = .56, Pt = .90, Sc = .86, Ma = .76.

The third set of reliability coefficient is reported for all the scales except K. The subjects were psychiatric patients who were administered complete and shortened versions of individual Forms within three days by Holzberg and Alessi (1949). The test-retest coefficients are:

? = .75, L = .85, F = .93, Hs = .67, D = .80, Hy = .87, Pd = .52, Mf = .76, Pa = .78, Pt = .72, Sc = .98, Ma = .59.

It is difficult to describes in brief the studies which furnish evidence regarding the validity of MMPI, an inventory which extensively used in both clinical and non-clinical settings. An atlas for the clinical use of MMPI contains 968 short histories of clinical cases with different profile codes. An extensive bibliography on validity of the inventory is also given in the atlas. A large number of special indices, configural patterns, sequential rules for the combination of scores have been proposed for proper utilization of personality data obtained with the help of MMPI. One can presume that there would be no abundance of methods for proper utilization of MMPI scores if the instrument was not found to be useful. The MMPI manual reports that a high scores on a scale has been found to predict positively the corresponding final diagnosis or estimate in more than 60 per cent of new psychiatric admissions. It is to be noted that this percentage is not for normal-abnormal differentiation; it is rather derived from differentiation among various kind of clinical cases. However, serious doubt regarding the source of variance of MMPI scales has been created by the findings of studies of item endorsement and social desirability values (SDSVs) of MMPI (Edward's, 1966, 1970). Block (1965) furnished empirical evidence and argument to refute Edward's assertion that MMPI scales are measures of tendency to give desirable responses.

Interpretation of MMPI Profile

The ultimate purpose of administration of any test is to know about the individual, his dispositions, personality traits, psychological difficulties, and psychiatric diagnosis. The first step towards meaningful interpretation of MMPI test protocol is to prepare a psychogram or profile. Before we describe in some detail the interpretation of MMPI profile, we should mention some general principles of profile interpretation to be followed in the interest of correct assessment of the subject:

1. When interpretation is likely to have a bearing on the subject's social position, only accredited persons should venture to do the task.

2. A deviant profile should not lead to hasty conclusion regarding the presence of abnormality. One should collect more information about the person.

3. Psychiatric symptoms are not usually found to be pure or independent of one another.

4. An individual's profile is not his permanent clinical picture. Marked changes in his configuration of scores at different point of time may reflect changes in his reactions to environmental pressures which may not remain uniform at different point of time.

A specimen of the standard MMPI profile sheet is given on the next page.

The profile is divided into two parts vertically. One part is for the plotting of raw scores on the validity scales and the other part is for plotting raw scores for the clinical scales with K correction, if any. At the bottom of the profile there are rows for entering raw scores, portion of K to be added to raw score, and corrected raw scores obtained after adding the K scores.

Visual inspection of profile is the first step towards interpretation of scores. It is always preferable to look first at the points representing validity scores. Studies have been conducted to discover the elevation of different validity scales in clinical profiles which reach or exceed T score of 70. Such studies tell us that in the presence of high elevation of validity scores, the scores on the clinical scales are likely to be adversely affected. Having prepared profile and considered the validity scores one can proceed to interpret MMPI scores using any one but preferably a combination of the methods mentioned below:

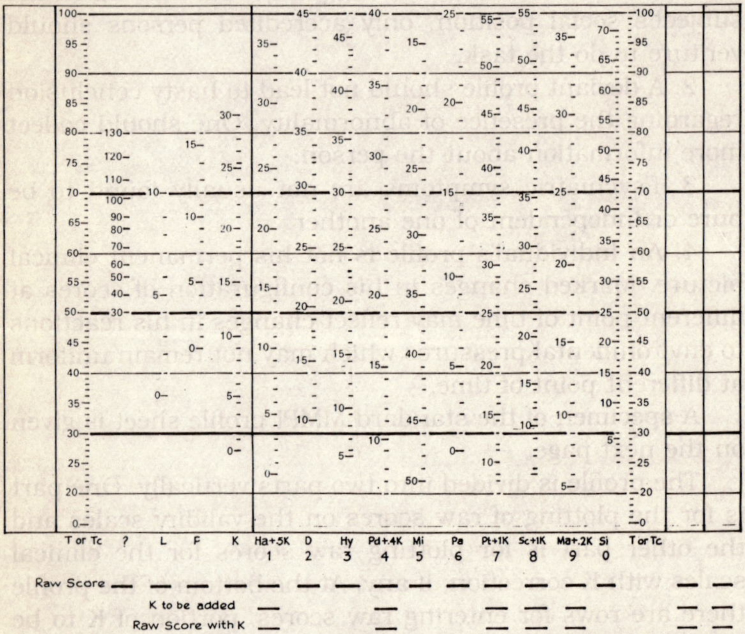
T or Tc
?
L
F
K
Hs+.5K 1
D 2
Hy 3
Pd+.4K 4
Mf 5
Pa 6
Pt+1K 7
Sc+1K 8
Ma+.2K 9
Si 0
T or Tc
Raw Score
K to be added
Raw Score with K

1. Scale-by Scale Interpretation

A perusal of the profile informs the interpreter of the distribution of the scores on different clinical scales. He can discover what are the scales on which an individual has got high scores and the scales on which he obtained low scores. Having found the scales on which the individual has got high scores, the interpreter may proceed to describe the person mentioning the characteristics of the criterion group which was used in the derivation of the scale. For example, if the individual has more than T score of 70 on the first scale, the interpreter may suspect that the individual has abnormal concern with his body functions and may be reporting physical symptoms without been really suffering from physical ailments. One can also use findings of studies on personality characteristics associated with high and low scores on different scales. One comprehensive source of such information are different volumes of an MMPI handbook prepared by Dahlstorm, Welsh, and Dahlstorm (1960).

2. Special Indices and Sequential Rules

Depending on the purpose of assessment and the kind of information which one wants, the interpreter may select special indices or sequential rules which would be applicable to get the desired information from the scores. Some of these indices and rules are applied to raw scores and some make use of T scores. Some important indices are:

Index of Pathology (Ip)

This index was proposed by Sines and Sliver (1963). In this index T scores of the subject on Pa and Sc scales are combined to yield the value which can vary from 1 to 10; 1 representing low level of pathology and 10 representing highest level of pathology. Different weights are used for the combination of two scores for male and female subjects:

$$\text{For Males: Ip} = .10\ \text{Pa} + .06\ \text{Sc} - 6.26$$

$$\text{For Females: Ip} = .08\ \text{Pa} + .10\ \text{Sc} - 7.36$$

Delinquency Index (De I)

Weighted T scores on five scales are combined to obtain

this index which can give both positive value and negative value. The positive value indicates presence of delinquency patterns and negative values indicate non-delinquency (Rempel , 1958, 1960).

This index is as below:

$$\text{De I} = .0695\ \text{F} + .0116\ \text{Hs} + .0578\ \text{Pd} - .0782\ \text{Mf} + .0256\ \text{Sc} - 2.0169$$

Choynowski Diagnostic Functions. A set of six linear weights has been devised for separating normals from neurotics, normals from schizopherenics, normals from psychopaths, and each of the three clinical groups from each other. The functions make use of T scores on all the ten basic clinical and validity scales except Cannot Say.

3. Profile Coding and the use of Code Books

With the realization that individual scores should not be considered in isolation because the meaning of equal score on the same test obtained by two persons would be modified by their standing on other scales, and also that certain kind of person have typical configurations, profile coding and code books are found to be much helpful in the interpretation of scores. Two most frequently used systems of profile coding are high-point and low-point coding proposed by Hathway and complete coding devised by Welsh. In both the systems scales are identified by their serial numbers.

Hathway Code

The serial number of scales are written in descending order of T score values greater than 54. A prime (*) is inserted after the last serial number which has T score of 70 or more. The scales which have equal T scores or which differ by one point are underlined. A dash is introduced after high points and then the serial numbers of scales with T scores below 46 are arranged in ascending order. Right to this raw scores of L, F and K scales are written with colon (:) in between the scores. If the raw score of L is equal to or greater than 10 or if raw score of F is equal or greater than 16, a capital X is placed immediately after the code of clinical scales to indicate invalidity of the profile.

Welsh (Total) Code

Serial numbers of all the scales are arranged corresponding to their T scores arranged from high to low. Appropriate elevation symbols are introduced to indicate the range in which T score fall. T score over 90 are followed by *, 80 to 89 followed by ", 70 to 70 by ", 6069 by -, 50 to 59 by /, 40 to 49 by : 30 to 39 by #, all scores below 30 appear right to # . Right to the code for the clinical scales is the code for validity scales arranged in descending order of T scores and marked by the same elevation symbols as the clinical scales. Two scales having equal T scores or differing by one T score are underlined.

For the purpose of illustration Hathway and Welsh codes for the scores given below are prepared:

Clinical Scales	Hs	D	Hy	Pd	Mf	Pa	Pt	Sc	Ma	Si
Serial number	1	2	3	4	5	6	7	8	9	0
T scores	40	91	49	39	35	68	75	72	61	50

Validity Scales	?	L	F	K
T Scores	50	40	73	46

278'69 - 541 1:13:10 : Hathaway Code

2 * 78'69 - 0/3 1: 45 # F'P/KL : Welsh Code

After profile coding one can use various codebooks which contain descriptions based on the correlates discovered to occur with various code combinations. Some well-known code books are Hathway and Meehl's Atlas (1951) for the clinical use, Hathway and Momachesi's (1961) Atlas for the counselling of high school students. The Counsellor's Handbook for the interpretation of MMPI profiles by Carkhuff, Barnett, and McCall (1965), Mark and Seeman's actuarial Atlas. As already reported (chapter II), many computer programs are available for obtaining complete automated interpretations and reports of MMPI.

Critical Evaluation of MMPI

MMPI has all merits and demerits of an empirically developed instrument. Its scales do not have homogeneous items. Lack of relevance of content of items to what the scales measure, particularly those items which ask the subject to report about the religious beliefs and private life has been so offensive that it led to the debate on the invasion of privacy. Hathway (1964) had to explain the use of MMPI in the selection of policemen in response to a 'courteous' inquiry he received about the justification of asking for religious beliefs. The letter drew his attention to laws against inquiry about religious affiliation. The logic and use of empirical keying of scale became target of mockery in the form of items like, "I salivate at the sight of mitten", "I would enjoy the work of chicken flicker" (Korchin, 986).

The inventory was developed for the identification of subjects which give responses similar to the subjects included in different criterion groups employed in test construction. As the subjects used for the derivation of the scales were psychiatric patients of different categories, the instrument is anchored in psychiatric system though it has been used for the general description of personality and scales in the MMPI are now referred to by their serial number rather than by their names. Many people doubt that items which were found to be useful for psychiatric diagnosis would be successful for the assessment of characteristics of normal personality.

Overlapping of items and inadequate size of the original normative sample which was representative of Minnesota population of 1930s are inherent defects of the MMPI which cannot be removed and only alternative is the revision of the MMPI. However, any attempt to remove certain items from the scale, or to add new items or to reconstruct the inventory would render useless the treasure of information collected in the form of Atlases, Code books, special indices, etc. Nevertheless, the fear of loss of information or availability of indices, code books, computer programs, etc., should not be an excuse for unmindful use of the interpretive material based on subjects drawn from one culture in another culture. It is not proper to expect that the MMPI can be used in India or any other country which has sizable population of English knowing people. It is true that items of MMPI are in simple English but there are many items with phrases, expressions, or idioms which would not convey the same meaning to non-Americans. Vernacular version of MMPI used with non-English speaking subjects is still more objectionable without the evidence of equivalence of the original and translated versions.

Like other questionnaires, MMPI is not free of the influence of different sources of response distortions. The scales are not balanced in regard to number of True-keyed and False-keyed items and evidence is furnished to the effect that frequency of endorsement of items is associated with social desirability of the items. It is claimed that scores on different MMPI scales can be predicted with the help of a social desirability (SD) scale consisting of 39 items keyed in socially desirable direction (Edwards, 1957). The interpretation of the first factor extracted from intercorrelation of MMPI scales and the SD scale as the marker of the first factor is the proclamation not acceptable to Block (1965) who observed that the logic advanced for equating MMPI first factor with social desirability can be adopted to arrive at totally opposite conclusion that the first factor of MMPI represents a personality dimension that is vital to an understanding of the SD scale.

PGI Health Questionnaire N-2

We are describing the PGI Health Questionnaire as an example of empirical approach but are aware of the fact that test constructors often fail to adhere to a single strategy which would be most appropriate to the purpose of test construction. We have described the JMPI as an example of rational theoretical approach because it did not make use of different criterion groups for item selection. Now we are describing N-2 as an example of empirical approach in spite of the fact that N-2 is made up internally consistent rather than heterogeneous items. This questionnaire devised by Verma and Wig (1976), is a measure of neurotisism in simple Hindi. It is an improvement over PGI N-1 which was mainly Hindi version of Cornell Medical Index, CMI, (Broadman, Erdman and Wolf, 1949). The N-2 Questionnaire was constructed because: (1) items of N-1 were suspected to be specific to the culture of the U.S.A. where the CMI was developed; they were not spontaneously reported complaints of neurotic patients among people of India; (2) there was no provision of lie scale which is indispensable for the detection of tendency to give socially desirable responses; (3) there were 38 items in the N-1 with the result that low scorers were not discriminated from each other and high scorers could not get high score due to inadequate ceiling.

The N-1 and N-2 Questionnaires were named as Health Questionnaires because subjects were found to be more cooperative if they were made to believe that they were giving responses to questions about their health rather than to the questions apparently related to their present problems. As regards the definition of neurotisism, Verma and Wig (1977) quoted the following definition given by Cattell (1965), "those personality characteristics which actually differ significantly between judged neurotics and normals". For the authors of N-2 Questionnaire, normals are those not seeking active psychiatric help at present nor they sought in the past. Both definitions are suitable for the empirical approach to test development.

The items included in the N-2 Questionnaire were obtained from two sources:

(a) Symptoms reported by departmental heads and senior consultants of different special clinics and medical units of the Nehru Hospital. Every unit/department was requested to give a list of five complaints which adult neurotic patients have been communicating to them. The symptoms were to be listed in Hindi or Punjabi.

(b) Case records of patients attending the psychiatric clinics of the Nehru Hospital during January 1971 and December 1971 (one calendar year). Out of 587 neurotic patients in the year 1971 there were 349 patients for whom the records of complaints in their own words were available and they became the source of initial pool of items for N-2.

The above two sources provided 70 good items but in the initial try outs 50 items related to neurotisism and 10 items related to the tendency to lie were tried out on 65 normal volunteers and 35 neurotics in age range 10 to 39 years. The subjects were required to mark those items which were applicable to them and to leave those items which were not applicable to them. Much difference was observed in the mean scores of the two groups on the set of neurotic items (Normal male mean =7.86, normal female mean =8.06; neurotics mean =28.51). The mean of Lie scores for the two groups were 3.67 and 4.94, respectively. The scores were also found to have high correlation with other measures of neurotisism.

For item analysis data were collected from 300 normals and 100 neurotics. The internal consistency of items was determined using Moray House E1/3 method described in the Publication No. 6 of the Bureau of Psychology Allahabad. For the calculation of E1/3 values for each item the subjects' scripts were arranged in descending order of their scores and divided into six parts S_1, S_2, S_3, S_4, S_5, and S_6. Item analysis chart was prepared showing frequency of item endorsement by the subjects belonging to each part. In addition to the criteria of comprehensiveness and practical consideration, three different criteria could be used for item selection. The most important quantitative criterion is the calculation of E1/3:

$$E1/3 = \frac{(S_1+S_2) - (S_5+S_6)}{N/3}$$

Where S_1, S_2, S_3, S_4, S_5, S_6 refer to frequency of item endorsement in the part of the sample specified by the subscript and N is the Number the sample size.

The value of E1/3 is roughly equal to Phi coefficient. All the 50 items of the neurotic set were found to be satisfactory not only on the basis of difference in percentage of endorsement by normals and neurotics but also on the basis E1/3 index. Three different methods of determining reliability were employed for finding the reliability of PGI

Health Questionnaire N-2. The coefficient of reliability (Flangan's formula) was found to be .84 for the N scale and .92 for the L scale. Coefficients of internal consistency for N and L parts were found to be .95 and .91 respectively. The test-retest reliability calculated for a sample of 65 neurotics was found to be .83 for N and .76 for the L scale. The fact that mean score of the neurotic group was found to be three and a half times as high as of the normal group is presented as the evidence of the validity of the scale. A table of norms is provided for converting raw scores into standard scores with mean of 50 and SD. of 10.

The PGI N-2 scale is an instrument which can be administered on those who are not well educated and who would be disgusted if they have to answer a lengthy questionnaire. But it cannot do more than differentiating neurotics from normals. One has to interview the person to decide whether he is suffering from anxiety neurosis or hysteria. Moreover, in spite of the fact that the test constructors were interested in developing criterion-related instrument, they relied more on item-total correlation analysis than on the discriminative index of the items. In the process of developing the instrument the authors of the questionnaire could use all the good 70 items so as to have 50 good items instead of retaining every item they subjected to item analysis.

5

Factor Analytic Approach to Personality Assessment

Like rational-theoretical approach, factor analytic approach is interested in developing internally consistent scale in which items are homogeneous. But unlike the former, it does not rely on the common sense or theoretical insight of the test constructor in deciding what is to be measured and what items are to be used for the measurement. Moreover, while rational-theoretical approach does not go beyond ascertaining internal consistency of items, factor analytic approach requires that all items in a scale should have one common source of variance. Factor analytic approach is used in devising scales which measure unitary traits.

We can illustrate the meaning of unitary trait with the help of analogy of a closed box containing pure gold. In this analogy item is like box and gold is like a unitary trait. We can think of another box which contains a mixture of gold, stone, coal, iron, silver, etc. Continuing with the analogy we can put only one thing in the box but this preplanned loading of a trait in items is not possible. At the best we can guess what is indicated by different items and then using factor analysis can ascertain whether our guess is correct. The job of factor analysis is to discover the clusters of items sharing the same source of variance and saturation of individual items on the discovered source of variance.

Factor Analysis

Factor analysis is a multivariate statistical method which

makes use of co-variance of variables to find out how apparently different variables can be reduced to minimum possible number of variables preserving all original underlying sources of variance. It helps in removing redundancy in measurement by simplifying complex and diverse relationship existing among a set of variables which are seemingly unrelated but linked through common sources of variance. Factor analysis answers the question as to how many minimum essential dimensions are required to describe certain kind of objects. We know that a line can be described in terms of only one dimension (length), a paper in terms of two dimensions (length and breadth), and a room in terms of three dimensions (length, breadth and height). We cannot see a space having more than three dimensions but mathematically a space of more than three dimensions is possible. What is achieved by factor analysis by way of reducing the number of variables, is shown below. Let there be six variables X_1, X_2, X_3, X_4, X_5, and X_6. Two hypothetical structures of relationship among the six variables are as below:

Three-Factor Solution			**Two-Factor Solution**	
Factor I	Factor II	Factor III	Factor I	Factor II
X_1	X_3	X_1	X_1	X_2
X_2	X_4	X_2	X_3	X_5
X_5	X_5	X_3	X_4	X_6
X_6	X_6	X_6		

The three-factor solution classified the variables in three clusters. It is to be noted that except X_4 all the variables occur in more than one cluster. The two-factor solution shown above classifies the variables in two clusters so that every variable has loading on only one factor. Obviously this solution more 'simple' than three-factor solution.

It is easier to explain the nature of factor analysis with the help of geometrical/trignometric representations. Correlation between any two variables can be represented as angle of separation between the vectors representing the two variables. A vector is a line that has a given length and direction. The relation of co-efficient of correlation with vectors and the angle of separation between the vectors is given by the following equation derived by Thurstone (Guilford, 1954, p. 483):

$$r_{ij} = h_i h_j \cos\Phi_{ij}$$

Where r_{ij} = correlation between variables i and j

hi, hj = legth of vectors of variables i anf j

Φ = angle of separation between vectors i and j.

If both h_i and h_j are equal to 1 the entire correlation is determined by angle of separation between the variables. The cosine of angles is a ratio obtained by dividing the base by hypotenuse (b/h). The value of cosine falls in the range of 0 to 1.0. It is 1.0 for 0°, 0 for 90°, and –1 for 180°. When separation between vectors exceeds 90°, the value of cosine becomes negative.

If we have all possible correlations among a set of variables (in the case of six variables there will be 15 rs) we can make angles between the vectors of all pairs of variables and then cut them with the help of a pair of scissors. The relationship between the variables may be such that the sectors representing the relationship may or may not be put together in two-dimensional space. The number of dimensions required to join the sectors are the number of factors required to describe the underlying structure. Once the underlying dimensions are identified, variables can be described as points located in the space generated by the dimensions. Each variable shall need as many reference points for the description as there are dimensions. If many variables have same location in the dimensional space then one of the variable can represent the cluster.

There are two basic assumptions of factor analysis:

Assumption 1: A set of intercorrelated variables has common factors running through them so that an individual's scores can be represented more economically in terms of these common factors (Frutcher, 1967). We can represent an individual's standard score on a test j (P_{ji}) as sum of the products of individual's score on each uncorrelated trait measured by the variable and factor loading of the variable j on the trait. Let P_{ji} represent an individual standard score on the test J, a_{j1}, a_{j2}.......a_{jk} factor loadings of test J on the factors running through it, X_{1i}, X_{2i},........ X_{Ki} as individual's standard scores on the traits (factors) underlying the scores of the individual on the factors running through the variable J. The assumption can be expressed by the equation:

$$P_{aji} = a_{ji} X_{1i} + a_{j2} X_{2i} + \ldots\ldots\ldots a_{jk} X_{ki}$$

The above expression seems to make the task of assessment more troublesome because score on one test is to be broken into a number of components. However, the redundancy-reducing nature of factor analysis shall be appreciated later on.

It is to be pointed out that underlying common factors do not account for the total variance of a variable. The total variance of a variable may be divided into three parts:

Common Variance: The part of reliable variance of the measure which correlates with other variables is known as common variance.

Specific Variance (s): The proportion of reliable variance of a measure which does not correlates with other variables is known as specific variance.

Error Variance (e): Chance variance due to such sources of error as sampling, measurement, non-standardization of conditions of testing, physiological and other changes within the individual, and other influences which contribute to unreliability of the measure are collectively known as error variance. Error variance is assumed to be correlated with reliable variance.

The terms defined above help us to understand not only the first and second assumptions but also other terms used in factor analysis such as factor loadings or saturations which are square root of common variance; communality (h) of a variable which is sum of independent common variances; and uniqueness (U) of a variable which is the portion of total variance due to specific variance and error variance and is not shared with any other variable. It can be obtained by subtraction of common variance from the total variance taken to be 1.

Assumption II: The second basic assumption of factor analysis is that correlation between two variables j and k can be considered to be contributed by the nature and extent of their common factor loadings. It is sum of product of loadings of J and K on the common factors (Frutcher, 1967):

$$r_{jk} = a_{j1}\, a_{k1} + a_{j2}\, a_{k2} + \ldots\ldots\; a_{jn}\, a_{kn}$$

Factor analysis can be used for exploratory as well as for confirmatory purposes. When we do not know how many independent dimensions are needed to describe something, e.g. personality, we can start with measuring the objects in all possible respects and then can do factor analysis to determine the number of dimensions required to account for the variance shared by the measures. We may have some theoretical hypotheses regarding the nature of dimensions required for the proper description of a set of objects and then proceed to verify whether the matrix of intercorrelation among the measures correspond to the hypothetical factors. Factor analysis carried out for the first purpose is known as exploratory factor analysis; factor analysis carried out for the second purpose is known as confirmatory analysis.

There can be one more way of classifying factor analysis depending on the nature of intercorrelation matrix. In the most frequently used R analysis, the matrix of intercorrelation is obtained by first measuring sample of subjects in respect of a number of variables and then finding intercorrelation among the measures. In Q kind of analysis we discover how persons (not variables) covary. We, therefore, start with matrix of intercorrelation among subjects and then analyze this matrix to find clusters of individuals. The P type of analysis helps us to study fluctuation within a single individual. The subjects are assessed with respect to a number of variables not once but at different occasions (for example, every 10th day) and then correlation among the variables measured at different times is obtained and used in factor analysis.

Steps in Factor Analysis. Factor analysis involves obtaining intercorrelation among the variables, making choice of method of factor analysis, estimation of communalities, decision regarding number of factors to be retained, rotation of axes, and interpretation of factors. Let us consider each step in some detail:

Matrix of Intercorrelation

The most popular method (which is also most satisfactory method) of calculation of intercorrelation among the continuous variables is Pearson's Product Moment Correlation (r). Most consistent results are obtained when the distributions of measures are normalized. However, raw scores can also be used and satisfactory results can be obtained if the assumptions underlying the r are satisfied. Biserial and Rank Order correlations may also be used as the estimate of Product Moment Correlation (Frutcher, 1967, p. 201). Tetrachoric coefficient can be used when sample is large and splits on variables are not too extreme. With certain corrections for removing the effect of difference in split, Phi coefficient can also be used. But in no circumstances more than one kind of correlation is to be used to get a matrix to be factorized.

Choice of Method of Analysis

From amongst the available methods one has to select the method of analysis which serves his purpose best. The Centoroid, Principal axes, Maximum Likelihood, Little Jiffy, Minimum Residual Analysis, Rao's Canonical factoring, Alpha Analysis, and Image Analysis are well-known methods of factor analysis. Computer software packages, SPSS, BMDP, and SAS are available for most of these methods. According to Dillon and Goldstein (1984, p. 85) two general conclusions can be drawn regarding the comparability of different methods:

1. All methods lead to identical results if communalities of the variables are closed to 1.

2. If the matrix of intercorrelation to be factorized has large number of variables, the estimation of communalities and choice of factor analysis procedure assume less importance.

Estimation of Communalities

The diagonals of a matrix of intercorrelation have to have the values of correlations of variables with themselves. The decision to estimate the correlation of a variable with itself is related to the choice of method of factor analysis. We have already referred to the fact that each variable is made up of two parts, common variance and unique variance and also to the fact that the communality of a variable is related to the variance shared by a variable with other variables. It is, therefore, evident that the estimation of communalities of different variables is an important step. Dillon and Goldstein (1984) have mentioned two approach to the estimation of communalities:

(1) Approach in which only few of the correlations are used,

(2) Methods which utilize the entire correlation matrix.

The first approach includes the use of highest observed correlation of the variable in the diagonal. This method is not found to be useful for small-order correlation matrices. Estimation of communality of a variable using two variables which correlate highest with the variable and average correlation of the variables with other variables in the matrix of intercorrelation are the methods suggested by Dillon and Goldstein (1984, p.72). The first of the two methods can give rise to estimation of communality more than unity. In such a case communality is set at .99 or 1.0.

Two methods that make use of the entire matrix of intercorrelation are the use of squared multiple correlation of a variable with all the remaining variables in the matrix and the iterative procedure in which the first analysis uses unity or any other estimate and communalities obtained after the first analysis are used in the second analysis. The procedure is to be repeated again and again until communalities do not change.

Number of Factors to be Retained

To understand the problem of number of factors to be retained we can use the analogy of the process of sifting what is substantive from what is waste/impure/unknown. The analogy would become more applicable if it is added that the person who is to sift is not told what is to be regarded as useful. In such a situation the decision to continue with the extraction of factor or to retain certain number of factors is to be based on:

(1) contribution of a factor in accounting for the common variance, and

(2) ascertaining whether the residual does or does not contains variance which is due to chance, errors of sampling, errors of measurement, unstandardized conditions of testing, physiological and other changes within the individual, and other sources of unreliability.

One of the popular criteria used in decision regarding number of factors to be retained is "root greater than one" criterion originally suggested by Kaiser (1958). According to this criterion all factors which have more than 1 Eigen value are to be retained. The rationale of the criterion is that any factor should account for more variance than any single variable in the standardized test score space.

Another well-known procedure for deciding the number

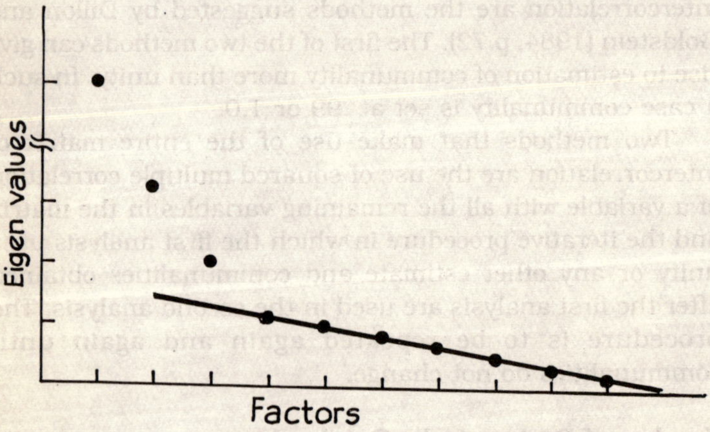

The scree test

of factors to be retained is the Scree test suggested by Cattell (1966). The test is named after rubble at the bottom of a cliff. In this test all Eigen values are plotted in order of their determination in the process of extraction. The graph is observed to identify the point of infliction which is the point at which an elbow in the curve is noted. One can identify this point by going to the bottom portion of the curve of Eigen values to see where they form straight line. There are two problems in using the Scree test: (1) There may be no obvious point of infliction, (2) there may be several breaks making it difficult to decide which break reflects the correct number of factors.

Horn's (1965) procedure removes the difficulties associated with the Scree test. The procedure is described by Dillon and Goodstein (1984).

Rotation of Axes

Extraction of factors is to be followed by rotation of axes. Factorization locates the axes without consideration of meaningfulness of clusters of variables on a factor. The purpose of rotation is to relocate axes from the arbitrary location determined by the method of analysis to the position which makes the factors more interpretable. This is achieved by making factors less complicated by minimizing the loadings of some variables and minimizing the loadings of other variables. Thurstone (1947) has given the following criteria for simple structure:

1. Each variable should have one loading close to zero.
2. There should be as many variables with zero loadings on a factor as there are factors.
3. When every pair of factors are considered, there should be several variables with sizable loadings on one member of the pair but not on the other.
4. When four or more factors are extracted from a matrix of intercorrelation, a large number of variables should have negligible loading on any pair of factors.
5. On any pair of factors only small number of variables should have substantive loadings.

While rotating axes one can make choice between orthogonal and oblique rotations. In orthogonal rotation the factors are placed at right angle of each other. This yields a rotated factor matrix in which factors are uncorrelated among themselves. When factor axes are not kept at right angle and are rotated independently of each other we have oblique rotation.

Different methods of performing orthogonal and oblique rotation are available. Three popular methods are Varimax, Quartimax, and Equimax. They differ in defining what constitute the simple structure. The most popular method is the Varimax which seeks to rotate axes so that the variation of the squared factor loadings for a given factor is made large. Computer program for Varimax rotation is available in SPSS, BMDP, and SAS packages.

Five popular algorithms for oblique rotation are: Oblimax, Quartimax, Covarimin, Biquartim, and Oblimin. Covariam is oblique analog of Varimax.

Many factor analysts do not regard simple structure as the best choice for the rotation of axes. Rotation can be performed to achieve the following:

1. To bring factors in agreement with clinical findings/psychological hypotheses.

2. To locate axes to agree with the successfully established factors.

3. To produce the pattern of loading congruent with general psychological expectations.

Eysenck (1952) is one of the most important critic of rotation of axes to simple structure when factor analysis is employed to discover the dimensions of temperament, character, attitudes, interests, and so forth. He observed that an investigator in the field of personality who has not much knowledge about what is to be measured cannot afford to take a number of variables and intercorrelate them in an effort to bring order out of chaos (p. 69). According to Eysenck (1952) there are two alternatives for the discovery of 'psychologically real influences' with the help of factor analysis:

1. Devising possible ways of overdetermining the analy-

sis of the given correlation matrix so that only one set of real factors emerge.

2. Propound a psychological hypothesis about what source traits are operating in the variables and then determining how far the factors can correspond to the hypothetical dimensions.

Cattell (1946) prefers the first alternative. He points out that in the absence of well-defined procedures and guidelines for testing the hypothesis invented about a particular factor, factorization attempted to match the hypothesis would lead to nothing except the confirmation of hypothesis. Cattell (1946), therefore, suggested reliance on general guiding principles for the mathematical analysis to get a unique solution. Recognizing the difficulty in hypothetico-deductive method of analysis but still believing that progress in the study of dimensions of personality depends on the invention of hypothesis, Eysenck (1952) evolved the procedure of "Criterion Analysis" which is a combination of hypothetico-deductive method and factor analysis. In this method two criterion groups (for example, normals and neurotics) are taken and their responses to the same set of items (which are expected to discriminate between the two groups) are separately subjected to correlational analysis. The two matrices are used for the extraction of factors. Correlations between the criterion and each one of the items are also obtained to get the entries of the 'criterion column'. The factors loadings found in two analyses are tabulated side by side along the item-criterion correlations.

The columns of factor loadings and the criterion column are closely scrutinized so as to find the pairs of factors on which the items have similar pattern of loadings for certain pairs of factors. Having discovered the similarity of the pattern of loadings for certain pairs of factors, item-criterion correlation entered in the criterion columns are also considered. The correlation between the criterion column (i.e. correlations of each of the items with the dichotomy of the criterion) and loadings of the factor specified to match the hypothetical dimension gives the evidence of correspondence of extracted factor(s) to hypothetico-deductive dimension involved in the dichotomy.

Interpretation of the Factors

Factor analysis provides mathematical answer to the question in how many groups given variables can be put on the basis of their sharing a common source of variance? It also answer the related question, what are the variables which have high loading on a factor? Once these questions are answered, we have to understand psychological nature of the extracted factors. At this stage we are guided by our rational consideration and theoretical insight. The attempt to understand the nature of extracted factors begins with the perusal of the matrix of factor loading obtained after the rotation of axes. We can examine each column of factor matrix and then encircle all the substantive loadings in that column. We then prepare a list of variables in order of the magnitude of their loadings on the factor. If we have included some markers in the variable used in factorization, we can interpret a factor with the help of the markers which are found to have high loading on the factor. As pointed out earlier, markers are those variables whose psychological nature is known because in previous studies they were found to have substantive loadings on a recognizable factor. When marker variables are not used or when they are not helpful in understanding the nature of extracted factors, we have to understand the psychological substance of the variables with high loading on a factor and then name the factor in the light of our understanding. However, this naming is only tentative. Correlational and experimental studies have to follow for the collection of evidence of the construct validity of the scales comprising items with high loading on the factors which they have to represent. It is to be noted that "The procedure of naming factors is always rational or clinical and empirical validity evidence must be accumulated before it can be concluded that behaviour domain involved in the factor is same as that typically described by that name". (Lanyon & Goodstein, 1971, p. 86).

Factor Scales

The purpose of this section is to describe personality questionnaires developed by R. B. Cattell and H. J. Eysenck not only because the questionnaires developed by them are most widely used but also because they are the examples of American and British traditions of the use of factor analysis in the construction of personality questionnaires. While describing the scales we will be able to mention the steps in the construction of personality questionnaire which can be followed by any one who is interested in the following factor analytic approach. Before we present the description we would acknowledge the contribution of others in applying factor analysis for the study of personality.

Among those who used the approach for the study of personality are: Guilford and his associates, Thurstone, and the collaborators of Cattell, and Eysenck. Doing factor analysis of questionnaire items, Guilford and his associates developed three separate inventories of factors: STDGR (Guilford, 1940), GAMIN (Guilford and Martin, 1943a) and the Personnel Inventory (Guilford and Martin, 1943b). A single inventory covering ten of thirteen traits of the original three inventories was developed by Guilford and Zimmerman (1949). The instrument is known as the Guilford-Zimmerman Temperament survey. It covers general activity, restrain vs. rhathimia, ascandance, sociability, emotional stability, objectivity, friendliness, thoughtfulness, personal relations, and masculinity. There are also two empirically derived falsification scales similar to validity scales of MMPI.

Thurstone (1949, 1951) Temperament Schedule is based on factor analysis of Guilford's data. Thurstone found that only seven instead of thirteen factors identified by Guilford were sufficient to describe personality.

Sixteen Personality Factor Questionnaire (16 PF)

The 16 PF is an omnibus instrument containing sixteen scales. The factors were initially identified in the L medium and then in Q and T media. The questionnaire can be used for the measurement of sixteen primary and eight secondary factors. The construction of the 16 PF was undertaken after the discovery of primary source traits of personality by Cattell (1946, 1947, 1948, 1950) who insisted measurement of personality traits is to follow the discovery of the source trait of personality. Source traits are the underlying unitary entities that cause surface manifestations of behaviour. Surface traits are clusters of observable attributes encoded in the ordinary language.

The whole design of the instrument and its parallels at younger age such as HSPQ, CPQ, is different from the questionnaires which measure rationally defined characteristics, e.g., Adjustment. It is also different from inventories of surface traits or syndrome, e.g. MMPI. The research that lead to the discovery of source traits measured by the 16 PF was guided by certain canons to ensure that factors appear in all the three media, they are found over the whole development range and are independent of any preconception about the personality structure. In addition to its anchoring in fundamental research, the 16 PF has the following features (Cattell, Eber and Tatsuoka, 1970):

1. *Comprehensiveness.* The 16 primary and eighteen secondary factors provide all the information which one would like to have in placing an individual in the dimensional space of personality. In the interest of comprehensiveness of coverage of personality it is advisable that the practitioners in applied field attack the problem with a "wide net" instead of focusing on certain traits.

2. *Availability of predictive information.* Research centered on primary personality factors, their age trends, their origin in heredity and environmental influences, their response to therapy, their effect on interpersonal processes make the instrument useful for the prediction of certain criteria with theoretical confidence and understanding. Systematic research has accumulated profile types and specification equations for various clinical diagnostic and prognostic groups and occupations.

3. *Linkage of 16 PF with parallel forms at younger age.* Studies on developmental continuation of trait structure

have provided the linkage of the 16 PF with its parallel forms at younger age levels such as High School Personality Questionnaire (HSPQ), Child Personality Questionnaire (CPQ), Early School Personality Questionnaire (ESPQ), and Pre-School Personality Questionnaire (ESPQ).

4. *Continuity of research towards improving the instruments.* During decades of research on personality and its measurement by Cattell and his collaborators not only reliabilities and validities of the scales have been improved but six different forms of the test A, B, C, D, E and F are made available. The vocabulary demand for the different forms vary from ordinary newspaper-literate adults to very simple less than that of average adult. With the availability of different forms one can improve reliability and validity of the test by using more than one form.

Construction of 16 PF. As pointed out earlier, the construction of the 16 PF followed the study of structure of personality. To discover the unknown source traits of personality, Cattell (1946) conducted factor analysis of ratings of subjects on trait descriptive terms in English language. His logic was that words contained in a dictionary refer to the individual differences perceived by the common man generation after generations. Reducing Allport-Odberts' (1936) list of 4,500 trait names, taken from the Webster unabridged dictionary, to 171 terms, Cattell did cluster analysis that led to the identification of 35 surface traits.

The surface trait variables were expressed as bipolar rating scales. Factor analysis of the L data generated with the help of the rating scales led to the identification of fourteen factors. Cattell proceeded to verify the existence of the fourteen factors and the discovery of other factors operating in the questionnaire medium. The research on self-rating personality descriptions from which the 16 PF emerged was based on the population of items derived from:

1. A survey of all well-known questionnaires, value, and interest scales which led to the discovery of 20 factors as of 1946.

2. A pool of items covering 15 factors that were emerged

in the study of the L data.

An initial pool of 1,800 self-descriptive items collected from the above two sources was put to "parceled factor analysis" and the extracted factors were rotated to oblique simple structure. The analysis led to the verification of most of the L factors and other factors hypothesized on the basis of the survey. There were seven factors which were not found in the L data. However, Cattell preferred to include in the test twelve factors which emerged in both L and Q media and four factors which were struck only in the Q medium. Research is going on for the extension of the test in the pursuit of the "seven missing factors".

To have 10 to 13 items per factor scale, form A and B, additional items were picked up from items known to correlate with the factor in the survey or by item analysis against the separate factors. Attempt to improve the measurement of factors continued by rechecking the factor structure by cross validation and intensification. The term intensification is borrowed from photography to refer to the process of raising the saturation of items on the required factor and reducing irrelevant correlations. The following canons were followed in the construction of revised (1956) version of the 16 PF:

1. A large pool of items is contributed by six people in the light of all that is known about the number and nature of primary personality factors.

2. The items are submitted to two persons of different background to eliminate uncommon words and the terms that are too long, ambiguous, or tied to matters too specific in place and time.

3. Two population samples are taken, one from upper and another from lower half of the range for which the test is intended. Separate correlation matrices are obtained for the two halves.

4. Items with extreme cuts (under 10 per cent in one end category of the three) in either samples are eliminated before the calculation of correlation matrices.

5. The two matrices are separately factored and rotated

to simple structure.

6. Items are picked up for each factor having highest loadings on the required factor and if possible suppressing loading on other factors.

7. To get suitable mean and variance and grading on each factor, the cuts (alternative response frequencies) must be examined. The choice of items by cuts should give means that is central on the scale range and should provide maximum scatter as well as equal means and variances for A and B forms.

8. An even balance of 'Yes' and 'No' answers must be chosen from surviving items to score positively on each factor to avoid response set effect.

9. The items should be symmetrically divided between forms A and B as to factor loading, mean, variance, 'Yes' and 'No' answers etc. as determined above.

10. The scale must be standardized with the usual attention to stratified sampling.

In view of limited capacity of the computer available in 1956 to handle a very large matrix, all the 347 items of the old and 126 new items were parceled into 75 groups. There were 30 parcels of old and 45 parcels of new items. The 75 × 75 matrix was centroid factored and rotated to simple structure with great care. Items of old 16 PF which had correlation of .2 or less on the old and new factoring were replaced by better items. The 16 PF measures the following factors:

Factors	*U.I.No.*	*Low Sten (1-3) Description*	*High Sten (8-9) Description*
A	U.I. (L&Q)1	Sizothymia A, A- (Reserved, Detached, Critical, Aloof, Stiff)	Affectothymia, A+ (Warmhearted, Outgoing, Easygoing, Participating)
B	U.I.(L&Q)2	Low Intelligence, B- (Crystallized, Power Measure, Dull)	High Intelligence, B+ (Crystallized, Power Measure, Bright)

C	U.I.(L&Q)3	Ego Weakness or Emotional Instability, C- (Affected by Feelings Emotionally Less Stable, Easily Upset, Changeable)	Higher Ego Strength, C+ (Emotionally Stable, Mature, Faces Reality, Calm)
E	U.I.(L&Q)5	Submissiveness, E- (Obedient, Mild, Easily Led, Docile, Accommodating)	Dominance or Ascendance, E+ (Assertive, Aggressive, Competitive, Stubborn)
F	U.I.(L&Q)6	Desurgency, F- (Sober, Taciturn, Serious)	Surgency, F+ (Enthusiastic, Heedless, Happy-go-lucky)
G	U.I.(L&Q)7	Low Super Ego Strength or Lack of Acceptance of Group Moral Standards, G- (Disregards Rules, Expedient)	Super Ego Strength or Character, G+ (Conscientious, Persistent, Moralistic, Staid)
H	U.I.(L&Q)8	Threctia, H-(Shy, Timid, Restrained, Threat-sensitive)	Parmia, H+ (Adventurous, "Thick-skinned", Socially Bold)
I	U.I.(L&Q)9	Harria, I- (Tough-minded, Rejects Illusions)	Premsia, I+ (Tender-minded, Sensitive, Dependent, Overprotected)
L	U.I.(L&Q)12	Alaxia, L- (Trusting, Accepting Conditions)	Protension, L+ (Suspecting, Jealous)
M	U.I.(L&Q)13	Praxernia, M- (Practical, Has down to earth concerns)	Autia, M+ (Imaginative, Bohemian, Absent-minded)

N	U.I.(L&Q)14	Naivete, N- (Forthright, Unpretentious)	Shrewdness, N+ (Astute, Worldly)
O	U.I.(L&Q)15	Untroubled Adequacy, O- (Self-assured, Placid, Secure, Complacent)	Guilt proneness, O+ (Apprehensive, Self-reproaching, Insecure, Worrying, Troubled)
Q1	U.I.(Q)16	Conservatism of Temperament, Q1- (Conservative, Respecting Established Ideas, Tolerant of Traditional Difficulties)	Radicalism, Q1+ (Experimenting, Liberal, Analytical, Free-thinking)
Q2	U.I.(Q)17	Group Dependency, Q2- (Socially Group Dependent, A "joiner" and Sound Follower)	Self-Sufficiency, Q2+ (Self-Sufficient, Resourceful, Prefers, Own Decisions)
Q3	U.I.(Q)18	Low Self-Sentiment Integration, Q3- (Uncontrolled, Lax, Follows Own Urges, Careless of Social Rules)	High Strength of Self-Sentiment, Q3+ (Controlled, Exacting Will Power, Socially Precise, Compulsive, Following Self-Image)
Q4	U.I.(Q)19	Low Ergic Tension, Q4- (Relaxed, Tranquil, Torpid, Unfrustrated, Composed)	High Ergic Tension, Q4+ (Tense, Frustrated, Driven, Overwrought, Fretful)

The labeling of factors is done at two levels: (1) the technical terminology, giving new acronymic names to new concepts; (2) universal index for each factor using numbers to name or describe it. The factors are listed according to amount of variance accounted by them.

The scores on the primary factor scales can be combined to obtained what Catteli, Eber and Tatsuoka (1970) prefer to call second-stratum rather than second-order factors. The second-stratum factors may be viewed as broader influences contributing for the intercorrelation among primaries. Some of these factors emerged as primary factors in the analysis of objective tests. One can also obtain scores for the third-stratum factors which account for inter-correlation among second-stratum factors. Thus, it is possible to bring out personality structure as a series of strata, twenty to thirty factors at the primary stratum, seven to a dozen at second stratum, and four or so at the third stratum. The following is the list of second-stratum factors measured by the 16 PF test:

Standard Index	*Bipolar Title*	*Chief Primaries Involved*
QI	Invia-vs.-Exvia	A+, E+, F+, H+
QII	Adjustment-vs.-Anxiety	C-, H-, L+, O+, Q3-, Q4+
QIII	Pathemia-vs.-Cortertia	A-, I-, M- (E+, L+,)*
QIV	Subdueness-vs.-Independence	E+, L+, M+, Q1+, Q2+
QV	Naturalness-vs.-Discreteness	N+ (A+, M-, O–)*
QVI	Cool Realism-vs.-Prodigal Subjectivity	I+, M+, L-
QVII	Low Intelligence-vs.-High Intelligence	B+
QVIII	Low Super Ego-vs.-Superego/ Strength.	G+, Q3+, F-

* For women in addition to primaries not included in parenthesis.

Forms A, B, C and D of the 16 PF have provided three response options and accordingly scoring is done by assigning 0, 1 or 2 score except for Factor B, intelligence, where scoring is 0 or 1. For items comprising forms E and F scoring is 0 or 1. Generally, total raw score for a factor is obtained by adding score assigned to response to all the items contained in the factor scale. However, it is possible to weight every item according to the V_{fe} (Beta) weight assigned to it from its correlations with each factor. A simpler method, known as computer synthesis method, is proposed for scoring in which each factor is scored on the items in its own scale and all other scales are also weighted to get the factor scores. Necessary tables for weighting scores in sten are provided to get computer synthesis scores in sten, (Cattell, Eber, and Tatsuoka, 1970). Sten scores of an individual are multiplied by values indicated by column heading listed in each column to get his computer synthesized score for the source traits.

Reducing the effect of sabotage and motivational distortion

While a detailed account of different sources of contamination of scores are discussed in a separate chapter, we have to discuss the ways of dealing with different sources of response distortion in the case of the 16 PF. Cattle, Eber and Tatsuoka (1970) have distinguished three different sources of response distortion in self-evaluation Q data: (a) deliberate sabotage which occurs if the subjects select response alternatives randomly or make an attempt to deceive; (2) unconscious motivational distortion occurs when the subject assumes a particular test taking role, e.g., as a patient or candidate for a job; (3) ignorance about himself, e.g., vague self-concept. In addition to the three kinds of response distortions, the instrument used for assessment contributes method variance which can be found with the help of multitrait-multimethod analysis proposed by Campbell and Fisk (1959).

Detection of Sabotage. Assuming that attempt to sabotage the testing programme will be evident in the spatial regularity which makes no psychological sense, Cattell, Eber and Tatsuoka (1970) suggested the following procedure to find whether sabotage has brought out significant change in an individual's score:

1. Obtain an individual's sten scores on each of the 16 PF factors by spliting the scales into halves A and B (or odd number and even number items)

2. Estimate the score on the second (or even) part as below:

$$\dot{B} = Ar + 5.51\ (1 - r),$$

where A is the score on the first part.

r is the correlation between the two halves which can be taken as .45 if actual coefficient is not known.

3. Obtain $\dot{B}$ - B = d

Where B is the score on the second part.

4. Find the sum of d for each factor; $S = \Sigma d^2$

5. Sabotage is suggested at

5% level if S > 83

1% level if S > 102. (both for r = .45)

Motivational Distortion. According to Cattell, Eber, and Tatsuoka (1970) motivational distortion is to be regarded as skill in playing various roles. These skills can be measured with the help of motivational-skill tests and are be regarded as source traits (TRs) beyond the factors measured by the 16 PF. Distortion d, in situation J for individual i, on source trait x can be conceived as:

$$D_{xij} = b_{j1}\ T_{1i} + \ldots + b_{jk}\ T_{ki} + b_{jR}\ T_{Rj1} + C_{xj}$$

Where R_j is the role, e.g., a patient, or job applicant, which is simulated in situation j, and C_{xj} is a constant showing average distortion by every one in that situation.

The specification equation given above can be used only when a lot of research has been conducted to discover the constant C_x to be added or subtracted for each major type of situation (J). Based on Meredith's (1986) data a table is provided for estimating the extent of distortion due to major sources: (a) maximum faking to give socially desirable responses; (b) bending self-concept to fit the "ideal self". The C and D forms of the 16 PF contain MD items to provide the MD scores to be used as temporary device of rough correction. The MD items are those items which: (a) themselves show shift from anonymous to job-seeking situation, and (b) correlate most with the shifts on the primary factors in the same situational change. The factors which are found to change most are A+, C+, F+, G+, H+, L-, M-, O-, Q2+, Q3+, and Q4-.

Standardization

The groups employed for standardization of the 16 PF are: (1) American adult; (2) Undergraduate university students, and (3) High school seniors. The samples were obtained with stratification according to (a) social status, (b) geographical area, (c) age, and (d) urban rural distinction. Percentage of subjects in each combination of the four categories was the same as in U.S. Census.

Tables are provided for converting raw scores to normalized standard ten (n-sten) scores which have a mean of 5.5 and standard deviation of 2. The n-sten transformation ensures that population scores are normally distributed, Mean and Median coincide, and units are equal. In view of significance of difference in men and women, separate tables are provided for the two genders. The magnitude of age difference is not as much as sex differences and for this reason age corrections for raw scores are provided (Cattell, Eber, and Tatsuoka, 1970, p. 72)

Reliability and Validity

Different types of reliability coefficients reported for the 16 PF are:

Dependability coefficient is the correlation between the administration of a test when time lapse is less than sufficient for change to occur (4 to 7 days). The range of dependability coefficient for form A is .83 (for factor H) to .61 (for factor N). In the case of form B the range is from .89 (for factor H) to .60 (for factor N). Higher dependability coefficients are obtained when forms A and B are combined. Stability coefficient refers to the correlation between two administrations of the same test when interval between testing and retesting is sufficient for people themselves to change (2-3 months). It is found that traits Q3, M, N, and L are more liable to fluctuation with change in the psychological state than are others. Homogeneity is not regarded as a desirable characteristic of factor scales. Cattell and Tsujioka (1964) are of the opinion that homogeneity is to be kept down to a moderate or low level in the interest of suppressor action into factor scales and the avoidance of "blown-up specifics". Not much information is provided regarding transferability, i.e., consistency when the test is applied to different populations. The equivalence coefficients for test forms for nine of the sixteen traits are of moderate level.

Evidence is furnished regarding the three main forms of validity. Direct Concept (construct) validity. Indirect or Circumstantial Concept validity, and Concrete validity. A distinction is made between factor (concept) validity and trueness. While factor validity is indicated by the correlation of a factor scale with the pure measure of the factor, trueness is indicated by lack of contamination of the measure with other personality factors. Both concept validity and trueness can be determined with the help of comprehensive factor analysis. The range of coefficients of correlation of factor scales with the respective pure measure is .35 (scale B) to .92 (scale H), for form A; .40 (scale B) to .87 (scale H) for form B; .46 (for scale C) to .76 (scale E) for form C; and .54 (scale B) to .75 (scale Q1) for form D. Except for factors scales M,N,O, and Q2, of some of the forms, A, B, C, D, validity coefficients (correlation with pure factors) are as high as can be expected from the scales containing as many items as the scales have. It is to be pointed out that the main problem in factor-analytic test construction is the suppression of contaminating variance which undermine the validity of measures of different factors. The computer synthesis procedure and the method of "variance reallocation" can be used for dealing with the problem of contamination and enhancing validity of the scales (Cattle, Eber, and Tatsuoka, 1970, p. 37).

The indirect evaluation of conceptual validities of the 16 scales can be done by asking the following question in relation to each scale. "How well do the correlations of this scale with a representative sample of concrete natural criteria (or, simply, other diverse psychological variables) agree with those which the conceptual criterion itself is expected to have with these relevant variables?" (Cattle, Eber and Tatsuoka, 1970, p. 38). This procedure is like a detectives effort to verify the identity of an impostor. The detective has to put questions about the persons and places the real person is expected to know and the decision about the identity of suspected impostor would depend on whether answers of the individual are correct or incorrect. Generally we say that indirect evidence regarding the properties of A depend on A's relation with not-As. However, the problem is that the number of not-As is infinite. It is, therefore, suggested that (1) the scale in question be correlated with other scales, and (2) the correlations of the pure source trait measured by the scale with other pure factors are obtained. Now the relationship between the two sets of correlation coefficients is indirect evidence of the validity of sixteen scales. Cattell, Eber and Tatsuoka (1970) who used the above method have reported that except factors N (r = .63) and M (r = .74) all the coefficients of indirect validity are more than .80.

There can be no exhaustive evidence in regard to the concrete validities of the 16 PF test because the criteria to be predict are unlimited. However, the test has been used to predict many concrete performances — school achievement, clinical disorders, psychiatric disorders, etc. Cattell, Eber and Tatsuoka (1970) prefer to call concrete validity as relevancy. The three important methods for making the 16 factors scores useful for educational, industrial, and clinical practice are: Method of Profile Belonging, Specification Equation, and Adjustment Specification Equation. These methods are discussed below in detail.

Technique for Prediction and Diagnosis

In order to make proper use of factor scores, it is important for the psychologist to have insight into the nature and changing effects of the factors with time and circumstances. The insight combined with the statistical methods to be described lead to better decision about the person.

Adjustment or Type Placement Method

We can assess the suitability of a person for certain

occupation or classify him in certain diagnostic group by finding how far he is similar to the typical person in the occupation group or the diagnostic category. For this we have to obtain ideal profile of the occupational or diagnostic group. Usually the pattern of mean scores of the members of the group is used as an ideal profile. The index of profile similarity (r_p) can be found to determine the similarity of profiles to be compared. The adjustment method presumes that an optimum value exists on each factor score. The method does not provide information as to how much effective a person be in doing a job. The average profile of people already in an occupation may not be the profile of the best worker. The model of adjustment approach is easier and the approach is preferred by clinicians as it is applicable in a variety of situations.

Effectiveness or Fitness by Performance Method

Setting equations in which the predictors are sixteen-factor scores and the criteria are goodness of performance on different jobs, one can specify the performance in terms of weighted combination of the factors which determine each criterion. A typical specification equation is as below:

$$P_{ji} = b_{jA}\ T_{Ai} + b_{jB}\ T_{Bi} \ldots +B_{jQ4}\ T_{Q4i}\ (+\ b_j\ T_{ji})$$

Where P_{ji} is the performance of individual in situation j, b's are the loadings of factors, which are represented by T's.

T_j is put in parentheses for the reason that there is no way of finding i's score on it (in situation J) and for this reason P_{ji} is an estimate, not an exact figure. The value of T_{ji} is simply omitted in the calculation of P_{ji} (Cattle, Eber, and Tatsuoka, 1970).

The values of b's to be used in the equation can be obtained by doing criterion analysis. Criterion analysis involves factoring of the criterion measures along with predictor variables. Instead of factoring, one can determine the contribution of each variable with the help of following procedure: administer the 16 PF to the group for which the criterion measures are obtained; correlate each factor score with the criterion measure; now one can set multiple regression equation and get the weights for each factor score. However, weights obtained in this manner will be lower than those obtained by criterion analysis. Moreover, weights obtained with the help of criterion analysis are 'true' values (not affected by unreliability or in validity of the given factor scales. Such weights are permanently useful as they can be used with factor scores obtained with the help of better editions of factor scales. (Cattle, Eber, Tatsuoka, 1970, p. 147)

Adjustment Specification Equations

As adjustment equations are more difficult to obtain; we can have specifications on the basis of easier-to-obtain profile data. The steps in obtaining adjustment equations are as below:

1. Obtain Z_i by finding the difference in the mean of the criterion/X_i group and mean of the factor in general population U_i and divide this difference by the standard deviation of the factor score in the general population. When raw scores are converted into n-sten scores, the value of U_i is 5.5 and the value of S.D. is 2. Thus we have:

$$\Delta_i = \frac{\overline{X}_i - \mu_i}{2.0}$$

We shall have 16 values of Δ, Δ_1, Δ_2,.......Δ_{16}.

$$\Delta = (\Delta_1, \Delta_2, \Delta_3, \ldots\ldots\ldots \Delta_{16})$$

2. Inverse the matrix of intercorrelation for 16 PF in general population, i.e., get R^{-1} matrix

$$Z\,R^{-1} = b = (b_1, b_2, b_3, \ldots\ldots\ldots b_{16})$$

3. Now we can have complete equation for predicting an individual's readjustment in the given occupation g.

$$Y'_g = b_{ig}\,A + b_{2g}\,B\ldots + b_{16g}\,Q_4 + ag,$$

where b_{ig}'s are calculated in step 2 and ag can be computed as

$$ag = 5.5\,(1 - b_{1g} - b_{2g} - \ldots\ldots - b_{16g})$$

Having obtain Y_g score for a person we have to decide his suitability for the occupation. For the occupations having large number of people the mean Y'g for each occupation is the suitable reference point. The smaller the number of people in an occupation, the higher is the value of mean, Y'_g (Cattell, Eber and Tatsuoka, 1970, p. 153).

Qualification (Weighting) Grid

This a non-linear method of combining factor scores of an individual for determining his suitability for certain occupation. The Grid has ten rows, one for each sten score, and sixteen columns giving weights for each factor corresponding to the stens. Sixteen weighted scores for a person are added to get the total weighted score. The total can be converted into Qualification Level. There are four levels of qualification: under qualified, minimum qualified, well qualified, best qualified. Range of total weighted score are provided for putting an individual in any one of the Qualification Levels:

Total Weighted Score	*Qualification Level*	*Interpretation*
0 to 29	Under qualified (U Q)	Not recommended for placement in this job area.
30 to 47	Minimum qualified (QLI)	Recommended only in tight labour market.
48 to 69	Well qualified (QL2)	Better than average risk for this job area
70 to 80	Best qualified (QL3)	Excellent risk for this job area.

Evaluation of the 16 PF

Factor analysis does not involve completely determined procedure. We have already mentioned the six points of disagreement among factor analysts. As the factors extracted from the same matrix of intercorrelation by different factor analysts are not likely to be the same, a doubt is created whether the 16 factors are the genuine dimensions of personality. Putting aside the controversies regarding the methodology of factor analysis, we can appreciate the comprehensiveness of 16 PF and the precautions (see canons) taken in the construction of the instrument. The criterion evidence and the values and constants for vocational selection and clinical diagnosis make the instrument of high practical utility (see the preceding section).

Eysenck Personality Questionnaire (EPQ)

Like 16 Personality Factor Questionnaire and other Questionnaire of its family, Eysenck Personality Questionnaire and its predecessors were outcome of factor analytic studies of personality conducted by H.J. Eysenck and his associates. However, unlike Cattell (1950) Eysenck preferred to extract few large number of small trait-level factors. Eysenck proposed a hierarchical model of personality in which habits are the least generalized units of behaviour. Habits combine to form personality traits and traits are combine to form personality types.

Eysenck began his factor analytic study of personality by using objective measures of personality such as motor dexterity, dark vision, body sway and the like. The subjects were normal and neurotic patients. The first book which gives the details of the study was published in 1947 under the title Dimensions of Personality. In later factor analysis of personality measures, Eysenck used samples of school children, mental defectives, and unskilled factory workers. The data were also generated by using as diverse instruments as ratings, inventories, and Rorschah Inkblot Test. The three factors which were discovered and confirmed with the help of the method of criterion analysis were identified as: Neuroticism, Introversion-Extroversion and Psychoticism. The rotation of axes was done orthogonally not blindly but to a theoretically meaningful position. The three dimensions of personality are briefly described as below:

Neuroticism: Those who are high on this dimension are anxious, depressed, suffering from guilt feelings, have low self-esteem, are tense, irrational, and emotional. Those who have low score on the measure of neuroticism tend to respond emotionally only slowly and generally weakly, and return to base line quickly after arousal; they are calm, even-tempered, controlled and unworried.

Etraversion-Introversion

Those who are high (extroverts) on this dimension are sociable, lively, active, assertive, sensation-seeking, carefree, dominant, surgent, ventursome, tends to be aggressive persons and lose their temper quickly, and, they are not always reliable persons. Those who are introvert are retiring sort of persons introspective, fond of books, are reserved and distant, take matters of daily life seriously, plan in advance, seldom behave aggressively, are reliable, and do not loose temper easily.

The typical introvert is retiring sort of person, is introspective and reserved. He keeps his feelings under close control, does not loose his temper, "looks before he leaps", and places great value on ethical standards.

Psychoticism: This factor was identified in factor analytical studies of personality reported in 1952. Those who are high on the dimension are aggressive, cold, egocentric, impersonal, impulsive, antisocial, unempathic, creative, and tough-minded. The common belief that schizophrenics are exaggerated introverts and manic-depressive patients exaggerated extroverts, is not supported by empirical findings. However, there is evidence that manic - depressives are less "psychotic" than schizophrenics.

Eysenck (1975) proposed that while discussing the results of inventory with lay person it is preferable to refer neuroticism as emotionality and psychoticism as tender mindedness.

Eysenck made a valuable contribution by showing that neuroticism and psychoticism are two different dimensions of personality. The question which brings the issue into focus is, "Is a neurotic condition or syndrome a less severe manifestation of the same personality trait that lead to psychosis." This question was answered with the help of criterion analysis. It was shown that tests defining the dimension of psychoticism differentiated between normals and psychotics but not between normals and neurotics. Similarly, tests defining the dimension of neuroticism differentiated between normals and neurotics but not between normals and psychotics.

Prior to developing Eysenck Personality Questionnaire, Eysenck developed three questionnaire, Maudsley Medical Questionnaire, (Eysenck, 1952), Maudsley Personality Inventory (Eysenck, and Eysenck, 1962) and the P.E.N. (Psychoticism - Extraversion - Neuroticism) Questionnaire. Earlier attempts were confined to measuring the N and E-I dimensions. The EPI was provided with a 9-item Life-Scale for detecting subjects' attempt to give fake responses. Other changes were made for various psychometric reasons, the main being: (a) reduction in correlation between factors, (b) elimination of items having high loadings on two or more factors, (c) to increase reliabilities of the scale in question. While there is evidence that intercorrelation among different versions of the instrument developed by Eysenck is satisfactory, there aroused a controversy regarding the inclusion of subtrait impulsivity in either the dimension of E-I or Psychoticism. While in the EPI the subtraits of sociability and impulsivity were included in the E-I dimension, the subtrait of impulsivity has become the part of psychoticism in the EPQ.

The P, E, and N scales included in the EPQ were developed through a series of about 20 factorial studies using slightly different items selected partly on the basis of previous studies and theoretical considerations. The Eysenck Personality Questionnaire incorporates a new P-scale containing 25 items besides having a 23-item N scale, "1-item E scale and 21-item L-scale to detect tendency to "fake good" and some degree of social naivete. Eysenck and Eysenck (1975) have described in detail the evidence of validity of the P scale. They have concentrated on two methods: (1) use of criterion groups, and (2) study of correlation of the P scale with variables which they are expected to have positive or negative relations.

In a study conducted by John Griffiths (Cited by Eysenck and Eysenck, 1980), the EPQ scale was ministered on eighty normals, thirty-seven nuerotics, and fifty-one psychotic men and women. The P score was found to be independent of E and N and it distinguished between psychotics and normal and psychotic and neurotics but not between neurotics and normals. The neurotic and psychotic groups were retested after psychiatric treatment for one and three months in between testing. The findings showed: (1) drop of P score of improved psychiatrics on retest; (2) improved psychiatrics showed significantly higher E on first test; (3) non-improved psychiatrics obtained significantly higher P score than improved psychiatrics.

Eysenck and Eysenck (1980) have mentioned a study carried out by A Rahman in which 116 males and 188 females diagnosed as neurotics were studied. Psychiatrists were asked to give prognosis ratings at the beginning and end assessment at the time of discharge following psychotherapy. The EPQ was also administered at both the occasions. Analysis of the data showed that P correlated with length of treatment for both males (r=.21) and females (r=.36). The assessment at the end of study gave significant correlations with P for both sexes (male r=.28, female r=.43). Applying attenuation, it becomes evident that P scores are related to failure to benefit from treatment.

Turning to abnormalities which do not have psychiatric nomiculature Eysench and Eysench (1980) referred to the study by Sergraves, and Zacune (1971), in which groups of drug users and controls were compared. All drug groups were significantly higher than control group on the P scale. The findings also suggested that drug users are similar in personality to psychiatric groups, and that P (predominantly) and N are involved in the causation of their behaviour. This conclusion is also borne out by other studies. Eysenck and Eysenck have given a table showing P,E,N, and Anxiety scores of male and female cannabis users divided into categories of occasional takers, regular takers, and all takers (who use other drugs also). A perusal of the table shows that drug taking is related to psychiatric abnormality; with both P and N implicated, the former rather more than latter.

Experimental studies have also furnished evidence regarding the validity of the P scale. Those who score high on P scale are found to have difficulty in persevaration of set in vigilance task. A large number of experiments have been conducted to test the hypothesis that psychiatrics are characterized by unusual associative connections and poor control. The findings were in expected direction: It is also reported that on weigl colour form scoring test psychotics tend to choose colour as the basis of discrimination more frequently than did normals.

In addition to the large scale factor analysis that was used to develop the EPQ, attempts have been made to recover the factors extracted by Eysenck and Eysenck (1976) and to find other psychometric characteristics of the scales contained in the EPQ. Loo carried out a psychometric investigation of the Eysenck Personality Questionnaire. The purposes of the study were: (a) to determine internal reliabilities of the scales, (b) to find independence of the scales, (c) to verify primary factor structure of the questionnaire, and (d) to find higher order factor structures. The study employed 139 female and 123 male university students in age range from 18 to 25 years. The internal reliabilities as determined by calculating Cronbach's Alpha Coefficient were found to be as below:

Scales	*Reliability for Male Sample*	*Reliability for Female Sample*	*Reliability for Total Sample*
P	.43	.44	.50
E	.82	.82	.82
N	.84	.84	.82
L	.62	.75	.71

The reliabilities coefficients are in line with those reported in the manual except in the case of the P scale. The P scale was found to be of more heterogeneous than it was for the normative sample. It is pointed out that higher reliability of the P scale reported in the manual was due to a higher proportion of zero scores, the scales were found to be independent of each other; not more than 5 per cent variance was shared by the scales. However, in the female sample the P and L scales were found to share 9 per cent of variance. With respect to the third purpose it is reported that 16 primary factors extracted in Loo's study were similar to the factors extracted from the EPI by other investigators. It was the addition of the P scale in the EPQ that led to the extraction of many primaries reflecting its items. It was also found that although the overall scales were independent, there were several factors which were heterogeneous with respect to scale items. The study of higher-order factor structure led to the identification of the following second-order orthogonal factors: Emotionality, Paranoia, Cautio-cooperation, Social Extraversion Anxiety, and Psychotherapy. The impulsivity factor, which is regarded to be a component of Extraversion was found to the factor of Psychopathy along with primaries containing items from the P scale. The items are related to highly deviant behaviour typifying aggressive and antisocial behaviour. The third - order analysis yield two orthogonal factors Anxiety-Paranoia and Emotionality-Psychotherapy. There was evidence to the effect that P is simply another measure of Emotionality.

Normal Sample

The EPQ was administered on large samples of males and females. However, the samples were not random samples. Beginning from age 16 and going up to age of 69 years class intervals of five years (16-19, ..., 60-69) have been made and means, S.D.s for P, E, N, and L scales are mentioned for each age class interval. Means and S.D.s for a large number of occupational groups are also provided. Mohan, Eysenck and Eysenck (1987) have provided evidence regarding the efficiency of the EPQ across cultures. They have reported means and S.D.s of different scales calculated from the data 2050 respondents including Indian students and foreign students in Indian universities.

6

Evaluation of Personality Measures

In the preceding chapters we have discussed the three strategies of personality assessment and the manner in which they proceed to select items so as to assess individual differences with respect to certain personality characteristics. In this chapter we propose to discuss different statistical methods which can be used to obtain item statistics needed to decide the suitability of an item for inclusion in a psychological test and to discuss the methods of determining the reliability and validity of scores obtained with the help of a measuring device.

Importance of Item Analysis

A personality questionnaire is made up of a number of items because response to a single item does not provide reliable individual score and it is not helpful in finding individual differences which can be obtained only when responses given to a large set of items are summated to get individuals' total scores. The test theory which regard score as summation of item scores helps us to understand the relation of item statistics with distribution, mean, variability, reliability and validity of test scores. Generally, two statistical aspects of items are considered, difficulty level and indices of item discrimination or item validity. The first statistics is generally obtained for ability tests which measure individual differences in maximum performance but it is also used in personality questionnaire with other names such as proportion of keyed responses (p_i), commonality, or eccentricity of cut.

The mean, standard deviation, and intercorrelation of items have bearing on the shape of distribution of total scores. If average item mean proportion of keyed responses (p_i) is high, the distribution of test scores is negatively skewed; if item mean is low the test scores are positively skewed. Intercorrelation of items has influence on kurtosis. With the increase of item intercorrelation, the distribution grows flatter, to platykurtic from mesokurtic, to rectangular, to bimodal, and finally U-shaped. With perfect intercorrelation and medium difficulty, half of the subjects would make perfect scores and half would make zero score (Guilford, 1954). The relation of mean of total scores on a test, (M_x) mean score in each item (M_i), and proportion of keyed responses (p_i) is given by the following expression (Guilford, 1954, p. 358):

$$M_x = \Sigma M_i = \Sigma P_i$$

Guilford has given a general formula which gives the relation between total variance and item variance and covariance (Guilford, 1954, formula 13.33, p. 358):

$$\sigma^2_t = \Sigma p_i q_i + 2 \Sigma r_{ij} \sqrt{p_i q_i p_j q_j} \quad \text{(where } j > i)$$

where p_i refers to proportion of subjects giving correct (keyed response) to a particular item (i), $q_i = 1 - p_i$ and r_{ij} is the correlation between each item in turn and every other item (where subscript is numerically higher than i). It may be noted that $p_i\ q_i$ is variance of item i and $p_i q_i\ p_j q_j$ is covariance between items i and j.

Item statistics bears relation with reliability and validity of test scores. If all items have equal difficulty (p_i is the same) and intercorrelation between different pairs of items (r_{ij}) is also equal, we have essentially parallel items and can use Spearman-Brown formula to estimate the reliability of total scores. Richardson (1936) has shown that average correlation between items is related to the average item-total correlation:

$$\bar{r}_{ij} = \bar{r}_{it}$$

where $\bar{r}_{ij}$ is average correlation between items and $\bar{r}_{it}$ is average item-total correlation.

Kuder and Richardson (1937) proposed a method of determining reliability based on consistency of responses to a test broken into as many parts as there are items. This formula, known as Kuder-Richardson formula 20 (K-R 20) makes use of summation of items variance pq. Other variations/modifications of K-R 20 also make use of item statistics.

The predictive validity of test scores depends on the correlation of items with the criterion and internal consistency. In order to have high predictive validity we have to have a set of items which are highly correlated with the criterion and have low intercorrelation among themselves. The following equation shows the relationship between test score and criterion and average item-criterion and item-total correlation for the items of uniform difficulty or equal pi values (Guilford, 1954, formula 13.37 p. 361):

$$r_{tc} = \frac{\bar{r}_{ic}}{\bar{r}_{it}}$$

where $\bar{r}_{tc}$ = correlation between test score and criterion

$\bar{r}_{ic}$ = average correlation between item and the criterion.

$\bar{r}_{it}$ = average correlation between item and total score.

For high predictive validity average item-criterion correlation should be high and average item total-correlation should be low. It is to be pointed out that if the purpose of constructing a measuring device is to assess individual differences in respect to a unitary trait, we have to select items which have high item intercorrelation because homogeneity is the hall mark of this kind of tests.

The proportion of endorsement of keyed responses to an item is also related to number of discriminations that an item can make. If out of 100 subjects only one subject has given the keyed response, the item discriminates one person from each of the 99 persons and as such only 99 discriminations are possible. Similarly, if percentage of keyed responses is 10 and non-keyed responses is 90, 10 × 90 = 900 discriminations are made. The maximum number of discriminations are obtained when we have an item to which 50 per cent responses are keyed and 50 per cent are non-keyed. The number of discrimination in such a case are 50 × 50 = 2500.

Many indices of item discrimination are proposed. Because a test is to be a measure of individual differences, it is to be comprised of items which can discriminate between the persons who have different levels of a personality trait. If the purpose of developing an instrument is to identify membership of certain criterion group, every item should be able to discriminate between those who belong to a criterion group and those who do not.

Methods of Obtaining Item Statistics

While the decision to make a univocal, internally homogeneous measuring device or to develop a questionnaire made up of heterogeneous items good for the prediction of an external criterion depends on the purpose and strategy of assessment, the choice of statistics depends on the fact whether responses to items and the variable against which items are to be validated are continuous, really dichotomous, or purposefully dichotomized continuous variables. The assumption of normal distribution of the response and criterion variables is also an important consideration in the selection of appropriate statistics. From the point of view of method and procedure we can distinguish between two kinds of item indices: indices of discrimination between high and low groups, and correlational indices of item validity.

Indices of Discrimination

A common practice in item analysis is to compare the frequency of keyed responses given by upper (U) and lower (L) criterion groups. As pointed out earlier, these criterion groups can be obtained by specifying the cutting points on the distribution of total test scores of a sample from the population for which the scale is being developed. Alternatively, the two groups may be recruited on the basis of external criterion such as psychiatric diagnosis or supervisors ratings. When the first alternative is preferred the U and L groups are usually obtained using P27 and P73 as the cutting points. It has been demonstrated by Kelly (1939) that when test scores are normally distributed, upper 27 per cent and lower 27 per cent of the distributions is the most appropriate choice in view of the problems created by more extreme classification allowing use of smaller portion of the tryout sample and less extreme classification (with median as the cutting point) which makes it possible to use entire data but reduces the extent of difference between the U and L groups. Having obtained the two groups, an item analysis chart of the frequency of keyed responses of the U and L groups to each item is prepared as shown below:

items	*U*	*L*	*Discrimination U – L* D
1.	90	76	14
2.	86	83	3
3.	98	50	48
4.			
n			

In the above example the U and L groups are presumed to have 108 subjects each and the tryout group to have 400 subjects. It is often preferable to convert the frequency of keyed responses into proportions dividing the frequencies by number of subjects in the group, U or L. In that case value of 1 or -1 would indicate that all the members of U or L group have given keyed response while none of the other group gave the keyed response. The value of D would be zero if the proportion of U group (p_u) and proportion of lower group (p_l) giving keyed responses is equal. Many important properties of D are reported: (1) D is directly proportional to the difference between the number of correct (number of keyed responses in U versus number of non-keyed responses in L) and number of incorrect (number of non-keyed responses in the U versus the number of keyed responses in the L groups) discriminations (Ebel, 1965; Findley, 1956); (2) D is related to reliability of the scale; the higher the mean D, the higher the reliability of scale (Ebel, 1967).

(3) The value of D, like other item discrimination indices, is related to the proportion of keyed responses. When proportion of keyed responses is either 100 or 0, the value of D is zero. It is maximum when the proportion of keyed responses is 50. Many other variations of D are proposed. Using the difference of p_u and p_l. One can calculate critical-ratio or can apply chi-square to find significance of difference between p_u and p_l. When number of subjects in the upper and lower groups are the same one can apply chi-square formula proposed by Guilford (1941):

$$\chi^2 = \frac{N\,(p_u - p_l)^2}{4pq}$$

where p is arithmetic mean of p_u and p_l, q is 1–p.

Guilford (1941) has presented an abac for finding whether the difference $p_u - p_l$ yields significant chi-square. Guilford (1954) pointed out that critical-ratio and chi-square are sampling statistics whose purpose is to test hypothesis. However, they can be used to compare the items as to discriminative power where N's are equal. The segregation of subjects on the basis of their giving or not giving keyed response to an item is also used for determining item discrimination index. One can then determine the significance of means of the two groups M_p and M_q. However, one should take precaution against spurious overlap of item score with the total. To take care of the overlap, Guilford suggested the use of $M_p - M_q - 1$ for testing the significance of difference. A variant of the mean-difference index is $M_p - M_q$ divided by σ_t standard deviation of total scores (Vernon, 1948) which is designated as d. The d index favours the selection of items deviating from the median of proportion of keyed responses.

Correlational Indices

Correlational indices are used for finding correlation between responses of items and either total test score or some external criterion. The choice of appropriate method among the following depends upon the nature of criterion and response to individual item: Tetrachoric Correlation (rt), phi Coefficient, Biserial Correlation, point Biserial Correlation.

Tetrachoric Correlation

This is a variety of product-moment correlation used when both the variables to be related are dichotomies but there is good reason to assume that both the variables are essentially continuous and would be normally distributed if exact measures were obtained and frequency distributions were prepared. For the calculation of r_t a 2 × 2 table is prepared and the following four different pairs of frequencies are counted and tabulated: A, those who are high on both variables X and Y; B, high on variable X and low on variable Y; C, high on variable X and low on variable Y; and D, low on both the variables X and Y. The tabulation and the formula used for the calculation are given below:

		−	+	
Y	+	− + B	+ + A	A + B
	−	− − D	+ − C	C + D

$$r_t = \text{Cos}^\circ \left[\frac{180^\circ \times \sqrt{BC}}{\sqrt{AD} + \sqrt{BC}} \right]$$

In the above formula, the value of BC is replaced by AD in the numerator if BC is greater than AD. The sign of r_t is positive when AD entries are more than BC entries and it is negative when BC entries are more than AD. Having obtained the angle, value of cosine can be read from trignometric table (table j in Garrett, 1958, p. 439). The value of r_t can also be estimated by using ratio AD/BC or BC/AD, depending upon whether AD is greater or BC is greater. As pointed out earlier, the sign of r_t would be negative if BC is greater than AD. Getting the ratio we can go to table K in Garrett, (1958, p. 440) to get the value of r_t. However, there is no need to calculate the vlaue of r_t because an abac designed for use in item analysis is prepared by Mosier and McQuitty (1940) for which only p_u and p_l are to be found. A graphic abac is given by Guilford (1954) which can be used when total-score distribution is dichotomized at the median and the sample is preferably as large as 400. Knowing p_u and p_l we can read values of r_t from this abac.

Phi Coefficient (Φ)

This is used when both the variables are genuine dichotomies and it is not proper to assume that they represent underlying normal distribution. A 2 × 2 table like one used for the calculation of r_t is prepared for calculating phi coefficient. The cells of the table are designated in the same way as in the case of rt. The formula for the calculation of phi coefficient is as below:

$$\Phi = \frac{AD - BC}{\sqrt{(A + B)\,(C + D)\,(B + D)\,(A + C)}}$$

The significance of phi may be determined by converting it into chi-square and going to the table of chi-square with df = 1. The significance of phi can also be determined by finding its standard error which is given by the formula

$\frac{1}{\sqrt{Np}}$ (Garrett, 1958, 391).

Guilford (1941) has given a simplified formula for calculating phi which makes use of p_u, p_l and p_q:

$$\Phi = \frac{p_u - p_l}{2\sqrt{pq}}$$

An abac for determining the value of phi with the help of p_u and p_l is also provided by Guilford (1954, p. 429). In addition to lack of requirement of assumption concerning the nature of distribution, phi can be calculated by taking any tail proportions — .5N, .27N, .25N. This makes it possible to use same abac regardless of tail proportions. However, the value of phi is greater for more extreme categorization of subjects. Perry and Michael (1951) have given a formula which can be used for estimating the value of phi that would be obtained if .5N was used in the tails instead of whatever cut, .25N or .27N was used. The formula is reproduced by Guilford (1954, formula 15.15, p. 432).

The biserial r (r_b)

It is used when the criterion (either total test score or external criterion) is continuous and response to item is dichotomous. The score of those who has given the keyed response to an item are separated from those who have given non-keyed response and two frequency distributions using same class interval are obtained. A combined frequency distribution is also obtained. The method of calculation is described in all standard text books of psychological statistics.

The value of r_b can be obtained by using an abac prepared by Flanagan (1939) which is reproduced by Guilford (1954, p. 428). The abac is to be used when middle 46% of subjects are eliminated and p_u and p_l values are obtained for the subjects belonging to upper and lower 27% of the distribution. Knowing p_u and p_l one can read the value.

The point-biserial r (r_{pbis})

Like r_b, r_{pbis} is to be calculated when one variable is continuous and the other is dichotomous but the two-category split cannot be regarded as representing an underlying normal distribution upon which an arbitrary division has been imposed; it is rather a discret grouping.

An abac for estimating r_{pbi} is provided by Guilford (1954, p. 429). The abac is to be used when one variable is divided at the median of the distribution and p_u and p_l are obtained. Unlike r_b, r_{pbis} is influenced by the departure of proportion of keyed responses from .5; with the increased departure the value of r_{pbi} becomes smaller.

Measures of Item Reproducibility

While discussing rational-theoretical and factor analytic

strategies of personality assessment we referred to the fact that to develop a measure of a trait we should select homogeneous items. If items of a scale are homogeneous it is possible to map the pattern of response to every items by knowing the total score of a person. Loevinger (1947) offered the following definition of homogeneity: "In a perfectly homogeneous test, when items are arranged in the order of difficulty, if any item is known to be passed the probability is unity of passing all previous items. In a perfectly heterogeneous test, the probability of an individual passing a given item a is the same whether or not he is known already to have passed another item b" (p. 13). In the case of personality scales the term difficulty occurring in the above excerpt is to be read as probability of item endorsement.

The important methods of determining reproductibility of an item are Loevinger's Hit Index, Jackson's Plus Percentage Ratio and Phi Coefficient (see White and Saltz, 1957).

Reliability

The National (American) Committee on Test Standards (1966) defines reliability of a psychological test as accuracy (consistency and stability) of measurement. Determination of reliability of an instrument requires that at least two sets of scores are obtained for the same sample of subjects. The two measures may be obtained by testing the same sample of subjects by administering the equivalent/parallel forms of the same instrument immediately one after another and finding correlation between the two sets of scores. The test should be administered by the same person and the testing situations should also be identical. The correlation would provide the information about stability of test scores. To obtain information about stability we have to administer the same instrument after an interval of time. The correlation between scores obtained on two occasions provides information regarding the stability of the measure.

In order to understand the meaning and importance of reliability we have to distinguish between true score variance and error variance as two components of obtained score:

$$\sigma^2 = \sigma^2_t + \sigma^2_e$$

Where σ^2 = variance of obtained scores
σ^2_t = variance of true scores of a group
σ^2_e = variance of error of measurement.

The relation shown above presumes that error of measurement is unrelated to the magnitude of true score. The components of true and error variance help us to define reliability as below:

$$r_{11} = 1 - \frac{\sigma^2_e}{\sigma^2}$$

We can define reliability of a test as the proportion of variance in test score which is due to true differences between individuals in the quality being assessed. The increase of error component in the obtained scores of an individual leads to decrease of reliability of the measuring instrument. A distinction is made between constant and random errors. Constant errors are those errors which contribute equally to the scores of every individual either positively or negatively (e.g., +2 or -3) pushing up or down the obtained scores above the level of true scores. Random errors do not operate in the same direction; some time they add and some time they subtract different quantities from true scores. In the absence of constant error an individual's true score can be obtained by finding the mean of scores obtained by him at different occasions because sum of random errors is zero. Constant errors come in the way of determining true scores. However, due to their constancy constant errors are of little importance when comparison is to be made between individuals.

What should be considered an error? Answer to this question is of basic importance in deciding the method of determining reliability of an instrument. Lindquist (1951) has mentioned six different kinds sources of variance in test scores. While determining reliability of a measure it is important to decide as to which fractions of variance should be thought of as true and systematic variance in quality or quantities being measured and which should be thought of error variance. The possible sources of variance are:

Lasting and general characteristics of the individual

This includes level of one or more general traits which operate in a number of tests; general skill and technique of taking test; general ability to comprehend instructions. These lasting and general factors present a problem of validity. Unless the author of the test makes use of them, he would make an attempt to minimize them by providing clearest possible instructions and ensuring minimization of secondary cues related to the choice of a response alternative.

Lasting but specific characteristics of the individual

The specific characteristics may be specific to a test as a whole and its parallel form and also to a particular item. The variance contributed by specific characteristics of the subjects is definitely systematic variance but there remains the problem of variance associated with particular format of a scale and particular sampling of items. What we are measuring is to be defined either in terms of an area of content, form of test or particular set of items, or combination of these?

Temporary but general characteristics of the individual

This includes health, fatigue, motivation, emotional strain, external conditions, etc. It seems that variance contributed by temporary factor is not to be treated as systematic variance but if one is interested in knowing how consistent an individual's score is from day to day, week to week then we cannot ignore the influence of temporary factors. When a test is to be used for the prediction of future criterion we have to pay due attention to consistency of score over an extended period of time.

Temporary and specific characteristics of the individual

These characteristics may be divided into two broad categories:

(a) Specific to a test as a whole which include comprehension of the specific task, specific tricks or techniques, level of practice on the specific skills required, and momentary 'set' for a particular test.

(b) Specific to particular test items which include fluctuation and idiosyncrasies of human memory, unpredictable fluctuations in attention or accuracy.

Systematic or chance factors affecting the administration of the test or appraisal of test performance

Under this category are included conditions of testing such as adherence to instructions, freedom from distraction, unreliability or bias in scoring of responses, etc. Mental set at the time of testing also influence individual's score.

Variance otherwise not accounted for (chance)

It is not possible to account for all the variance in a set of test scores. The variance contributed by unknown scores is allocated as error variance without any controversy.

The variance which cannot be attributed to any source is the variance which no one would regard as systematic variance. While there may be controversy as to which of different sources of variance be treated as systematic or error variance, variance due to chance is the variance which undermines the reliability howsoever it is defined.

The classical concept of reliability based on the notion of single source of true variance is not found suitable by those who are interested in the generalizability of obtained scores. Cattell (1964) suggested the restructuring of the concept of reliability because according to him the concept suffers from an absence of common sense, logic and psychological perspective. He, therefore, introduced a generic and superordinate term, test consistency, which includes reliability, homogeneity, and transferability. The consistency of a test is to be evaluated in three possible senses:

1. *Across occasions:* Applying same test to the same sample on different occasions we can determine reliability subsumed by consistency.

2. *Across tests:* Not considering different occasions but making use of the data collected on the same occasion from the same people and studying consistency across individual items is the procedure of determining homogeneity.

3. *Across people:* When the same test is applied on the same kind of occasions to different sets of people for the purpose of ascertaining whether there is agreement in the meaning of scores, we are studying transferability.

Distinction is made among three kinds of reliabilities on the basis of varying combination of sources of error. The main sources of retest variability are: (a) variation in scores when a test is administered by different persons on the same sample, (b) variations in the scores assigned by different scorers to the same set of responses, (c) remaining unknown conditions of subjects' decision in the test situation.

The three sources can be combined in several ways, each defining a distinct type of reliability. Of major importance are: dependability (immediate retest), administrative reliability (across administrators), and the conspection (across scorers). The last term is a combination of 'con' and 'spectrare' which means to observe together.

Study of consistency of meaning of test scores across people is a new psychometric parameter introduced by Cattell (1964).

Transferability is like hardiness of a plant which can withstand changes of climate. It can be determined by finding correlation between two persons from the application of the same test over a series of occasions where they are experiencing exposure to exactly same series of stimuli. Transferability is a test's constancy across the typical range of age, subculture, status, etc., which a test is likely to encounter.

Methods of Determining Reliability

We propose to give the details of different methods of determining reliability. Consistency and stability which are two aspects of classical concept of reliability can be obtained by using one or more of the following procedures:

1. *Test-Retest Reliability.* The same person administers the same scale on the same group of subjects under identical conditions after a definite interval. The interval is to be

selected after consideration of reducing possibility of recall of responses given on the first administrating and on set of genuine change that is likely to occur over years. The measures of characteristics which fluctuate day to day are not likely to be stable and for this reason it is not proper to determine test-retest reliability. However, it is essential to determine test-retest reliability of those measures which are to be used for the prediction of certain future criterion.

2. *Equivalent-Form Reliability.* Administering two equivalent forms on the same group of subjects after a short while we can find agreement between the two sets of scores with the help of Product Moment Correlation. However, this procedure can be used if really equivalent forms are available. Equivalent or Parallel forms are those forms which have identical source of true variance, equal means, equal intercorrelations among items of the scales and there is no overlap of error variance. Equivalent forms are difficult to construct and often not available.

3. *Split-Half Reliability.* When a test has no parallel forms and due to certain reasons it is not proper or possible to administer it twice we can divide items of the test in two equal halves and find scores of each individual for the two halves. While breaking a test in two halves, one should be aware of the fact that a single test is to be broken into equivalent forms. Once two sets of scores are obtained, Product Moment Correlation can be found between two-halves of the test. The correlation is to be corrected because it gives reliability coefficient of an instrument containing half of the items of the original instrument.

The effect that lengthening or shortening of a test will have on its coefficient of reliability can be estimated by Spearman-Brown formula given below:

$$r_{nn} = \frac{r_{rtt}}{1 + (n - 1)_{rtt}}$$

where r_{nn} = the reliability of test after increasing its length n times of original

r_{tt} = obtained reliability of a test having a given number of items

n = the number of times (multiple of original number of items) length of an instrument is to be increased.

It is noted that new items to be added in the scale are to be equivalent of the original items. When reliability of full test is to be estimated from the reliability of one-half of the instrument, the Spearman-Brown formula becomes:

$$r_{tt} = \frac{2r_{hh}}{1 + r_{hh}}$$

Where r_{hh} = correlation of half tests.

An alternate method for finding split-half reliability is given by Rulon (1939). To apply this formula the variance of difference in scores obtained by each subject on two halves of a test and total score are to be found. The formula is in accordance with the definition of reliability in terms of proportion of true variance in the total variance.

3. Interitem Consistency Coefficient

This kind of reliability is based on consistency of responses to all the items comprising an instrument. It is like split-half reliability with the difference that here the test is assumed to be broken into as many parts as are number of items. Interitem consistency coefficient is suitable for homogeneous tests but not for heterogeneous tests. There are different methods of determining this kind of reliability including methods for determining reproducibility of a scale. The most popular method of determining interitem consistency is that developed by Kuder-Richardson (1937). This method uses item statistics, proportion of correct or keyed responses (p) and proportion of incorrect or non-keyed responses (q), and variance of test scores. Kuder-Richardson formula 20 (K-R 20) is given below:

$$r_{tt} = \left(\frac{n}{n-1}\right)\left(\frac{\sigma^2_t - \Sigma pq}{\sigma^2_t}\right)$$

where p = proportion of keyed responses

q = 1-p

σ_t = Standard Deviation of the scores of subjects on the whole scale.

n = number of items in a test

The values of p and q for every item are multiplied to get the product pq and then added and substituted in the formula. Because the K-R 20 requires considerable labour, K-R 21 is proposed which makes use of average of p and q (p, q). The formula is given below:

$$r_{tt} = \left(\frac{n}{n-1}\right)\left(\frac{\sigma^2_t - n\bar{p}\bar{q}}{\sigma^2_t}\right)$$

In the above formula we can use M_t/n as $\bar{p}$ and $(n-M_t)/n$ as $\bar{q}$. This enables us to make use of mean of the total score instead of using item statistics.

The formula becomes:

$$r_{tt} = \frac{n\sigma^2_t - M_t\,(n - M_t)}{(n-1)\,\sigma^2_t}$$

The K-R 21 provide lower bound estimate of r_{tt} which is lower than value obtained by formula 20. Both K-R 20 and K-R 21 can be used when scoring is 1 and 0. Ferguson (1951) has extended the formula for the situations in which more than two response weights are used. It is to be mentioned that K-R reliability is the mean of all the possible values of split-half reliabilities obtained by splitting a test in as many ways as possible.

Cronbach's (1951) alpha coefficient is an important method of determining interitem consistency. The formula for the calculation of alpha can be used even when scoring of responses is different from 1, 0. The formula is given below:

$$\alpha = \left(\frac{n}{n-1}\right)\left(1 - \frac{\Sigma V_i}{V_t}\right)$$

where V_i = variance of part i of a test

V_t = variance of total scores
n = number of parts

The parts can be as small as single items; they can also be two halves as in the cases of split-half reliability.

In the section of item analysis, we have referred to Loevinger's index of item homogeneity and Jackson's plus percentage ratio for an item. We have also mentioned that Loevinger's Index and plus percentage ratio can be obtained for the test as a whole. The index and the ratio provide information about interitem consistency. A formula for determining coefficient of homogeneity for a test is given below (Loevinger, 1947).

$$H_t = \frac{N\ (\Sigma X^2_t - \Sigma X_t) + \Sigma R^2_i - (\Sigma X_t)^2}{2N\ (\Sigma iR_i - \Sigma X_t) + \Sigma R^2_i - (\Sigma X_t)^2}$$

where H_t = coefficient of homogeneity
N = number of subjects
X_t = total-test score
R_i = number of correct responses to ith item
i = ordinal number of item in an increasing order of difficulty/decreasing order of proportion of keyed responses.

Loevinger (1947) advised that the above formula should be used when N is more than 100.

The different kinds of reliabilities discussed above regard different sources of variance as error. The sources of variance which are treated as error variance are specified below (Anastasi, 1982, p. 118):

Type of Reliability Coefficient	*Error Variance*
Test-retest	Time sampling
Alternate-Form (Immediate)	Content sampling
Alternate-Form (Delayed)	Time sampling and content sampling
Split-Half	Content sampling
Kuder-Richardson and Alpha coefficient	Content sampling and content homogeneity

It is customary to group factors influencing test reliability into: (1) Sources of variance in individual scores, and (2) factors in construction of test themselves. We have already mentioned factors falling in the first group. The factors belonging to the second category are of the nature of precautions that have to be taken by a test constructor to devise a good instrument. Some of these factors are:

(1) Number of items in a test should be large. The Spearman-Brown formula indicates the importance of increase in length of a test for its reliability.

(2) The range of proportion of keyed responses to items of a test should be large. Reliability of a test depends upon the number of discriminations that can be made on the basis of responses to every single item. From this point of view the best items are those which are given keyed responses by 50 per cent of the subjects.

(3) Scoring of items should be objective and the scoring system should be such that each item is scored independent of other.

(4) Homogeneity of test material is related to better reliability.

(5) To ensure better reliability of an instrument one should be careful in the formulation of items as the following characteristics of items are likely to undermine reliability of a test: the emotional tinge of words in items, length of items, unusual or difficult words, poor sentence structure, and faulty and inadequate instructions.

An important factor influencing the size of a reliability coefficient which is not mentioned above is the variability among the subjects who are employed for determining reliability coefficients. With decreasing variability, reliability is like to go down so much so that if all the subjects have got the same score, the reliability coefficient shall be close to zero.

Validity

Scores provided by a psychological test are not better than numerals scribed by a child who is learning writing alphabets and numbers unless they can be assigned some meaning. If scores have to carry meaning, the scale used for obtaining it should be valid. Calling a scale a measure of sociability or anxiety is not enough to regard test score as the indicator of the characteristic which the test is named to assess. There should be some evidence independent of the opinion of the test constructor as to the genuineness of the meaning given to the test scores.

It is not easy to collect evidence regarding the validity of a test that would be found trustworthy by every one. The main reason for this is that a test does not possess singular validity and one can always assert that the kind of evidence as regard to validity of a test is not the one in which he is interested. Depending upon the situation and intent of the user, a test would vary in degree of validity. Thus, it is important to consider the numerous aims of testing if one wants to understand the problem of determining validity of an instrument. A test can be used for the following purposes:

1. Assessment of an individual's performance at present in a universe of situations that the test has claimed to represent. For example, a measure of aggression may be interested in the responses of an individual to all the aggression-arousing situations.

2. To forecast an individual's future standing on a variable of particular interest that is different from test. For example, a prognostic instrument may be used to predict the changes of recovery from certain kind of mental disorder following certain kind of psychotherapy.

3. To find as to how much a hypothetical trait or quality (construct) is possessed by an individual and is reflected by his responses adding up to the total score.

It is to be pointed out that it is not always the case that a test is used for only one purpose. A test requiring the subjects to indicate similarity between two objects may be used to assess abstract reasoning, extent of brain damage and prediction of academic achievement. However, one can be interested in any one of the above aims of assessment and the relevant aspect of validity of an instrument. Corresponding to the aims of assessment we have following kinds of validity: content validity, criterion-related validity, and construct validity.

Content Validity

A psychological test has limited number of items through which it intends to assess all the manifestations of a psychological trait. All the possible situations and stimuli (items) which are relevant to the expression of a particular test constitute the domain of the trait-indicating behaviour from which a sample of items is selected to comprise an instrument. It may be so that the selected items do not cover all the aspects of the trait to be assessed, that is, the sample of items is not a representative sample of the domain to be covered.

Though it is true content validity is more important for achievement tests, its important for personality questionnaire cannot be ignored. Content validity, it may be argued, is an inbuilt quality of rationally derived instruments because rational strategy is based on the correspondence between the response (True or False) given by a person to an item and his actual feeling and behaviour. If a depression scale contains items related to mood disturbance, psychomotor retardation, loss of interest in daily activities, etc., what else evidence is needed as to the validity of the instrument? However, one should not forget that the purpose of psychological testing is to predict real life correlates of test scores. Thus, adequate coverage of the content may be a necessary but not sufficient condition for validity of a test.

Concurrent and Predictive Validities

Psychologists are employed to select personnel, diagnose, and to help in decision making in many other situations where information about individual differences is an essential ingredient of decision making. Predictive validity, refers to the accuracy with which we can say on the basis of an individual's score how he would behave in a real life situation. For determining predictive validity of an instrument we have to define the criterion behaviour and to have a reliable assessment of individuals in respect of it. Though the selection of criterion is related to the purpose of assessment, it is relevant to illustrate the nature of predictive validity by mentioning some common criteria used for determining predictive validity of different psychological tests:

1. Academic achievement or job performance.
2. Contrast groups.
3. Ratings by peers, teachers, instructors of specialized courses, and job supervisors.
4. Contrast groups such as those of students participating in certain extracurricular activities and those who do not participate, membership or non-membership in certain occupational group, etc., have been used for the validation of interest and personality inventories.
5. Psychiatric diagnosis.
6. Scores on previously available tests.

Whatever criterion one prefers for the validation of a psychological test, he has to take precautions against the following imperfections or biases in the criterion (Brogden and Taylor, 1950):

(1) *Criterion Deficiency.* Omission of pertinent elements from the criterion.

(2) *Criterion Contamination.* Introducing extraneous elements into the criterion. An example of criterion contamination is the effect of knowledge of subjects test score on the criterion rating by the raters who happened to know their score.

(3) *Criterion Distortion.* Improper weighting in combining criterion elements to arrive at composite criterion.

(4) *Criterion Scale Unit Bias.* Inequality of scale unit in the criterion.

The distinction between predictive and concurrent validities depends upon the time of availability of criterion measure. The criterion to be predicted may be available concurrently with the administration of the test to be predicted or it may be available after a certain period of time, for example on job performance of selected candidates shall be available after six months. As a matter of fact, psychological test may be used not only for the prediction of a current event but also for the postdiction of effect of an event that has previously occurred but could not be measured directly as it required considerable effort. An example of postdiction is the assessment of values and needs of a group of subjects acquired after exposure to socializing influences which could not be studied when they were occurring. It is to be noted that diagnosis involves either postdiction or the assessment of present status of the subject.

Predictive and concurrent validities are not of the kind which are determined once for all time to come. Criterion related validity of an instrument is to be found even when the same or similar criterion is to be predicted for a different group of subjects. This is so because much variability in validity coefficients is observed (Bennett, Seashore, and Wesman, 1974). One of the reason of variation in validity coefficients is the use of 50 or even lesser number of subjects in validation studies (Schmidt, Hunter and Urry, 1976).

Coefficient of predictive validity is an important but not the only determinant of accuracy of prediction. We have discussed the role or selection ratio, base rate, and reliability of the criterion measures as other important determinants of accuracy and utility of prediction.

Construct Validity

This kind of validity is related to the third purpose of psychological testing, i.e., to find as to how much a hypothetical trait or quality is expressed in the responses of the subjects to items comprising a scale. When the main purpose of assessment is not the prediction of certain criterion and decision making but to assess certain characteristic of theoretical importance, the author of a test finds himself in a difficult situation as there is no specific criterion to be predicted for the demonstration of the fact that a test measures what it purports to measure and yet evidence is to be furnished that a test measures what it intends to measure. The kind of evidence which is furnished in such a case is known as construct validity.

The importance of construct validity lies in more than furnishing a way out to the dilemma of furnishing empirical evidence in respect of validity of an assessment device without relying upon a non-specific criterion. Protagonists of construct validity assert that it is the scientific validity while content and predictive validities are essentially two kinds of administrative validities (Loevinger, 1957). It is argued that when validity of a test is defined as the correlation of the test with some criterion, it cannot be a fixed or unitary characteristic of a test.

Since 1920's construct validity was relied upon by those who developed personality inventories without practical orientation of prediction of specific criterion. However, the term was introduced in 1954 in the technical recommendations of American Psychological Association (APA, 1954). Both APA which introduced the term, and Cronbach and Meehl (1958) who elaborated the nature of construct validity, have emphasized that construct validity is involved when one is interested in answer to the question, "What constructs account for variance in test performance?" and finds it difficult to either define the construct operationally or select a criterion for validation of a scale.

To have a better understanding of the nature of construct validity, we have to understand the meaning of construct. According to Cronbach and Meehl (1955), "a construct is some postulated attribute of people, assumed to be reflected in test performance" (p. 283). Construct validity provides us information regarding the proportion of variance of test score variance that is attributed to construct (Cronbach and Meehl, 1955, p. 289). Construct, the postulated attribute, is assumed to have three characteristics: (1) the postulated attribute is reflected in test performance, (2) it has predictive properties, (3) meaning of construct is given by the laws in which occurs. The third characteristic of a postulate implies the existence of theory and complete set of laws, termed as nomological network. The laws in a nomological network may relate (a) observable properties or quantities to each other; or (b) theoretical constructs to observables, or (c) different theoretical construct to one another. However, Campbell (1960) made a distinction between two types of construct validity trait validity and nomological validity. The distinction is made on the basis of the level of development of the theory involving the construct. If the theory is as rudimentary as not going beyond indicating a hypothetical syndrome, trait or dimension of personality, the validation of the test measuring the construct would be trait validation. When a nomological network exists and it is evoked for determining the validity of an instrument, nomological validity is ascertained.

Procedures of Construct Validation

Construct validation is not to be identified by particular methodology; it is a holistic approach to test validation. Much of research on tests of personality is construct validation. Thus, construct validity does not call for a new scientific approach. The following methods can be used for investigation of construct validity of a scale:

1. *Group differences:* In order to find validity of an assessment device hypotheses are formulated regarding the behaviour of those who are high on the characteristic measured by the test and those who are low. If the difference exists in the expected direction we may conclude that there is evidence in favour of construct validity of the instrument. Studies in which scores on Taylor Manifest Anxiety Scale (MAS) is used as a measure of drive and the effect of variation of drive level on performance is investigated, are the example of construct validation.

2. *Correlation matrix and factor analysis:* Administering the test to be validated (test A) and other measures of the same construct or other theoretical construct(s) with which it expected to be correlated on a group of subjects, we can have evidence regarding the construct validity of the test.

However, when the correlation(s) is different from what was expected this may be so either because the test is not valid or because other measures do not tap what they are supposed to tap. The matrix of intercorrelation may be factor analyzed and the magnitude of factor loading of the instrument along with the factor loading of other theoretically relevant variables of the same factor would furnish evidence regarding construct validity of a measuring tool. One can explicitly test hypothesis regarding a construct by using Eysenck's (1950) procedure of criterion analysis.

3. *Studies of internal structure:* If an instrument is supposed to measure a unitary trait, its items should be intercorrelated with each other. Even low correlations, if consistent would give evidence of the existence of generalized tendency to behave in a certain manner. Item-total correlation, Kuder-Richardson formula, measures of reproducibility of responses are the methods of studying internal structure. Negative item-total correlation may support construct validity provided that the items with negative correlations are irrelevant to the postulated construct and serve as suppressor variables.

4. *Studies of change over occasions:* If a characteristic is theoretically expected to be stable, the stability of test scores (retest reliability) may be relevant to construct validation. If the theory in which a construct occurs stipulates the change in the quantity of the construct under certain circumstances, one can conduct experiments in which experimental treatment is given to influence the scores. If the change is in the expected direction, we have evidence in support of construct validity. Some common experimental interventions which have been used in validation studies are: Change of examiner in projective testing, alternative instructions (tell truth vs. make good impression), and coaching to improve performance on mental tests.

5. *Studies of Process:* Evidence regarding the construct validity of an assessment device can be obtained by studying the process involved in making a response. If, for example, a test measures mathematical competence but the

analysis of errors show that they were caused by erroneous reading of the questions, we may suspect that the test scores are contributed by reading competence. Another example of the study of process is the analysis of empathy, the ability of judge to predict what responses would be given by person who the judge happens to observe for a short while. Cronbach (1955) has shown that empty scores depend on several attributes of judges including assumed similarity, and other components of interpersonal judgment (mentioned in the second chapter). Thus, accuracy to predict another person's scores cannot be considered as the evidence of construct validity of the measure of empathy.

Keeping in view the fact that variance of scores obtained by a measuring device may be contributed not only by the construct but other sources such as intelligence, response styles and response biases, and the particular method (instrument) of assessment, Campbell (1960) has recommended that the following additional evidences are to be obtained and included in the report on construct validity.

1. *Correlation with intelligence tests:* If a measure of personality, which is not expected to be correlated with intelligence, is found to be correlated with intelligence test, it may imply that the contribution of the construct is being obliterated by intelligence.

2. *Correlation with social desirability:* While the role of social desirability in influencing test responses and scores is discussed in detail elsewhere, it is to be pointed out that if a test is highly correlated with desirability, it would not be the measure of construct it purports to measure.

3. *Correlations with measures of acquiescence and other response sets:* Here again the logic is same as in the case of desirability. Different kinds of response sets are discussed in chapter VII.

4. *Self-descriptive and stereotype keys for interpersonal perceptual accuracy tests:* Evidence for the validity of measures of empathy, interpersonal perception, social competence and the like is furnished in the form of accuracy to replicate the scores of a particular target person. But this

evidence is not sufficient; it is rather misleading (Gage, Levitt, and Stone, 1956; Cronbach, 1958). It is therefore, necessary that efforts to replicate the scores of particular social targets be compared with the use of self-descriptions and stereotype scores as predictors. Alternatively, such scores may also be based upon competence in differentiating among social targets rather than upon the absolute discrepancy in predictions for a single social target.

5. *Validity correlations higher that those for self-ratings:* We use personality tests instead of self-ratings because personality tests are believed to be better measures than self-ratings. It is, therefore, necessary to demonstrate that test scores are better predictor of the criterion measure than self-ratings.

6. *Multitrait-multimethod matrix:* Campbell and Fisk (1959) have proposed that in order to demonstrate construct validity of a measuring device, it is necessary to furnish evidence to the effect that the measure has high correlation with the variables with which it is theoretically expected to be related and at the same time it has low correlation with those variables with which it is not supposed to be correlated. The convergence and divergence can be studied by using different methods for the assessment of different constructs. Intercorrelations among the scores are tabulated in a multitrait-multimethod matrix. The four criteria suggested by Campbell and Fisk may be used to determine convergent and discriminant validity. The criterion are about the evidence of higher correlation among different measures of the same trait than measures of different traits involving separate methods. What Campbell and Fisk (1959) require from the test constructor is to generate from his learned conception or private construct not one operational embodiment but two or more. Each device is to be as different research instrument as possible. The test constructor is also expected to make explicit the distinction between his newly constructed variable and other variables.

Construct validation is inclusive of all other methods of validation. Messick (1980) argued that the term validity should be used in the context of interpretive meaningfulness of a test and other procedures of validation should be designated by more specifically descriptive labels; the content validity may be called content relevance, predictive validity be labeled as predictive utility, and so on. However, it is to be acknowledged that the process of construct validation is an open process because the theory may lead to new deductions and the measure of construct is to be found useful in testing new hypothesis. When in the process of construct validation, an investigator comes across negative evidence, he can interpret his results in three ways (Cronbach and Meehl, 1955):

1. The test does not measure the construct variable.
2. The theoretical network which generated the hypothesis is not correct.
3. The experimental design failed to test the hypothesis properly.

The notion of construct validity has been questioned by Bechtold (1959) and Sarbin (1968) on the ground of circularity of argument, disregard of "as if" for metaphorical nature of a construct and considering it to be something real, and lack of its utility for practical work. Some of these objections were anticipated and the initial discussion of construct validity may be used for countering the objections against construct validity.

We have discussed different aspects of evaluation of assessment devices. The technical aspects that have been discussed above are important but the main purpose of evaluation is to inform how effectively the instrument can be used for diagnosis, prognosis, placement and classification. It is, therefore, essential that the user is provided full information about the psychometric qualities of the instrument. The information is to be provided in the manual to be prepared after a thorough reading of Standard for Educational and Psychological Tests according to which a user is expected to be given details about the following :

General Information: This includes title of the test, publisher's name, date of publication, date of manuals, supplementary material, time required for administration.

Description of purpose and nature of the test : This includes statement of theory and purpose for which the instrument is developed, type of test (e.g., individual or group), for whom the test is devised, nature of content, type of items, instructions for administration and scoring.

Technical evaluation: This includes details about norms and standardization sample such as size, sampling procedure, availability of subgroup norms (e.g., age, sex, education, occupation, region). The procedure used for determining reliability, different kinds of reliability coefficients and the groups for which they are found are also to be reported. All the evidence bearing on the validity and the manner in which the assessment data obtained with the help of the devise can be put to use are to be reported so as to prevent improper use of the instrument.

It is to be recalled that personality assessment is more than measurement. The information about the purpose and technical qualities of an instrument does can ensures its proper use unless the user is not able have confidence in his understanding of the devise. The assessor is also expected to be aware of influences of various social and cultural factors on test results. His training should go beyond a knowledge of test theory, test construction, test administration, test interpretation, and personality theory. He should have knowledge of complexities of human interaction in psychosocial, interpersonal, and sociocultural spheres. The assessor who is engaged by an organization should have to pay due attention to adverse impact of any selection procedure on hiring opportunities of members of any race, sex, or ethnic group. In United States of America a selection rate for any race, sex, or ethnic group which is less than eighty percent of the group with highest rate is regarded as evidence of adverse impact of assessment programme.

7

Sources Confounding Personality Assessment

Psychological tests are devised to assess individual differences. A score is assigned to a person on the basis of his responses to the items included in a psychological test. The assigned score is expected to be solely determined by the trait which the test intended to measure. However, from the very beginning of psychological testing, psychometricians have been aware of the fact that scores obtained with the help of a psychological test may not be reliable and valid. It has become customary to report coefficients of reliability and validity and the methods which were used for determining them.

While no one would minimize the importance of reliability and validity in the choice of a better test for assessment, we have to go beyond these global requirements of a good psychological test if we want to know the sources of relevant and irrelevant variance. Let us take an example to explain the importance and implications of the question about the contribution of different sources in determining the responses of an individual to a set of items comprising a psychological test. The subject is asked to give 'True' or 'False' response to the following item, "I am afraid of high places." Should we accept 'False' response at its face value? It may be so that the subject wants to conceal his fear of high places, or he has a tendency to give 'False' response whenever he is in doubt about his behaviour, or he picked up the response without caring for the meaning of the item.

Different kinds of confounding determinants of responses on personality inventories are divided into two broad categories by Lanyon and Goodstein (1971), response styles and response sets. The distinction is based on the involvement of content in giving rise to confounding influence. Response style refer to the tendency to distort response in a particular direction regardless of the content of stimulus item. Response set is defined as "...conscious or unconscious desire on the part of the respondent to answer in such a way as to produce a certain picture of himself" (Rorer, 1965, p. 133). It is also to be pointed out that despite the conceptual distinction between the two confounding influences, it is difficult to decide whether the confounding source is a response style or response set. An account of the two kinds of confounding influences is given below.

Response Styles

Rorer (1965) defined response style as a "tendency to select some response category a disproportionate amount of time independent of item content" (p.136). Jackson and Messick (1958) began their discussion of content and style in personality assessment by drawing attention to the ubiquitous distinction between interpretation of behaviour in terms of (a) the content of "needs" and cognitive structures, and (b) characteristic styles of response and action. This distinction between what and how is illustrated with the example of an obsequious person whose deference is not only manifested in his act of yielding but also by the tone of his voice while performing the act of yielding. Though personality theorists have been aware of the distinction between the instrumental and stylistic aspects of behaviour, they could not draw attention to the role of style in determining responses to the items of a personality inventory until it was realized that scores obtained by the subjects are not fully determined by the personality characteristic which the inventory purports to assess. The following are sources of response distortion falling in the category of response styles as defined by Lanyon:

1. Acquiescence.

Lorge (1937) and Lentz (1938) were the initiator of work on this source of response distortion. But since their papers were not published in their entirety, Cronbach (1941, 1946, 1950) is given credit for the systematic study of acquiescence. He was concerned with the problem of guessing on objective tests used for the measurement of classroom achievement. Cronbach discovered that the usual practice of subtracting the number of wrong answers from the number of correct answers was not an effective method for removing the effect of guessing. This practice led to unequal penalization of students because the outcome of subtraction depends on the tendency of students to prefer 'True' or 'False' response alternative when they do not know the correct answer and have to guess. Cronbach made distinction between the students who showed the tendency to guess 'true' by calling them acquiescent and those who showed the tendency to guess 'False' by calling them critical. He predicted that acquiescent students would get high scores on the test which have True-keyed items and critical students would get high marks on the test having False-keyed items. The prediction was confirmed by empirical findings (Cronbach, 1941, 1942). In his later papers Cronbach (1946,1950) pointed out that acquiescence is a test-taking response set which an individual brings to testing situation. He defined acquiescence as, "any tendency causing a person consistently to make different responses to test items than he would had the same content being presented in different form. Acquiescence response style would be evident if two persons getting equal score on a test comprising multiple choice items get different scores when the same content appears in different form (1946, p. 476)."

Most of the studies of acquiescence response style are regarding its role in determining the scores on MMPI scales and the F scale. While the MMPI have unequal number of True-keyed and False-keyed items, all the items of the F scale are so worded that agreement with the items indicate authoritarianism.

The MMPI scales were devised for identification of subjects suffering from different kinds of psychiatric problems and every scale is expected to be independent of other. However, when scores on different MMPI scales are correlated and the matrix of intercorrelation is factorized, the first extracted factor is identified as acquiescence response style by Messick and Jackson (1961). They reviewed eight-factor analyses of matrix of intercorrelation of MMPI scores and then calculated rank order correlations between proportion of items keyed 'True' in each scale and the loading of items on the largest factor. The magnitude of rank order correlations was in the range of .52 to .91. Messick and Jackson (1961) concluded, "These strikingly consistent findings indicate that in most of the studies the largest factor on MMPI is interpretable in terms of acquiescence" (p. 300). However, Edwards (1970) would not agree with this conclusion. As we would see later on, he would interpret the factor in terms of desirability of responses.

Studies of the effect of acquiescence on the F scale illustrate the problems involved in the methodology of acquiescence studies. As the F scale is comprised of items worded in only one direction, study of effect of acquiescence required that the items be worded in reversed direction. The evidence regarding the involvement of response distortion could be obtained by correlating scores on the original and reversed F scale. Negative correlation between the two scores would be an indication of responses to items content and positive correlation between the scores obtained with the help of two versions would be an indication of acquiescence. The findings of the different studies are not unanimous; some are in favour of content and some in favour of acquiescence interpretation. The reason of the disagreement in findings is suggested to be the difference in the nature of reversal. Jackson and Messick (1958) referred to the fact that in their earlier study (Jackson and Messick, 1957) they retained extremely worded and cliche-ridden style of the F scale in their reversal and obtained correlation indicating presence of acquiescence because the subjects endorsed both original and extremely worded reversed statements. Christe, Havel, and Seidnberg (1958) obtained correlation between original and reversed items in content direction because they did not retained the sweeping generalizations of the original items in their reversals. Rorer (1965) whose refutation of response-style interpretation of personality scores is reflected in the title of his article, "The Great Response Style Myth", pointed out that there could be no valid interpretation of correlation of original and reversed versions of a scale like the F scale if the subjects are not contradicting themselves while giving 'True' responses to both versions. From the point of view of Rorer, the studies in which mean endorsement values of the original and reversed items were low but the correlation indicated the presence of acquiescence responding, should not be regarded as evidence in favour of acquiescence responding because False responses to the original and reversed items do not amount to contradiction.

The problem of identification of determinants of responses on the F scale items became more complicated with the distinction of two kinds of acquiescence processes, agreement and acceptance (Bentler, 1969; Bentler, Jackson and Messick, 1971). Agreement acquiescence is the tendency to agree with personality statements without consideration of the content; acceptance acquiescence is the tendency to accept any self-descriptive item whatever its content may be. An extreme acceptor would say 'True' to all items that describe personality characteristics (e.g., I am happy; I am sad) and would say 'False' to all items that deny characteristics (e.g., I am not happy; I am not sad). In the case of agreement acquiescence, positive correlation between the original and reversed versions is the demonstration of acquiescence, in the case of acceptance acquiescence positive as well as negative correlations would indicate acceptance acquiescence. The positive correlation would indicate acceptance acquiescence when subjects are asked to give response to pairs that represent presence or absence of a trait such as happy-sad, and not happy-not sad. Negative correlation would indicate the presence of acceptance acquiescence when the subject is presented positively and negatively worded pairs such as sad—not sad, happy—not happy.

While considering the confounding of content and response style in personality assessment one should be aware of the fact that acquiescence and other response styles do not have uniform influence on all the scales or all the items of a scale. They are elicited differently as the function of specific item content and certain characteristics of items such as ambiguity, desirability, etc.

Deviation Response Style

In our discussion of empirical approach we referred to Berg's deviation hypothesis to explain the possible reason of disregard of logical relation between the content of items and psychological characteristics which can be assessed by them. We are now discussing deviation response style which overshadow the content of personality inventories in determining individuals' scores. Attention toward this mode of responding was drawn by Berg, Hunt, and Barnes (1949) who observed that some persons have a tendency to give responses which are different from the responses given by most of the people. They also noted that this tendency to give deviant responses is general. The formal articulation of this point is deviant hypothesis which we have mentioned earlier.

While deviant response style may itself be useful for differentiation between different criterion groups, it becomes a source of response distortion when items comprising a personality inventory are considered as indicator of certain trait and responses to items (True/False; Yes/No) are considered to have correspondence with the trait indicating behaviour. When responses are not determined or partially determined by item content and partially by relative deviation response style, we have to consider this style as a source of confounding. However, it is to be pointed out that deviation hypothesis gives little importance to the use of relevant content in the measure of personality and the variance which can be attributed to the content. What is important for the deviation hypothesis is that due to past learning, inherited structures, or organic or psychological states some persons may share a pattern of response bias and this relative deviation may be utilized for psychological diagnosis and assessment. Minimizing the importance of content and highlighting the importance of response bias in personality assessment, Berg observed, "The available evidence indicates that items dealing with jobs, social activities, and adjustment, etc., are quite unnecessary for objective personality, interest and similar tests. One can use such content if he so desires; but he can equally well use abstract designs, sounds, list of foods, light, imagery questions, spiral after effect and the content of equally wide range".

In order to demonstrate the application of deviation hypothesis in the differentiation of criterion groups sharing relative deviation tendencies, Berg and his associates (1949) devised Picture Reaction Test (PRT) which has 60 abstract designs drawn with the help of a ruler and compass. In respect of each design the subjects have to select one response alternative out of the following: Like Much, Like Slightly, Dislike Slightly, Dislike Much. Comparing the responses of 700 normal subjects with the responses of different criterion groups, the following scales were developed: Delta for general neurotic disturbance, Psi for psychotic conditions, Sigma for schizophrenia, Chi for character disorders, and Psi-Chi for separating diagnostically psychotic conditions and character disorder states.

While Berg and his associates (1949, 1955, 1959) have suggested the utilization of deviation response style for making useful clinical differentiation, doubts are expressed regarding the content free nature of the PRT. Berg (1961) regards it an absurd proposal that since content of items is unimportant any item is as good as the other. The only implication of the assertion that item content is not important is that no particular content is important, and that for any given verbal item, one can find a design or sound that would be as well (Berg, 1961, p. 336). The success in the derivation of different scales with the help of abstract designs is considered to be evidence of the importance of content by Rorer (1965) who argued that since reliable scales have been developed and since individuals were not responding to a particular alternative, they must, on purely logical ground, be responding to the content.

Extreme Response Style (ERS)

This response style operates when subjects have to respond along intensity dimension and are given the choice to locate their response anywhere along a continuum such as Strongly Agree, Agree, Neutral, Disagree, Strongly Disagree. A subject's tendency to give extreme response is observed when he makes a choice at either end of the continuum, i.e., Strongly Agree or Strongly Disagree.

Many different measures are used for the detection of this response style. The F scale, the Dogmatism scale, Parental Attitude Research Instrument, Semantic Differential scales are the examples of the scales which have been scored for extreme response style. Since all these scales have content for measuring certain personality characteristics, it is difficult to isolate the contributions of their specific content and the extreme response style to the score obtained by a person. Only Berg's PRT and WRT are the instruments which are free of specific content.

While any instrument can be scored for extreme responding, it is better to make use of contentless items for developing a measure of extreme response style. Whatever may be the content of items, the scoring system of ERS measure may be as below:

1. Counting number of category at each end of the continuum.

2. Instead of one category at both ends, two extreme categories at each end may be included. For example, when a 11-point scale is used, we can count how many times responses are located in 1 and 2; 10 and 11.

3. Bimodality Index used by Peak et al . (1960) which is defined as average number of responses in categories 1, 2, 10 and 11 (on a 11-point scale) minus mean number of responses in the intermediate categories.

4. Deviation from mid-point of the scales in which mid-point is assigned a score of 0 and moving in both direction numerals 1, 2, 3, etc., are assigned to the steps approaching the two extremes as shown below:

Strongly Agree	*Moderately Agree*	*Agree*	*Undecided*	*Disagree*	*Moderately Agree*	
3	2	1	0	1	2	3

Studies reviewed by Hamilton (1968) show that test-retest reliability of ERS measures fall in range of .79 to .94 while internal consistency vary from .53 to .94. Generally, content-free measures of ERS were found to have higher reliability coefficients than such measures as the F scale which is content-laden. Hamilton also found evidence regarding generality of ERS but also noted that two variables are found to affect generality of ERS measures: (a) amount of content in the stimulus items, and (b) the similarity of item format in the ERS measures which are used in the study of generality of ERS. Sometimes a distinction is made between positive and negative extreme response style depending which side of neutral point the response is located. Attempts have been made to answer the question, "Do individuals who endorse the extreme category in one direction also tend to use extreme category in other direction?" Peabody (1966) and Brengelman (1959) furnished evidence of low positive correlation between positive and negative extreme responses.

Four different interpretations of extreme response style are offered. According to these interpretations when subjects are given opportunity to respond along an intensity continuum, there operates a tendency to make use of extreme response categories and if this tendency to make use of extreme response categories is not restrained by the content of items, it is likely to give information about the individual's style. Deviancy is the most obvious interpretation of ERS. It is suggested that ERS is the deviancy observed in the form of abnormal behaviour. In support of this contention Zukerman et al. (1958) furnished evidence of positive relationship between ERS and abnormality. ERS is also reported to be associated with the use of associative communality in word association (Arthur and Freemantle, 1966). But it may be pointed out that ERS is different from Berg's conceptualization of deviancy because according to Berg's (1957) specification, deviancy can be determined in statistical terms knowing the pattern of response of certain group. Intolerance of ambiguity as manifested by the choice of response categories which enable a person to be certain in his choice is another explanation of extreme response style offered by Brim and Hoff (1957). However, there is no conclusive evidence in this regard due to inconsistent findings. Consistent findings regarding the tendency of abnormal and maladjusted persons to give extreme responses, have given rise to the explanation of ERS in terms of Hull-Spence theory. Zax et al. (1964), who offer this kind of explanation, point out that high drive level of high anxious persons and associated excitatory potential find manifestation in the choice of extreme response categories. ERS can also be explained in terms of cognitive development. According to this explanation cognitive development proceeds from less differentiated cognitive structure to more differentiated cognitive structure and the choice of extreme responses is a manifestation of less cognitive differentiation. Evidence is furnished to the effect that young and old persons make more frequent extreme responses than adults. White and Harvey (1965) have shown the relationship between concretness and ERS. Lightet et. al. (1965), Zax et al. (1964) and Hesterly (1963) are the contributors to this point of view. One more plausible explanation of extreme response style is in terms of the stimulus material. O' Donovon (1965) furnished evidence to the effect that responses to meaningful material tend to be polarized while responses to meaningless material tend to fall in different categories and are unpolarized. But contrary evidence is furnished by the studies that show that individual differences in ERS do not disappear when items are ambiguous and subject's own stand on the stimulus material is controlled.

Findings regarding the consistency, generality, and correlation of ERS with other personality dimensions elevated it from the status of a source of irrelevant variance to that of a personality variable in its own right. We shall refer to a study conducted by Jain (1978) to illustrate the nature of evidence furnished to establish ERS as a personality variable. Using contentless PRT as a measure of ERS, Jain compared high and low extreme response groups with respect to their scores on the F scale and Security-Insecurity (S-I) inventory and their revered forms. He argued that high positive correlation of a contentless measure of ERS with other measures comprising meaningful items presented to the subjects in multi-response format and reversed forms of the meaningful items, would be evidence of consistent operation of ERS. Further, while evidence regarding the personality correlates of ERS would be provided by correlation of ERS measured by PRT with the measures of authoritarianism and security-insecurity, the evidence about ERS as a variable of personality in its own right would be in the form of low factor loading of ERS on 16 factors measured by 16 PF questionnaire. The findings of the study showed that ERS operates consistently in both contentless and meaningful measures; the relationship between measures of authoritarianism and security-insecurity on one hand and ERS on the other is curvilinear. The ERS has loading on a factor different from the sixteen factors measured by 16 PF questionnaire.

Response Sets

The two response sets which we are going to discuss are social desirability and faking. Social desirability is more similar to response style because it is spontaneous and unconscious choice of the response alternative which is pervasive and found to occur whenever an individual has to make a choice between the alternatives implying socially desirable and undesirable behaviour. Unlike social desirability, faking is an attempt to create impression which an individual believes to be useful in the context of assessment.

Social Desirability

If a subject is asked to give his responses to a set of items and responses given by him are used for the purpose of assessment of his personality trait(s), there remain the possibility that his responses are not a straightforward reflection of his personality because he may not be responding to the trait-related content of the item but to the element of social desirability which is mingled with the trait-relevant content. Attention to this kind of ubiquitous source of response distortion was drawn by Edwards (1953) who is of the view that any item of any personality inventory may be characterized in terms of its position on the dimension of social desirability. Edwards writes, "I am contending that regardless of multiple dimensional nature of personality statements with respect to content, it is still possible to describe each one in terms of its position on social desirability continuum... The importance of dimension rests in the fact that, if we know the position of statements, we can predict, with a high degree of accuracy, the proportion of individuals who will say, in self-description, that statements do describe them." This contention is based on empirical studies carried out by Edwards and his associates. In an initial attempt to determine the influence of social desirability on item endorsement, Edwards asked 86 males and 66 females to rate social desirability of 140 statements on a 9-point scale ranging from extremely desirable, through neutral, to extremely undesirable. The ratings were used for obtaining mean judged desirability values of the every item designated as SDSV. Another group of subjects was administered the set of items with the instruction to give True or False response to each of them. The probability of giving

True response, P(T), was determined for each item by dividing the frequency of True response by total number of responses to the item. The SDSV values and P(T) values of items obtained independently were correlated and the correlation was found to be as high as .97. Similar findings were reported by Kenny (1956), Zimmer (1954) and Hanley (1956).

A landmark in the research on the operation of social desirability variable in personality was the construction of the Social Desirability (SD) scale. One of the purposes of construction of an independent measure of social desirability was to meet the objection that the studies in which an independent measure of SDSV of items are correlated with their P(T)s, both values were based on the same set of items. In such a situation if the trait keying of items and SD keying coincide (e.g.,True response indicates both trait to be measured and social desirability response), the correlation cannot be considered to be between two independent variables. Another purpose of developing the SD scale was to have an instrument that would enable the assessment of individual differences in the tendency to give desirable responses.

With the development of the SD scale it became possible to conduct correlational and factor analytic studies regarding the contribution of social desirability in responses to items in personality inventories. Edwards reported that SD scores correlate with Guilford-Martin scales measuring Cooperativeness, Agreeableness, and Objectivity to the extent of .63, .53 and .71 respectively. The fact that the SD scale was found to have high correlations with different MMPI scales led Edwards and Walker (1961) to conclude that the SD scale can be regarded as a short version of MMPI because scores on the SD scale can be used to predict MMPI score with little error of estimate. The implication of this conclusion is that most of the variance of different MMPI scales can be explained in terms of desirability responding and what is left is nothing but error variance. More evidence in favour of desirability responding is furnished by factor analysis of matrix of correlation among MMPI scales. As loading of MMPI scales on the first factor were corresponding to the magnitude of coefficient of correlation of MMPI scales with the SD scale, Edwards and Walsh (1964, p. 59) observed, ".... the degree to which MMPI scales also have loading on the first factor or the degree to which they are correlated with the SD scale, they must be measuring the same trait as the SD scale regardless of the particular trait name which has been assigned to the MMPI scales."

As pointed out earlier, one-directional keying of the SD scale makes it susceptible to acquiescence and for this reason doubts are expressed that the correlation of this scale with factor loading on the first factor can be due to acquiescence rather than desirable responses (Messick and Jackson, 1961b). Edwards did not deny the possibility of confounding of social desirability and acquiescence but furnished evidence to the effect that largest factor is desirability rather than acquiescence. One kind of evidence is based on the logic that if the MMPI is administered with instructions which can minimize acquiescence responding and scores thus obtained are used for factor analysis, the largest factor extracted should be different from that obtained from scores provided by the standard administration wherein acquiescence operates. In order to minimize acquiescence responding, Edwards and Dier (1962) instructed one group of 120 subjects, who were administered MMPI under standard instructions a week before, to give socially desirable responses. Another group of 150 subjects was administered MMPI with instructions to give socially desirable responses. For each of the administration conditions—standard(S), desirable responding (SD), and undesirable responding (SUD) instructions—responses were scored for 58 MMPI scales. Three-factor analyses were done, one for each of the three conditions of instruction. To identify the nature of the first factor emerged in analysis, indices of acquiescence and desirability were obtained for each of the scales included in factor analyses. The index of acquiescence was based on finding the proportion of items keyed for True responding and the index of desirability was based on the proportion of SD keyed items. The correlation of the two indices with the first factor loadings of the variables were same for all the three conditions S, SD and SUD. If SD and SUD could minimize the influence of acquiescence responding, the correlation of acquiescence index would be found to be different in different conditions of administration. One possible explanation of the fact of correlation remaining the same could be confounding of acquiescence and desirability but evidence is furnished in support of desirability interpretation of the first factor. The SD scale was correlated with scores on each of the MMPI scales administered under S, SD and SUD conditions and the values of coefficients thus obtained were correlated with loadings of the scale on the first factor. It was found that both proportion of SD responses and 39-item SD scale could accurately predict the first factor loadings of MMPI scales regardless of variation of instructions.

Rorer (1965) and Block (1965) are the ardent opponents of response style and response set interpretation of subject's responses to the F scale, MMPI, and other personality inventories. Rorer did not deny that studies have yielded results that can be interpreted in terms of acquiescence and desirability responding but insisted that no conclusive evidence can be furnished unless the effect of content is eliminated (Rorer, 1965, p.142). The elimination of content becomes an impossible task because even contentless tests have some content.

Block's (1965) argument to contest the challenge of response set includes difficulty in the construction of content free tests, and possibility of content interpretation of what are supposed to be pure measures of response styles and response set, colinearity of desirability and characterological dimensions but heuristic failure of SD hypothesis, and relation of SD notion to personality dimension as demonstrated by the possibility of constructing "subtle SD Scale" with item in neutral range of desirability. Block pointed out that Edwards' SD scale is not comprised of heterogeneous items which would be needed to interpret responses in terms of social desirability. According to Block, the content of the scale reflects anxiety and tension and it is content homogeneity rather than social desirability which determines high correlation of the SD scale with MMPI scales. Block demonstrated the "untenable anomaly" of desirability hypothesis by showing that a set items neutral as to the social desirability correlate high with the first factor of MMPI which he designated as "Ego Resiliency". But Jackson (1967) is not impressed with the demonstration of anomaly of subtle SD scale because search of subtle scales in MMPI test construction has a long history and if there can be subtle pathological scale there can also be subtle SD scale.

Faking

When a person is instructed to read every item of a personality inventory carefully and then to choose one of the response alternatives which describe his behaviour most appropriately, he may either comply with this instruction or he may defy it depending upon his perception of the testing situation and the expectation regarding the use to which the outcome of assessment would be put to. If the person knows something bad about himself which if communicated to others would evoke negative attitudes towards him, he is not likely to make a genuine self-disclosure. Making use of what Goffman (1963) calls prestige symbols, and disidentifier, a person would try to conceal his real identity because he wants to avoid the negative consequences which he would have to face if his true identity is disclosed.

Faking good is not always in the interest of a person. Depending upon what would be in his interest, a person may either fake good or fake bad. If a person is being assessed for determining his suitability for the job he wants to have, he is likely to give the responses which would make him to appear the most eligible candidate for appointment. Similarly, a hospitalized psychiatric patient who wants to return to his home shall make an attempt to impress the staff with his simulated normal behaviour as well as simulated responses to formal assessment devices. However, if someone wants to escape from responsibility of his criminal behaviour or wants to avoid compulsory draft in the army, he may simulate psychiatric symptoms. For faking good and faking bad we have to assume that the subject knows what kind of responses would be helpful in creating the kind of impression he is trying to have. This implies that the subject has an understanding of the inferences that can be drawn from his responses to items of the inventory.

Personality assessment became concerned with the problem of faking when it was found that some known psychiatric patients have profile of scores similar to normal persons and some normal subjects have profile similar to the psychiatric patients. This created the problem of false positive and false negative. False positive subjects are those who are normal but their test scores show them to be abnormal. False negative are those who are abnormal but their test protocol shows them to be normal.

To understand the nature of faking and to develop the device which would be helpful in the identification of instances of faking, a number of studies have been conducted in which subjects were instructed to fake good or fake bad.

Gough (1954) was pioneer of studies on stereotypes of professionals and laymen about the self-perception and inner experiences of neurotic patients. Such studies help us to recognize the attempts of faking bad by normal subjects. Gough (1954) findings showed that normal dissemblers use of distinct set of items which makes it possible to differentiate them from known psychoneurotic patients.

A study conducted by Dicken (1959) deserves mention because it shows that faking is possible on an instrument like Edwards Personal Preference Schedule (EPPS). The forced choice format of EPPS items is an attempt to control social desirability of response. Four role playing groups employed in the study were: need order (ORD), need dominance (DOM), need change (CHG), and general impression (GI). The study was conducted to test the following hypotheses: (a) subjects motivated to simulate a personality trait are capable of inducing substantial changes in their EPPS scores; (b) substantial score changes will occur under role playing of a "good impression", despite of the attempted control of the SD factor; (c) subjects' groups that play different personality variable roles will obtain different simulated pattern; (d) the consistency score is not an effective index of simulation. All the hypotheses were confirmed. One of the important conclusion of the study was that the subjects can simulate even without specific information of the variables assessed by an instrument. This conclusion was based on the fact that the GI group which was not given specific information about role playing was successful in simulating "desirable" traits.

While Gough's study referred to above showed that both professional and normal laymen can give stereotyped responses, evidence regarding the inability of disturbed individuals to simulate the responses of normal persons is furnished by Grayson and Olinger (1957). It is reported that only 11 per cent of a group of psychiatric patients could fake a normal profile and also that when instructed to fake good they produced more deviant profiles and profiles of a different patterns of abnormality. A study conducted by Canter (1963) has shown that better adjusted persons are more successful in producing good faked profile of the California Psychological Inventory. The superiority of well-adjusted persons to simulate the MMPI pattern suggesting psychopathic personality was demonstrated by a study conducted by Lanyon (1967b).

Due to the fact that structured personality inventories are made up of items which are meaningful and for this reason would be more helpful in creating good impression, it is reasonable to believe that personality inventories are more susceptible to simulation but projective tests are not. The empirical evidence is not in agreement with the expectation. Although studies conducted by Fosberg (1938, 1941) showed that subjects instructed to make best possible impression through Rorschach responses were not successful in doing so, his findings are not considered to be valid on the ground that his statistical procedures were faulty. Evidence showing vulnerability of projective tests to impression management is furnished by Carp and Shavzin (1950), Feldman and Garley (1954), Henry and Rotter (1956).

Dealing with Response Distortions

Whereas it has been recommended that a considerable portion of variance of scores obtained with the help of personality inventories is contributed by response styles and response sets, we have to search for the ways and means that would enable us to eliminate or, at least, minimize the role of response distortions. Response distortions can be dealt with in the following manner:

1. Improvement of Test Design

An attempt can be made to restrict the operation of response distortions by including in the test the kind of items which do not provide the opportunity of response distortions. Different steps can be taken to deal with different kinds of distortions:

(a) To minimize the possibility of acquiescence, the test constructor can formulate items in such a way that the scale is balanced with respect to True-False keying of items. However, finding the items which are worded in both the directions becomes difficult because the structure of English and many other languages is such that it is difficult to present the same content in such a way that "True" response to some items indicate the same trait as "False" response to some other items. Failing to collect equal number of items worded in opposite direction, a test constructor may make an attempt to write the reversal of the original items. But this attempt may run into difficulty because such a simple way of reversing an item as by adding the prefix, "It is not the case that..." or "It is not true that..." alters the style, length and complexity of the items (Rorer and Goldberg, 1965). Failure to find an appropriate antonym and the disregard of distinction between logically contradictory and contrary statements are other problems of balancing the scale in respect of True-False keying for the purpose of removing acquiescence.

(b) Prior scaling of items in respect of social desirability and then using only those items which have social desirability scale values (SDSVs) in the neutral range of the desirability-undesirability continuum is one of the ways of minimizing the impact of desirability. An attempt is to be made to avoid extremely desirable and extremely undesirable items because a scale made up of items which have bimodal distribution of SDSVs is more susceptible to desirability responding than a scale made up of items with flat distribution of SDSVs (Wiggins, 1973).

Devising the scales in which desirable responses and trait relevant responses are in opposite direction is another suggestion given by Edwards. Edwards (1963) recommended that, "....we might seek items such that socially desirable response is the keyed response in scales designed to measure socially undesirable variables. For scales designed to measure socially desirable variables, we would, of course, attempt to find items for which the socially undesirable response is keyed" (p.115).

Use of a forced-choice format for items seems to be most effective way of dealing with the social desirability. This approach helps in developing scales which are relatively uncorrelated with individual differences in rate of SD responding. Edwards Personal Preference Schedule (EPPS) makes use of this format of items and requires subjects to read a pair of statements and select one which describes him better. The statements are paired in such a way that both have approximately same SDSVs but the differ in describing two different needs. It is assumed that since statements included in a pair having equal SDSV, the choice between them would depend on the need which they depict. However, even forced-choice format is not able to eliminate faking.

(c) Deliberate effort to fake good or fake bad may be minimized by using the subtle items. This makes it difficult for subjects to understand how the items and the responses which the subjects would give to the items are related to the kind of impression which he wants to create. Seeman (1952) defined item subtlety in terms of "meaning" property of test stimuli and suggested a method of giving experimental form to the concept of subtlety. According to Seeman (1952) subtlety refers to the degree to which "meaning" can or cannot be arbitrary assigned in a priori fashion to test items (p. 278). The criterion of subtle items is to be lack of success of the naive subjects to assign the item to the diagnostic category/trait/context to which they belong and that in ability to specify the direction of scoring. The usefulness of subtle items depends on their power to discrimination between external criterion groups. Duff (1965) conducted a study in which the measure of subtlety was percentage of judges correctly identifying both the item's scale and keyed response. In regard to the relationship between item subtlety and discriminating power it is reported that only 40 per cent of the most subtle items, as compared to 90 per cent of obvious items, discriminated between appropriate criterion groups. For moderately subtle items the percentage of discriminating items was intermediate to the two percentages. Duff concluded that, "By requiring that items exhibit at least a minimum level of obviousness in addition to empirical discriminating power, it would be possible to develop scales which continue to function and at the same time are not completely susceptible to conscious manipulation" (p. 569).

The usefulness of subtle items in a scale was demonstrated by Gynther, Bukhart, and Hanovitz (1970) who divided items of Pd scale into obvious, neutral, and subtle categories and then used three sets for the prediction of conformity. Multiple-regression analysis showed that while neutral items made no contribution in addition to already existing relationship between obvious items and criterion, subtle items made a small but unique contribution in the prediction.

The distinction between subtle scale and obvious items seems to suggest that subtle items are the items which have low face validity. But Holden and Jackson (1979) have made the following distinction between subtlety and face validity of items: Whereas face validity involved the ability of a test respondent to relate item content to a hypothesized behavioural dimension, item subtlety is concerned with the respondent's ability to relate item content to its actual, keyed scale. Therefore, with respect to the test respondent, face validity can be defined as contextual relevance of an item. Whereas item subtlety can be viewed as lack of an obvious substantive link between an item and its underlying construct (p. 461).

(d) Attempt to fake can be checked if the purpose of testing is concealed from the subjects. This can be done by not printing the name of the test since it can help the subjects to understand how they would be evaluated on the basis of their responses to test items. Because it is rather difficult to enlist the cooperation of the subject without informing them the purpose of testing, the test can be given some general name which does not reveal the real purpose of testing. However, going through the items a subject can understand what the tester wants to know about him and he may accordingly alter his responses to create the kind of impression he wants to have. The use of some items which distract the subject from gradual accumulation of the purpose of testing, is one of the provisions which can be made for preventing the subject from faking. Such items are known as fillers or buffers because they appear in a scale only for the purpose of concealing the meaning of test items and are not considered in scoring. Let us consider available empirical evidence regarding the utility of filler items. Kestebaum and Hammersla (1976) conducted experiments to find whether filler items can be effective in accomplishing the following: concealing purpose of testing which results in different scores than would be without use of such items, and preventing social desirable responding and faking. The first experiment conducted by Kestenbaum and Hammersla was regarding the difference in mean I-E scores when Rotters's Internal External Control scale is administered with or without the presence of filler items. The finding showed that the two means do not differ significantly and it was concluded that if a scale is poorly constructed with regard to social desirability few filler items are unlikely to prevent faking.

The second experiment was conducted to find whether instructions to create good impression on prospective employer are likely to have different effect when a scale has/has not filler items. The experiment used 2 × 2 × 2 design in which combinations of male/female, fillers/non-fillers, and good impression/standard instructions were made for the purpose of finding the effect of the three variables on changes in I-E scores. The findings of the study showed that neither filler items nor altering instructions influenced I-E scores. Moreover, filler items failed to obscure knowledge of what the scale measures. Sex differences were found in knowledge and certainty. Female were more successful in discerning the purpose of the scale but they were less certain than male of their conjecture regarding the purpose of the scale.

Strahan and Wilson (1976) used items of Neuroticism-Extraversion (N-E) questionnaire as buffer in a study of subjects' insight in the purpose of Marlowe-Crowne SD scale. There were three experimental conditions created by variation of mixing of items. After the administration of the questionnaire the subjects were given a measure of insight in the purpose of the questionnaire. Trait judgment protocols given by the subjects were sorted out into insight and non-insight categories. It was found that buffer items could not affect the means of the MC scores and that 'insight' and 'non-insight subject' do not differ in the MC scores. Though it is evident that presence of buffer items does not influence MC scores, Strahon and Wilson warns against the generalization of the findings by pointing out that ineffectiveness of buffer items is specific to the conditions of the study the particular buffer items, the population sampled, the characteristics of questionnaire administration.

2. Detection of Response Distortions

We have discussed the methods of identification of items which are not likely to be influenced by response biases and response sets. Many well-known personality inventories have been developed without making an attempt to make use of items which are less likely to be susceptible to response distortions though some of them are provided with the devices which help us in determine whether responses given by the subjects contain information about personality characteristics and whether it would be worthwhile to interpret the scores. The MMPI has four validity scales which are used for examining the presence of evasiveness, lying, lack of comprehension of items and other factors which influence responding to such an extent that if subject's scores are interpreted despite their presence, the assessor is unlikely to arrive at a valid description of subject's personality. While MMPI validity scales are described elsewhere, we shall describe the scales for the detection of acquiescence, social desirability and attempt to create good impression.

Detection of Acquiescence

If we have obtained an individual's score with the help of an instrument which is susceptible to this kind of response style, we can administer a measure of acquiescence of the subject and if that measure shows that the subject has a tendency to acquiesce, we can legitimately suspect that this tendency might have operated in determining the score on the personality scale. A measure of acquiescence is to be made up of items which are contentless because if items have content it would not be possible to decide how far subject's responses are due to acquiescence and how far they are due to the content of items, a confounding effect which we really want to discover.

In order to minimize the role of content-determined responding on an acquiescence scale one can use either (1) contentless items like those used by Berg, et al. (1949), or (2) include items which if endorsed in a particular direction would indicate logically untenable position. One of the extensively used and carefully developed measure of acquiescence is Frick's (1957) Response Bias or B scale. Other measures of acquiescence on MMPI are Hanley's (1957) Bn scale, Wiggin's (1962) Rb scale, and Ars scale devised by Shaffer (1963). All these scales are similar to the B scale in derivation and have a common feature of being neutral in social desirability.

Detection of Desirability Responding

A large number of scales are available for the detection of social desirable responding. In some of the measures of desirability the distinction between desirability and deliberate attempt to make a good impression on others is blurred. Two important measures of desirability are Edwards (1957) SD scale, and Marlowe-Crowne SD scale. Edwards SD scale was developed with an initial pool of 150 items drawn from L, F, and K scales of MMPI, and Taylor Anxiety scale. The items were rated by a panel of judges in respect of desirability of content. There was unanimity among judges for 79 items. A subsequent version of the scale was developed containing 39 items which were found to discriminate between high and low scorers on 79-item set. Two shortcomings of Edwards SD scale are: (1) single direction of keying of items which makes the scale vulnerable to acquiescence, and (2) pathological content of items which makes the scale a measure of tendency to admit maladjustive symptoms.

The construction of C-M scale began with a collection of 50 items describing desirable or undesirable behaviour with low probability of being true of all people and having minimum of pathological or abnormal implications. The low probability criterion was in accordance to the point of view that social desirable responding is a tendency to conform to social stereotype of what should be acknowledged and what should be rejected in self-description. The minimum-pathology criterion was for the removal of the possibility of a subject getting high score on the SD scale by giving False responses to items describing in the maladjustive symptoms which are actually of low frequency. If minimum pathology criterion was not applied then it would not be possible to distinguish an attempt of presenting oneself in favourable light from genuine denial of abnormality.

The C-M SD scale is given more meaning and interpretation than tendency to conform stereotype of good behaviour. It is regarded as a measure of need to achieve approval from others. The research in which C-M SD scale has been used led Crowne and Marlow (1964) to conclude, "The behavioural correlates of the tendency to avoid self-criticism and to choose self-evaluative statements which summatively portray a stereotypically acceptable self-image are complex: they occur in the contexts for beyond the confines of the test situation" (p. 189).

Gough (1954) whose pioneer research on dissimulation has been referred in a previous section devised a Dissimulation Scale (DS) which can be used for differentiating faked neurotic records from the records of known neurotics. A set of 14 items were found to discriminate neurotics from students of abnormal psychology and professional staff members instructed to give responses to MMPI pool of items in the same way a person experiencing a psychoneurotic reaction would do. A neurotic configuration with raw score 35 or above would be suspected to be a case of attempted faking, while such a record with 15 or less score on the DS score would be an assurance of no attempt of faking.

Thirty-three items Mp scale developed by Cofer, Chance and Judson (1949) was derived from an investigation in which both good and bad malingering instructions were employed. The Mp scale provides a check on the tendency to answer the MMPI with the intention to create favourable impression. A raw score of 20 points was found to be the cutting point for judging dependability of protocol for personological interpretation; that is if a subject gets Mp score less than 20, credence can be given to MMPI description of his personality. Among college students with score higher than this cutting point 86 per cent produced positively malingered records while only 4 per cent of bonafied records obtained with standard instructions were above that point.

A scale which can distinguish 'hits' from 'misses' was developed by Osbone (1969). This scale is known as Moderator scale (Mo) because it helps in the identification of records which provide less dependable clinical judgment. Two experienced staff members of the university of Minnesota Department of Psychiatry were asked to use a 31-item symptom checklist to judge MMPI profiles which were previously screened on validity-scale criteria (no more than 10 Cannot Say answers, L less than 10, F less than 21, and K less than 23). In each case the judges were to indicate five features which they expected to find by their interpretation of the MMPI. Depending upon the correspondence of actual and expected symptoms, the patients were divided into hits and miss category. Item analysis led to the identification of 38 items which separated hits from misses. The Mo scale comprising these 38 items was found to be negatively correlated with the F scale and all clinical scales except Hypomania. However, it seems to reflect variance which is independent of validity indicators.

Correction for subjects' attitudes which make a protocol of little use for the inference of personological characteristics, is illustrated by correction of concomittal response as indicated by Cannot Say scores and attempt of faking as indicated by K score of MMPI. While answering MMPI items many persons do not give any response to a large number of items. Inability to understand meaning of items, opposition to being asked to complete a test like MMPI, and attempt to create an impression by avoiding self-disclosure are some of the reasons of omitting response to certain items. Brown (1950) suggested an approach to make the MMPI protocol usable in the case of large scale omission of responses. The first step of this approach is to examine all the items and to find items which are not applicable to the subject. For remaining of the unanswered items the subject is given one-half of credit. Brown's proposal illustrates the correction following an attempt of defensiveness in responding. However, this proposal has the following limitations: the first step of the proposal amount to purification of MMPI scale for each subject and the second step involves giving some credit for a false response and some credit for the true response when he has not given either of the responses.

The addition of certain portion of subject's K score in raw scores on some of the clinical scales of MMPI is another illustration for making correction for defensiveness. More details about the K scale are given elsewhere. It is sufficient to point out that the purpose of adding a portion of K score (for example, .5 K to Hs scale) is to have better differentiation between a bonafied and fake record. Two points regarding the utility of the K scale for combating defensiveness are to be mentioned. One, the K scale would not be able to improve the predictive validity of a scale which is itself of low validity. Second, the weights of K scales for the correction of raw scores are expected to differ from population to population. Heilburn (1963) has reported a revised set of correction fractions to be used with MMPI scores of college students.

Suppression of Response Distortions

We have discussed the use of forced-choice format and K scale for dealing with the spurious variance of test scores contributed by different sources of response distortions. The suppression model is implicit in use of these devices for the elimination of "unwanted" predictor variance. However, the nature of suppression model becomes more explicit in the situation of prediction of a criterion. Dickens (1963) defined suppressor variable as "one which is significantly associated with a predictor, but essentially unassociated with the criterion for which the predictor is valid" (p. 699). The importance of association of the suppressor variable with predictors is that it can take away that portion of predictor variance which is not associated with the criterion.

It is true that like good men good suppressors are difficult to find but the effectiveness of measures of response styles and response sets in suppressing criterion-irrelevant variance has been demonstrated in a number of studies. When a test to be used as predictor, the test and a measure of response distortion are administered on a sample of subjects whose criterion behaviour is to be predicted. We can then find intercorrelation among the criterion, predictor and suppressor. If the intercorrelations are in accordance with the requirement of suppression model we may study the increment in the predictive validity of the predictor with the use of the suppressor variable; substantial improvement in prediction would lead us to retain the suppressor variable. Measures of response sets and response styles are able to suppress criterion-irrelevant variance because predictors also contain variance which is contributed by different kinds of response distortions and because this part of variance covary with the other measures of response distortion used as suppressor. The removal of irrelevant variance leads to improvement in prediction.

We have discussed in detail the different kinds of response distortions and how they could dealt with. Our purpose was to show the concerns of psychologists to make personality assessment independent of confounding influences. Though it may appear the person who is brought for psychological assessment is the culprit, we have to search for the reasons for his malingering which may or may not be deliberate. Dicken (1959) has suggested the following plausible reasons for high scoring on L scale: (1) deliberate faking with intention to deceive, (2) response in terms of ideal self-concept rather than candid self-appraisal; (3) honest but uninsightful self-assessment, and (4) genuine conformity to social norms.

While we have discussed different ways of dealing with confounding sources, we have not to ignore the fact that some response sets and response styles help us to understand the person and can be regarded as genuine personality dimensions. Block (1963) has observed: Confounding is a blade that, held too tightly, will cut it wielder. With the same logic advanced for social desirability as underlying (first factor) MMPI scales, one can argue that the (first) factor of the MMPI represents a personality dimension that is vital to an understanding of the SD scale" (p.69). Eysenck and Eysenck (1980) have put forward the evidence and argument to show that underlying the L scale there is some consistent personality attribute and that the notion of 'readiness to dissimulate' would not fill the bill. Regarding the L scale as a measure of conformity, Eysenck and Eysenck (1980) insist that a score can be evaluated under conditions where external motivating conditions are roughly equalized; when this is done, then the L score can be used as a measure of conformity. However, when conditions are motivating to dissimulating, the score becomes a proper Lie score.

Regarding the evidence of distortion furnished by studies in which subjects were instructed to fake bad one can argue that the difference of the scores under dissimulation instruction from that of ordinary administration is an indication that no malingering occurs in routine test administration. Further, the condition of anonymity does not produce changes in test scores as compared with name-signing condition. On the whole personality assessor is expected to be cautions rather than feel dejected in his enterprise.

8

Cross-Cultural Assessment of Personality

Like other sciences, psychology has been interested in general theories and laws which are applicable to human behaviour irrespective of time and place of its occurrence. At the same time it has also been interested in different sources of individual differences. This interest led to the comparison of samples drawn from different racial groups. What appeared to be such a simple design of study as administering the same measuring instrument to samples drawn from two racial groups and comparing their means, ran into difficulty when it was realized that same measuring device when used with two groups may not be tapping equivalent constructs or processes which it is expected to operationalize. This realization led to concern for development of a methodology which is more suitable for the studies involving comparisons between different ethnic groups.

The difficulties involved in the interpretation of findings of cross-cultural studies are due to competing hypothesis involving interaction of experimental and cultural variables and almost impossibility of controlling the variables that might make the two experimental setting comparable (Triandis et al., 1972). Differences between behaviour of samples drawn from different cultures may be contributed by the following : (1) the stimulus or task used in the study may not have same meaning for the subjects drawn from two cultures; (2) the experimental or testing situation may be differently perceived by the people from different cultures. For some people the situation may be that of showing respect to the experimenter, for others it may be a situation of antagonism; (3) the response alternatives set up by the experiment may be of high frequency in the ecology of one culture but of low frequency in the other culture.

Culture-alien and Culture-syntonic Measures

In order to have a better understanding of problems peculiar to cross-cultural assessment, we have to make a distinction between culture-alien and culture-syntonic measures. Culture-alien measures are the measures which have been developed in one culture but have been used in another culture for the assessment of the trait which they purport to measure in the culture of their origin. As tests of intelligence preceded the tests of personality, the use of culture-alien tests of intelligence became first issue of controversy regarding the suitability of tests developed in one culture for being used in another culture. The use of tests of intelligence and other abilities in an alien culture became an emotive issue because reports regarding higher intelligence of certain ethnic groups were advance as scientific, justification of colonial doctrine of White man's burden. According to this doctrine, the subjugation of 'inferior' people was 'in their own interest' because they were (believed to be) incapable of looking after themselves. Attribution of certain positive and negative personality characteristics to different groups may also be used as justification of certain political ideologies. But this is less likely to become the basis of certain political ideologies because personality traits are not as much popularly believed to be shaped by heredity as is intelligence. The problems related to culture-alien tests becomes more acute when scores obtained with the help of psychological tests are to be assigned construct referenced meaning rather than criterion-referenced meaning. The construct reference meaning has to do with the interpretation of test scores across culture and the source(s) of variation in test score. The following excerpt from Cole and Scribner

(1974) makes the distinction clear and brings out its implication: "So long as IQ tests were treated solely in terms of their ability to predict a child's performance (criterion-referenced meaning), arguments about the nature of the test need not arise. But as soon as we ask, what do IQ tests really measure (construct-referenced meaning), we enter an area of seemingly endless arguments and ambiguity" (p. 175).

The above excerpt strikes a note of caution against the use of a culture-alien measure because drawing of valid comparison would not be possible unless it is ensured that the test measures the same psychological variable in the alien culture as it does in the culture of its origin. However, when a test is to be used, for the prediction of a criterion in different cultures, one may not be interested in what it measures so long as it has applied utility. The argument regarding what the test measures may continue among those who are interested in understanding the nature and meaning of what is assessed by the test.

Imperative of Cross-Cultural Assessment

When the use of same instrument with different ethnic groups created the problem of meaning and equivalence why should we embark on such a hazardous course? The answer to this question has both pragmatic and substantive aspects.

Reasons for Using Foreign Tests

A test developed in one country may be used in another due to the following reasons :

1. The test was carefully developed, has all qualities of a good psychological test, has been found useful for certain purpose such as prediction of specific criterion or diagnostic classification of psychiatric patients. Because it would require expertise and financial resources to develop an indigenous instrument, a foreign instrument is borrowed and used for similar purpose as it served in the country of its origin.

2. It is believed that a test measures a characteristic which has similar manifestations in different cultures. Doubts are expressed regarding this assumption because it ignores emic-etic distinction. This pseudoetic approach may create a situation in which an emic approach developed in a Western culture is unwittingly assumed to be etic, and the trait indicators in the West are assumed to be the same as in the native culture.

3. Comparison is the sole of scientific method as it enables us to bring out substantial differences and similarities, covariation and cause. Culture and quality of life are hypothesized to be source of quantitative differences in psychological variables. The field of psychology which is interested in comparison of different cultural groups is known as cross cultural psychology. Since in psychology the term comparative has been traditionally associated with philo-genetic comparison, the term cross-cultural has been adopted to refer to the field which is interested in systematic comparison of psychological variables under different conditions for the purpose of specifying the antecedent processes that underlay the manifestation of behavioural differences. Because it is cross-cultural psychology which has been systematically concerned with the measurement of personality variables in different cultures, it is relevant to mention main purposes of cross-cultural research:

1. Utilization of naturally occurring variations. In cross-cultural research, cultural functions as 'experimental treatment'. Cross-cultural studies are non-manipulative in nature because they do not create the phenomenon which they study. The independent and dependent variables involved in cross-cultural research are culture and behaviour respectively. The term culture includes ecological and societal variables; behaviour includes inferred variables.

2. Cross-cultural research is interested in encompassing the total range of variability and all possible differences of human behaviour. This makes 'largesweep' as one of the salient features of cross-cultural research. It is believed that if a researcher has no opportunity to make observations in a

different cultural setting he would not realize that the behaviour which he observed in his own culture is a limited manifestation of variability of behaviour which he would be able to know if he undertakes cross-cultural studies.

3. "Cutting the Pie of experience" is one of the purposes of cross-cultural psychology (Triandis et at., 1972). Cross-cultural research is interested in gaining insight into social mechanisms employed in different cultures. Studies of subjective culture and ethnoscience are mentioned as examples of studies conducted for this purpose. Studying the key concepts typical of a culture is one of the approaches directed towards understanding subjective culture. Study of attitudes, roles, and values can also be helpful in understanding subjective culture.

4. Discovering general laws is one of the purposes of all scientific disciplines. This purpose is emphasized in one of the definitions of cross-cultural psychology: "Cross-cultural psychology includes studies of subjects from two or more cultures using equivalent methods of measurement to determine the limits to which general psychological theories do hold, and the kinds of modifications of these theories that are needed to make them universal" (Triandis et al., 1972, p.1).

If it is to be verified that certain generalizations regarding the antecedents and consequents are not confined to a single culture, we have to collect data from several cultures. However, collection of data which helps us to verify certain generalization about behaviour is so full of hazards that one who undertakes a cross-cultural study has to be careful about a number of biases, particularly confusion of the researcher's own perspective with universal perspective. The understanding of a phenomenon independent of narrow confines of culture in which the understanding is being generated, is known as *decentering*.

Importance of Equivalence

The definition of cross-cultural psychology given by Triandis, Malpass and Davidson (1972, p. 1) makes it explicit that equivalence of measuring instruments is one of the essential features of cross-cultural comparison. Any comparison which is not based on equivalent methods is likely to lead to as absurd a comparison as of body-build of subjects drawn from one culture with need-achievement of subjects drawn from another culture. Comparison requires comparability or dimensional identity. Comparison is meaningless if it is not possible to place two phenomenon on a single dimension. According to Berry (1980) there are two ways to ensure dimensional identity: *adaptation of universal* and *empirical demonstration* of equivalence. Universals may be adopted from biology, anthropology, or sociology. A list of human needs is an example of universals from biology; language, tool use, myth, etc. are examples of universals taken from anthropology; role differentiation, normative regulation of behaviour, and socialization are the example of universals adopted from sociology. Because the things listed above are found in every culture and no cultural group is without these things, they are known as universals.

Berry and Dasen (1974) have made a distinction among three kinds of equivalence: functional, conceptual, and metric equivalence.

Functional equivalence is not based on similarity of activities or any other apparent similarity. It can be demonstrated even when dissimilar activities are directed to deal with the same kind of problems or are engaged in for the same pursuit. The following excerpt makes the nature of functional equivalence clear :

"Thus, functional equivalence of behaviour exists when the behaviour in question has developed in response to a problem shared by two or more social/cultural groups, even though the behaviour in one society does not appear to be related to its counterpart in another society. These functional equivalences must pre-exist as naturally occurring phenomena; they are discovered and cannot be created or manipulated by cross-cultural psychologists. Without equivalence, it is suggested, no valid cross-cultural behavioural comparison may be made" (Berry, 1969, p.122).

Conceptual equivalence is related to the meaning of research materials or behaviour. The stimuli and the concepts used in research should have equivalent meaning if they are to be involved in cross-cultural comparison. The equivalence of meaning can be discovered by finding local meaning of concepts in cognitive system of people to be compared. Berry (1980) has mentioned three ways of obtaining this kind of equivalence : through translation equivalence, study of equivalence using semantic differential scales, and categorization of objects and experiences. Translation equivalence would be discussed in detail in another section of this chapter. Semantic differential scales make use of a sets of polar adjectives. Subjects from different culture are asked to describe a given concept, for example intelligence, by indicating its location in the space created by polar adjectives. The placement of a concept on bipolar scales by two cultural groups indicates extent of equivalence of the meaning of the concept. The use of semantic differential scales enabled Wober (1957) to discover that Kingrda concept of intelligence is different from the western concept of intelligence.

Categorization equivalence has been studied by ethnoscience or cognitive tradition of anthropology. It is demonstrated that division and structure of concepts and categories are different in different cultures. Categorization equivalent can be obtained by asking the subjects to sort out items, for example edibles, into different categories. The observed similarity-dissimilarity of classification would demonstrate the presence or absence of equivalence. Cognitive tradition of anthropology has made use of this method.

Metric equivalence is concerned with psychometric properties of data. It can be ascertained by the study of relationship of independent and dependent variables obtained in analysis of data collected from different cultures. This is known as subsystem validation. The stability of covariation among variables, regardless of the source of variation, is taken as an indication of metric equivalence. Another requirement of metric equivalence is the similarity of pattern of relationship among independent variables. Similarity of intercorrelation matrices and common factor structure can be used for the study of similarity of pattern of relationship among dependent variables. It is to be noted that unlike functional and conceptual equivalence, metric equivalence can be obtained after collection and analysis of data (Berry, 1980).

Emic-Etic Distinction

Emulating physical sciences, psychologists have been traditionally interested in the discovery of universal (pancultural) laws of human behaviour. But anthropologists have been subscribing to the position that each culture should be understood in its own framework. However, cross-cultural psychologists have realized the importance of emic-etic distinction because disregard of this difference may lead to pseudo-etic approach.

The emic-etic distinction was first proposed by Pike (1954, 1966) who derived the terms from phonemic and phonetic traditions of linguistics. While phonemics focuses on sounds, phonetics emphasizes general and universal aspects of meaning. The terms Emics and Etics are obtained, obtained from 'phonemics' and 'phonetic' respectively after dropping its root (phon). Gleaning from Pike's (1966) comments regarding the nature of emic and etic approaches, Berry (1980) tabulated the distinctive features of the two approaches :

Emic Approach	*Etic Approach*
Studies behaviour from within system	Studies behaviour from the position outside the system
Examines only one culture	Examines many cultures, comparing them with each other
Structure discovered by the analyst	Structure created by the analyst
Criteria are relative to internal characteristics	Criteria are considered absolute or universal

It is legitimate to adopt emic approach and record and discover valid culture specific principles of behaviour by using the constructs which are meaningful to members of the culture. A researcher may prefer the etic approach to create a system of analysis which is not specific to a particular culture and is intended to be universal. However, one cannot approve the use of pseudoetic approach which is an emic approach developed in Western culture but is applied to non-Western cultures as if the approach is etic rather than emic.

The emic-etic distinction can be illustrated by taking the example of n-Achievement. The concept is useful as it refers to realistic goal setting, exerting for the attainment of objectives and so forth. But the exact interrelation of n-Ach with other cultural patterns and practices is different in different cultures; it is not the same as in the USA where the concept was originated. It is interesting to note that whereas in the USA high n-Ach is likely to involve people in competition, in our country people accomplish more when they are put in the mental set of co-operation (Sinha, 1968).

Let us consider how the emic-etic distinction can be maintained in research. If the researcher is interested in both kind of data he can begin with a set of core items which are expected to tap etic aspect of the concept(s) relevant to certain aspects of behaviour. In addition to the etic core, emic items specific to each culture are to be collected or written. Obtaining subject's responses to both kind of items, one can undertake correlational analysis and expect to find high correlation among the etic and emic items but no relationship between these items.

Obtaining Culture Specific Items

Different methods are suggested to obtain culture specific items but because each method has shortcomings, a researcher is expected to combine as many of them as possible. The methods are :

1. Having collaboration with colleagues from other cultures who have knowledge of salient features of their

respective cultures. Culture specific items may be contributed and discussed by the collaborators drawn from different cultures.

2. Making use of 'informants' is suggested by Wesley and Karr (1966). Informants are to be the persons who lived in more than one culture where the study is to be conducted. The informants are to be questioned for the purpose of obtaining items relevant to each culture and also to obtain items which are appropriate for more than one culture.

3. Using such methods as sentence completion, free association and other techniques one can elicit culture specific items. The methods mentioned above can also be used for finding the common responses and responses occurring in the protocols of subjects belonging to one peculiar culture.

4. Study of anthropological literature on the cultures to be investigated is one way of finding similarities and differences in people's behaviour relevant to the issue under investigation. Human Relation Area Files (HRAF) can be used for finding information on a given topic. The HRAF organization informs readers about ethnographies on different cultures.

5. There can be no substitute of having first-hand contact with the culture which one intends to study. However, a casual visit would not be of much help. In regard to psychological studies Irvin (1968) observed: "To collect valid data, psychologists need adequate and sympathetic training in understanding a society system that is alien, complex, and conceptually different. Participant observer research will acquire greater scientific status, it seems, as a result' (p. 3).

Irvin's observations underscore the development of tradition of participant observation in cross-cultural psychology besides experimental, psychometric and correlational traditions of research.

The Importance of Translation in Cross-Cultural Assessment

The emic-etic distinction mentioned above makes it necessary that individuals belonging to different cultures should be assessed with the help of instruments which make use of the language and trait indicators of their specific cultures. However, there is no escape from determining the equivalence of research instrument/material to be presented to subjects drawn from different cultures because the main purpose of cross-cultural research may be to develop a pan-culture theoretical system. One may also be interested in verifying that emic measures specific to different cultures are linked with the same etic dimensions. It is to be noted that most of the psychological instruments developed in India are vernacular adaptations of the instruments developed in the U.S.A. and other Western countries. Not only because we expect that this tradition of pseudoetics will be continued in future but also because Indian is a land of cultural and linguistic diversity, students of personality assessment have to be familiar with the problems of translation of items. Before we discuss strategies and errors in interlanguage communication, let us refer to a study conducted by Valez-Diaz and Gonzalez-Regosa (1978) in which the Spanish version of the Clinical Analysis Questionnaire was examined to identify different kinds of errors. As many as 52 items of the Spanish version were found to have one or more of the problems specified below :

1. Awkwardly constructed sentence not written like Spanish but like English translated into Spanish.
2. Myraid errors in instructions : misplaced accent, inappropriate use of common words, misspelled words, words of little common usage, and awkward expressions.
3. Grammatical and syntactical errors in 36 per cent of the tests items.
4. Poorly written incomprehensive items.
5. Literal translation of colloquial expressions much as "I am at the end of the rope".
6. Ineffective dealing with negatives that make certain alternatives awkward and unintelligible.

Strategies and Errors in Interlanguage Communication

Before we take up the methods which have been suggested for ensuring equivalence of the original and translated versions, let us discuss strategies and errors found in the process of communicating the original content in foreign languages. Veradi (1983) suggested a framework for the investigation of translation competence. The system is known as Approximate System Analysis (ASA). According to ASA, in order to communicate in the target language a bilingual makes an attempt to construct an optimal message which has optimal form and optimal meaning. Lacking adequate interlanguage skills to communicate this optimal message, the communicator adjusts the message within the sphere of his encoding abilities. This adjustment may involve shedding some of the parts of optimal meaning. The user of a foreign language may adopt a number of strategies when he finds it difficult to express his meaning. A list of such strategies is provided by Tarone, Cohen, and Dumas (1983) :

1. *Negative transfer from native language.* Inappropriate but correct transfer may be observed in phonology (sound), morphology (rules), syntax (system) and lexicon (using native language words for words existing in the target language).

2. *Overgeneralization.* The application of rules of foreign language to inappropriate form or context is known as overgeneralization. Overgeneralization may be related to phonology, morphology, syntax or lexicon.

3. *Use of prefabricated pattern.* This occurs in syntactic domain. Prefabricated pattern is a regular patterned segment of speech employed without knowledge of its underlying structure. An example of this use of prefabricated pattern is, "What do you doing?" instead of "What are you doing?"

4. *Vowel insertion.* Unable to use unfamiliar vowel clusters in the target language, the communicator inserts vowels to pronounce the clusters.

The remaining six strategies to be described below are different means of getting around the target language rules or forms which are yet to be fully acquired.

5. *Topic avoidance.* The learner may not involve himself

in communication of a topic if he does not know the target language rules required to communicate. For example, uncertainty of appropriate technical vocabulary may lead to avoidance of discussion about the topic.

6. *Semantic avoidance.* This refers to the evasion of communication about the content which requires target language rules or forms not known to the communicator. However, the communicator may make an attempt to impart the message/information by talking about related concepts. An example is, "I like to swim" when the communicator is not able to answer the question, "What happened yesterday?"

7. *Appeal to authority.* Asking some one else to supply a form or lexical item which one does not know is known as appeal to authority. This strategy may be applied to deal with problems of phonetics, morphology, syntax, or lexicon.

8. *Paraphrase.* It is expressed in the form of rewording of message when a communicator finds it difficult to communicate the way he wants to do. Paraphrasing involves the use of an acceptable target language form in order to avoid a more difficult form of construction. Paraphrasing may be done by picking up a more frequently used high coverage superordinate words such as 'tool' when an inter-language communicator is not able to call the tool by its more specific name, i.e., wrench. Use of tool for wrench conveys less information than use of wrench, the exact name of the tool. Word coinage (for example, air ball for balloon) and circumlocution are other forms of paraphrasing. In circumlocution a description of a desired lexical item or definition in other words is presented. An example of circumlocution is 'a thing you dry hands with' when one is not able to use the word towel.

9. *Message abandonment.* After initiating a communication the inter-language communicator stops because he runs into difficulty with target language form or rule.

10. *Language switch.* In this strategy an inter-language communicator makes use of native words or expressions (untranslated). This is done to avoid difficult target lan-

guage form or to serve some social purpose (for example, a desire to fit with one's peers).

Difficulties and errors of different kind have been identified by social scientists who have to conduct research in an alien culture and those who have undertaken the job of translating the Bible in different languages. Elder (1973), who conducted a research project in different parts of India have identified three kinds of difficulties : lexical, contextual, and difficulties due to gap in written and spoken language.

1. *Lexical difficulty.* This difficulty is encountered when there is no word in the foreign language which has same connotation as a word in the original language. One can realize the difficulty faced by anthropologists who have to collect data from tribal people using language which has no dictionary. Even a good dictionary cannot be helpful in selecting a proper equivalent when such a simple word as 'friend' is to be translated into Spanish and German. In English 'friend' refers to a somewhat less intense and wider range of acquaintances; the German equivalent *frund* refers to a few deep personal associates; the Spanish word *amigo* refers to a very wide range of persons including those who were introduced a short while ago. Thus the answer to the question, "How many friends do you have" would not be an answer to the same question if the question is put in the three languages. Elder (1973) found it difficult to translate the following question in Hindi: "For a country to progress, it is necessary to find people whom the public can trust. 'Two equivalents of trust were considered, *Bharosa* and *Vishwas*, but neither of the two could put across what the English version wanted to know. *Bharosa* in Hindi denoted 'dependence' or 'reliance'; *Vishvas* connotes belief or faith with religious overtones. Both words were used in a field pretest and it was found that the respondents were confused. It took a field interview of about 15 to 20 minutes to explain the meaning of the question to a respondent and still it was not certain whether the exact meaning had been communicated.

2. *Contextual difficulties.* Even when lexical equivalence has been achieved it may not ensure contextual equivalence. The problem of contextual equivalence arises when such a simple question as, "Whom do you think was correct"? In Hindi there is no genetic pronoun 'you'. *Tum* or *Aap* is to be used with variation in verbs depending upon who refers to someone who is higher or lower in status. The change of verb ending to match gender of the verb's subject complicates the process of translation even more. The problem of contextual equivalence was experienced by Edler (1973) when he had to translate the following question for Hindu and Muslim respondents: "Priests and sacred books contain all truth...." For Hindus priests was to be translated as *pundits* and sacred books as *dharmik pustak*; for Muslims *Mulla* and *mazhabi kitab* were the respective translations.

3. *Gap between written and spoken language.* There is gap between language of conversation and language of written communication. Edler (1973) reported that when this difference was ignored by translators who had to translate the questionnaire in Tamil, the outcome was difficulty in communicating with the respondents who were to answer oral questions. The Tamil translation team could not avoid using polysyllabic words and big sentences. To make the questionnaire simple, the translators were told to imagine as if they were speaking to a 11-year old boy and write what they would orally ask him.

Errors found in translating Bible stories in different languages warn us against the possibility of making similar errors in translating material to be used in psychological studies. Missionary translators committed the following types of errors even after taking the help of 'informants' who were full members of the culture and had knowledge of language, the customs, and beliefs of the people (Williams, 1965) :

(i) *Error of exegesis:* This error occurs when a word conveys a meaning contrary to the specification by exegesis. An example of this kind of error is need to substitute word 'grace' if this word conveys the meaning "to bless with material blessing" while the study of exegesis reveals that the meaning to be conveyed is "the work of grace in conversion".

(ii) *Errors arising from terms the connotation of which the translator was unaware.* An example of this kind of error is the impression created that in the following sentences one of the many sons are being referred, "thy holy servant (son) Jesus...." To remove this impression the construction was modified as follows : "....your son Jesus, He is holy..." A very interesting example of errors arising from connotation of which the translator is unaware is that in Chuj 'They said.....' implies statement of truth. A contrary to fact participate is to be added if it is to be pointed out that what was said was not true. The sentence is to be, "They said untruthfully..."

(iii) *Errors arising from literalness.* Williams (1965) reported that 70 per cent errors in Bible translation are of this kind. There are three kinds of literal errors:

(a) *In translating a person.* The following expression created the impression that the speaker was referring to some other God, not one he worships: "The God of Abraham, of Isaac, of Jacob..." To convey the correct meaning the translated read "I am the Lord, but they plotted against me".

(b) *Lack of specific actor, goal, subject, agent, etc.* While doing literal translation the omission of 'by God' at the end of the following sentence created the impression that the devil shook the place; "The place in which they gathered together was shaken." Without addition of Jesus at the beginning of the following sentence it was not understood that Jesus was referred two in the passage as, "The holy and righteous one".

(c) *General literalness.* Examples of this kind of errors are as follows:

Translation following original order of clauses in the Spanish version, "You killed him, putting him on a cross," conveyed the meaning that the first act was of killing, and the second act "putting on a cross" followed the first. Consider the following sentence, "Abraham's descendants would be foreigners in a foreign land." This implies that they would lose their culture and change their way of life. The translation that conveyed the correct meaning was, "Abraham's descendants will live in a land belonging to foreigners".

The following examples of reactions of participant natives in translation and revision of the Gospel of Marks in Guhu-Samane of New Guinea shows that literal and semiliteral translations not only fail to convey the intended message, they also give rise to doubts, puzzlement, and even distress (Riohert, 1965) :

Source Form	*Reaction*	*Translated Form*	*Reaction*
No man puts new wine into old wineskins	Puzzlement : Why on put wine or any liquid into the skin of animals since skin just got rot quickly.	'No man puts wine into old gourds....'	Comprehension : It is concluded that for preservation of wine no one would choose old instead of new gourds. So the argument is not lost and puzzlement is removed.
"....uselessly (in vain) they worship me..."	Doubt : why should their efforts to worship God produce no result, try as they may?	".....with the front teeth of their mouth they worship me..."	Relief and Comprehension : The Idioms come from the picture of one who is making pretense at eating food, hence their deceit is apparent.
".... which shall not taste death until..."	Doubt and Distress. The original sentence suggests cannibalism to New Guinea natives.	"....which will not die until...."	Relief and Comprehension. The ordinary form of expression is clear. Attention from the message is not diverted.

Purpose and Methods of Translation

Ideas and information generated in one language are to be communicated to others in their own language for different purposes, such as sharing of information, propaganda, wider appreciation of poetry and literary work, curiosity to know about the unfamiliar life styles of different people, verification of veridocity of observations and their casual explanations etc. As translations have to serve different purposes, a translator cannot remain indifferent to the purpose of communication. According to Casagrande (1954) there can be four 'ends' of translation :

1. *Pragmatic Translation.* The main purpose of pragmatic translation is accurate communication of information to the people in their own language. Translation of technical manuals, manuals describing how to use and repair a machine are the examples of this kind of translation. In pragmatic translation there is no attempt to preserve other aspects (e.g. aesthetic form) of the original language. The purpose of pragmatic translation is served if translation of certain instructions enables the reader of translation to do as the reader of original version would be able to do.

2. *Aesthetic-Poetic Translation.* The purpose of this kind of translation is to preserve the original emotions, feelings, message and impact of the source in translated version.

3. *Ethnographic Translation.* The purpose of this kind of translation is to explicate the culture and context of the source in second language version. Translators are to be sensitive to the way the words are used in the culture where communication was originally formulated and the culture in which the translated version is to be used. Nida (1976) discussed this kind of translation under the heading 'sociolinguistic' translations. According to him a most compelling example of this kind of translation is the translation of passages from the Bible in every day language which were used by students protesting against social injustice in a Latin American country. The translation and the form in which it appeared (mimeographed on inexpensive paper used by the protesters) was in confirmation of cultural

context. The purpose of this kind of translation is the same as that of type of analysis of words in *Oxford English Dictionary*. In the dictionary the context of usage is illustrated by embedding a word in long passages with as much context as possible.

4. *Linguistic Translation.* This kind of translation is concerned with "equivalent meanings of the constituent morphemes of the second language" (Casagranda, 1954, p. 337). The operational machine translation system based on linguistic analysis of the source and target language is an attempt to have this kind of translation.

The above categorization of translation according to the purpose helps us to set the criterion regarding the quality of translation. It is apparent that the quality of translation is to be judged in relation to the purpose. However, translation done with a definite purpose can be judged on the criterion laid down for other kinds of translation. For example, linguistic translation may have some features of aesthetic translation and it can be evaluated in that respect.

The Importance of Source Text in Translation

The importance of the source text can be realized by the fact that the original material can be expressed in words and sentences which are easy or difficult to translate into another (target) language.

If in the source, content is expressed in the form of idioms, proverbs, and colloquial words, it would be more difficult to get an equivalent version of the source material in different languages. Metaphorical expressions in the source language often lead to amusing expressions in the source language. Consider the following item, "I eat, live and breathe my job" and its two Hindi translations, *"Mai kam per he khata, jeeta aur sas leta hun"*; *"Kam he mera odhna-bichuna hai"*. With the selection of a suitable idiom the second translation became more appropriate. Also consider the problem of translating the following item, "Barnum was right when he said every moment a sucker is born". We have to substitute 'Barnum' with the name of a person who is known throughout India and has the same image as Barnum has for American respondents. We have also to find the lexical and contextual equivalent of 'sucker'.

Experienced practitioners of the art of translation and researchers who investigated problems of translation have recognized the importance of context and redundancy in translation. More than one phrases referring to the same concept are helpful in better translation of the material. The significance of redundancy in all sorts of communication is highlighted in the following quotation from a proponent of information theory in psychology:

"It is reasonable to ask why we are so redundant. The answer lies in the fact that redundancy is an insurance against mistakes the only way to catch an error is to repeat. Redundant information is an automatic mistake catcher built into all languages". (Miller, 1953, p. 8).

The use of redundancy in cross-cultural studies employing questionnaire or interview schedule is recommended by Campbell (1968). He suggested that if possible every concept under investigation should be put into at least two differently worded questions. If the same results are obtained by using the two questions one can be sure that the results are not due to translation errors.

The importance of context for better translation is demonstrated in better translation of a word occurring in a sentence than when a word is translated as a single item. Longacre (1958) reported that long Biblical passages were easier to translate than short passages because long passages provide more context. Addition of clarifying words is noted to be a salient feature of translation procedure of the well known anthropologist Bronislaw Malinowaski (Phillips, 1960).

Besides the use of redundancy and context for maximization of translatability of research material, the following rules proposed by Brislin, Lonner and Thorndike (1973) are helpful in preparing easily translatable source version:

1. *Simple sentences.* Making use of vocabulary which is

known to all the communicators, one can have a simple source version for ensuring maximum translatability.

2. *Repetition of nouns rather than pronouns.* Use of nouns where pronouns can be used makes it easy for the readers/ listeners to understand what is referred to. Thus it is recommended that it is better to repeat a noun again instead of substituting it with a pronoun.

3. *Avoidance of metaphors and colloquialism.* A non-native bilingual may give the wrong meaning to an expression in his ignorance of the meaning of a metaphor, leading him to literal translation of the expression.

4. *Avoidance of passive tense.* If the source text is in English, avoidance of passive tense is recommended because many languages do not have his kind of sentences. Translation of passive sentences may be awkward or difficult to understand or incapable of preserving the original tone and tenor.

5. *Avoiding hypothetical phrasing or subjective mood.* Sentences expressing conditions, hypotheses, or contingency have to be translated in such a way that expression of condition is preserved in the target version. This makes the task of translation difficult.

Irrespective of the fact that translated version of a questionnaire is to be used for either criterion-referenced or construct referenced interpretation of obtained scores, an attempt is to be made to translate the source questionnaire into an equivalent version of the target language and then to determine the quality of translation using certain criteria. In the following sections we are going to discuss some important methods of translations, criteria for determining the quality, and factors which influence the quality of translation.

Methods of Translation

The following five methods are used for the translation (Campbell, Brislin, Stewart and Werner, 1970) :

1. Back-Translation

Translatable source material is to be prepared following the precautions mentioned above. Thereafter one bilingual person is requested to translate the original version into the target language. The target-language version done by the first bilingual is translated back into the source by another bilingual. The two source-language versions, the original one and the other translated back from the target language, are compared. The disparity between the two source languages forms,—original and back translated—are to be discussed with the two bilinguals. Such a discussion may lead the researcher to revise the original version to get identical items in the foreign and back translated versions. This process is known as decentering. For the preparation of equivalent versions, decentering accords equal importance to the source and target versions. The decentering may initiate the process of multistage iterative translations in which the original language version (01) is translated by a bilingual into the target language (T1). This T1 version is translated into the original language and this back translation (02) is examined by monolinguals who compare it with the original (01) version. This may lead to the necessary amendment in the original 01 version so as to make it more translatable. The amended source version (03) is translated into the target language to get T2 version. The T2 version is translated back and the processes of comparison with the original version, decentering and translation into target language is repeated till equivalence is achieved. An example of the use of back translation in preparing an equivalent version of original source material in English is the survey of attitude in Laos conducted by Fink (1963). Competent bilinguals who could translate from English to Laotian language were not available, but there were competent bilinguals who could translate from English to Thai or Thai to Laotian language. Fink, therefore, used the following successive translation procedure : English to Thai, Thai to Lao, Lao to Thai, Thai to English. The original English version was to be revised when the back-translated version was different from the original source version.

2. Bilingual Technique

In this technique the source and target versions are

administered on bilingual subjects and the responses given by them are examined for the evidence of discrepancy and/or difference of frequency. Instead of administering the whole set of items, the source and target versions may be broken into two parts and different groups may be administered different halves. This method makes it possible to use sophisticated statistics and to obtain evidence regarding the basic characteristics of the instrument such as split-half reliability. The use of an atypical group, bilinguals, in developing the instrument is the greatest disadvantage accruing from this method.

Brislin et al., (1973, pp. 38-39) have furnished an example of decentering in the translation of the following item: "I don't find it particularly difficult to get along with loud-mouthed, obnoxious people".

The item was to be translated in the native language of Guam and the Marianas Islands, known as Chamorro. As the terms 'particularly' and 'obnoxious' were not found in the back translation and the bilinguals informed that the target language lacks their equivalent, the first back translation was given to the bilingual and with this decentering process started. The target language, instead of the source language, determined the words of the English version. In the second back translation 'get along with' was replaced by 'talk with'. Another phase of translation and back translation led to the following English version for which word-for-word equivalence was obtained : "It is not hard for me to talk with people who have big mouth".

3. The Committee Approach

A group of bilinguals translate material from the source language to the target language. Translation done by one bilingual is examined by other bilinguals who have to point out mistakes. Brislin (1970) pointed out that committee members may not criticize one another and may unify against the researcher.

4. Pretest Procedure

Pretesting refers to field testing of translated material so as to determine comprehensibility of material. There is nothing objectionable against this procedure. However, the success of pretesting depends upon the competence of the interviewer doing it.

The success in getting equivalent versions of an inventory or questionnaire item is expected to be greater if the methods mentioned above are simultaneously employed and evidence obtained from one method is checked against evidence provided by other methods. One should take care of the fact that much depends on the translatability of the original version. Decentering is an important step in getting the natural sounding version in the target language.

Criteria of Good Translation

The purpose of translation of material used in research is to ensure the use of equivalent material in obtaining responses of subjects speaking different languages. Thus, equivalence of meaning is the most important aspect of translation which is to be used in the evaluation of quality of translation. Realizing this fact Treisman (1965) suggested the unit of translation quality is to be a unit of meaning. Meaning criterion was used by Carroll (1966) who asked the raters to evaluate translation quality on the basis of judgment of meaning. But Carroll did not a devise unit of translation quality. The body movement criteria was suggested by Miller and Beebe-Center (1956) and MacNamara (1967). Subjects have to read either source or target language version and to perform bodily movement as instructed in the communication. The similarity of bodily movement performed by readers of different language version is an indication of similarity of meaning of source and target language versions. Allport and Pettigrew (1957) made use of bodily movement in the study of presence or absence of Trapezoidal illusion. Zulu subjects had to make use of hand movement to indicate presence or absence of the illusion. It is to be noted that bodily movement cannot be the criterion when the material is such that it cannot be expressed through bodily movement. The use of answers to the questions after reading the source or target version is also suggested by Miller and Beebe-Center (1956) and Mac Namara (1967). The equivalence of an answer to the question after reading the original or translated version is an indication of the quality of translation.

Brislin (1970) used the following five criteria in his empirical study of effect of *content, difficulty level*, and *language variation* on quality of translation:

1. *Errors identified by monolingual judges.* The original and back translated versions are examined by monolinguals who are required to indicate disparity between the two versions. The following instructions given to the raters by Brislin (1970) make the nature of the criterion and the procedure of its application clear :

"Examine the second copy of the English against the original and write down any error that you may feel might affect the meaning between the two passages. That is, write down errors that might make differences in the meaning people would infer from reading only one passage. For instance, if the original is 'food' and second copy 'hunger', that might be a meaning error, depending upon the context. Examine the two English versions, and write down those errors that might affect meaning".

There are two methods of comparing meaning errors. In the first method errors identified by each judge are recorded and then correlation is calculated between (or among) errors found by two (or more) judges. The obvious shortcoming of this method is that the number of errors found by different judges may be same but they might find quite different errors. The second method has no shortcoming of this kind because in the second method, known as method of percentage overlap, percentage of raters finding the same meaning errors is obtained.

2. *Errors identified by bilinguals.* While in the first criterion monolinguals are asked to judge same language form and to find errors, the second criterion requires the bilingual judges to read both the original and target versions and write down meaning errors. Meaning errors identified by bilinguals can be compared with meaning errors found

by monolingual judges. This enables us to have a more direct test of original-target versions equivalence. Brislin (1970) reported the pretesting on this criterion has shown that bilingual rating of errors was very time consuming and also very difficult for raters.

3. *Answer to the questions on target language and back translated versions.* The purpose of this is to find if there is difference in number of correct answers given to the original and target version(s). If the difference is discovered one can make an attempt to know whether translation or back translation has created difficulties. In a study conducted by Brislin (1970) the subjects were required to specify exactly which combination of words in a given essay they used for answering a question.

As the subjects were given different essays to read, there could be the possibility of subjects answering questions on the basis of what they read on the previous essay. The requirement of specification of words combination was for the purpose of avoiding the possibility of answer being based on reading of previous essay. The specification requirement may also be useful for finding the nature of difficulties responsible for the discrepancy of answer to the source and target versions.

4. *Performance Task Criterion.* If the source version asks the subjects to do a certain task, then those who read the equivalent version should also be able to perform the same task. An interesting example of the use of performance criterion is given by Brislin (1970). The two colours could be distinguished by referring green as ".....like leaves on a tree" and blue as "like the sky". The performance task was to make pictures using green and blue pieces of paper. The Palauan version would be equivalent to the source version if it enabled the subjects to make distinction between green and blue colours inspite of non-availability of two different words for green and blue.

5. Administration of the Questionnaire. This criterion is similar to the criterion measure obtained by requesting the bilinguals to answer questions in the two languages they

know. Four groups of bilinguals are employed : Group I makes responses to a questionnaire in the source language; Group II gives response to a questionnaire in which first half of the questions are in the source and the second half in the target language; Group III gives responses to a questionnaire in which items in the first half of a questionnaire are in the target language and rest of the items are in the source language; Group IV has to give responses to a questionnaire which is entirely in the target language. Counting frequencies of responses and a getting total score for the entire questionnaire, we can have evidence regarding the equivalence of the source and target versions. Same frequencies of responses and same total for all the four groups would indicate equivalence of the two versions. Additional evidence can be obtained by finding correlation between the scores of groups II and III. Brislin (1970) regard criterion 5 as a variation of the bilingual technique and a method to check the adequacy of material translated by the back-translation method and tested with criterion one. He used this criterion for determining the equivalence of English and Chamorro versions of Marlowe-Crown Social Desirability Scale. Before the procedure for the application of criterion five was initiated, the scale was translated from English to the target language and back translated into English. Applying Bristin's first criterion it was found that there were many errors. This indicated the need to revise the source. One instance of need to revise the original version was absence of Chamorro word for 'take advantage of'. The revised source versions was translated into Chamorro and the amended target version was back translated into English. Before administration of the two versions to initiate the procedure for the fifth criterion, another review session was arranged for removing a few problems of translation.

Some of the findings of Brislin's study which have a bearing on the quality of translation deserve attention. Brislin found that the same source material when translated into different target languages would not yield equally good translation. This is due to the fact that one of the target languages, may share many words with the source language and also because some bilingual translators may be more familiar with certain language and culture. The content of material also determines the quality of translation.

Better translation of a passage is done if it contains the concepts which are familiar to the translator and it contains the details exceeding the requirement of context and redundancy.

Brislin's study also demonstrated that deliberate violation of the rules for enhancing translatability of material is likely to enhance difficulty level of the material in respect of rendering it into a target language. One can have better translation after giving practice and allowing the translator warm-up.

Adequately Good Translation

While the five criteria mentioned above laid down the procedure adopted in identifying errors in translation, there remains the question, "How good does a translation have to be before it is usable, or before a translation is judged as adequate"? To put the question differently, what would be considered as an indication of satisfactory translation? Brislin regards 8 errors per 300 words a satisfactory criterion. The following seven-step procedure is suggested by Brislin (1970) to obtain adequately good translation.

1. Preparation of the source material in simple translatable language. This can be done by following the rules mentioned above and ensuring the minimum level of difficulty with the help of Flesch Readability Score (Flesch, 1949) and Thorndike-Lorge Word Counts. Addition of redundancy to sentences and context to difficult ideas, and avoidance of detailed description are other suggestions for making the source material translatable.

2. Bilinguals who have interlanguage competence and are familiar with the content of the material to be translated are to be employed for translating the source material into the target language.

3. One bilingual is to be instructed to translate from

source to the target language and another from target language to the source. The translators should have the some practice before they are assigned the proper task of translation.

4. Several raters have to examine the original, target, and/or back-translated versions so as to identify the errors that led to differences in meaning. If possible, some other raters should be presented one of the versions and be requested to answer questions related to the content. Detection of errors may lead to the initiation of process of decentering, that is modification of the original, so as to make it more translatable. Decentering is to be followed by repetition of step three.

5. When meaning errors do not occur, the translated material is to be pretested with target-language speaking people. Insight gained during pretesting may be utilized for the revision of the source of translated versions. A bilingual is to be asked to examine the translation critically.

6. This step is taken for demonstrating the translation adequacy. Some bilingual are administered the source version, some the target version, and some are administered both versions. Calculation of means, standard deviations, and correlation coefficient can demonstrate the similarity of responses across the groups.

7. A report of experience using different criteria of equivalence is prepared. The verdict of translation adequacy derived from meaning-error standard and a simple pretest is to be compared with the verdict derived from more formal and time-consuming administration to the subjects (step six). The same verdict for many research projects would make the task of the future investigator simple because he would be expected to apply only meaning-error standard to do pretesting.

In our discussion of cross-cultural assessment of personality the problem of equivalence of communication in different languages has got much prominance. This may create the impression that cross-cultural assessment makes use of verbal content and nothing else. This impression is to be removed and it is to be mentioned that there have been attempts to use nonverbal culture fair or culture free material in testing abilities and aptitudes. However, there is growing body of evidence that nonlanguage tests may be more culturally loaded than language tests. The problem of translating nonlanguage content from one culture to another is highlighted by Ortar (1963) who observed, "on the basis of our results it appears that, both from the practical point of view and theoretical grounds, the verbal tests and items are better suited as intercultural measuring instruments than any other kind .... The "language" of performance is the cultural perception, but its "words" and grammar and syntax are not even completely understood, let alone organized in national entities" (p.232).

Anastasi (1982) has identified three approaches to the development of tests for persons brought up in different cultures :

1. Collection of items common to different cultures and validation of the test comprising such items against local criteria.

2. Developing a test within one culture and administering to individuals with different cultural background. While such a test is not to be regarded as universal yardstick, it can be useful for the prediction of local criterion within a culture and also for ascertaining cultural differences between the groups.

3. Developing different tests within each culture and validating them against local criteria.

When an instrument devised in one culture is adapted in another there arises problem of comparability of norms and equivalence of scores. A two-step procedure can be followed in equating the scales. The first step in the selection of anchor items appropriate for each both culture language groups. For this one can do item analysis and discard items showing item-group interaction. The second step is to include these anchor items in regular administration of both the versions. The score obtained on these anchor items are used as the basis of converting test scores to single scale (Anastasi, 1982, p. 347).

9

Utilization of Personality Data

We have already discussed how to make sense out of MMPI and 16 PF scores in chapters four and five respectively. In this chapter we propose to have a detailed discussion of different methods used for the utilization of personality data for the purpose of clinical diagnosis and prediction of a criterion. Assessment of personality, whether it is formal or informal is a purposive activity. We do informal assessment of others because we are interested in their as well as in our own welfare. If we find a friend worn out, depressive, sad, less friendly, hostile, etc., we may take steps to rescue him from his present phase of desperation; if we find our colleague hostile, annoyed, and with a lot of airs about himself, we may make an effort to change the colleague or reclaim our relations with him. Formal personality assessment is undertaken to help either the person, the sponsor of assessment programme or both and to make decisions that would not be as good in the absence of assessment as after making use of the information furnished by the assessment programme. The definition of assessment given by Sundberg, Snowden, and Reynolds, (1978) has acknowledged the role of assessment in making important decisions. They define assessment as the examination of individual characteristics used for decisions in person-society relationship. Cattell definition of personality also gives much importance to the utilization of personality data for the prediction of patterns of real life behaviour of an individual. It is to be that Cattell defined personality as "that which permits a prediction of what a person will do in a given situation" (Cattell, 1950,

p. 2). However, personality assessment would not be of much use without proper utilization of the data yielded by the assessment programme.

While data provided by measurement of physical characteristics can be utilized as such without any transformation, this is not possible in the case of personality data. Physical measurement is reported in terms of units of measurement such as grams, centimeters, etc., whereas personality data is in numerals without designation of units of measurement. It is, therefore, necessary that users of personality data be aware of the meaning and implications of different kinds of transformations which are required for giving meanings to numerals.

In the absence of units of measurement we can make use of personality data by relating it to behaviour in real life situations. Having knowledge about the expected behaviour of those who fall in different class intervals or range of scores, we can describe and/or predict the behaviour of those whose data are at our disposal. At this juncture, it is also to be mentioned that personality data may not be in the form of numerals; it may be in the form of verbal descriptions of behaviour in different situations of life. While there can be attempts to make use of every bit of information about an individual separately, one can also combine the pieces of information either clinically or statistically. Let us now consider the ways of utilization of personality data.

Use of Norms

Numerical data do not give any information until it is known what they refer to. Because psychological measures do not have units of measurement, we have to search for a point of reference (norm) which can, at least, give us standing of one person in comparison to others. Drawing a sample from a population and obtaining frequency distribution of the scores of this sample on the measuring device, we can locate the position of a certain person so as to find out whether his scores fall at the centre or toward upper or lower ends of the distribution. An individual's standing in a group may be expressed in two ways :

(1) In terms of units of standard deviations;

(2) In terms of ordinal position of the individual among the subjects included in the sample.

The first kind of comparison leads to standard-score family of transformations, the second to percentile-rank family.

Standard score (z). In this kind of transformation the difference of an individual's score (X) from mean ($\bar{X}$) is expressed in terms of units of standard deviation :

$$z = X - \bar{X} \ / \ S.D.$$

Positive values of z indicate that individual score falls above the mean of the normative sample; negative value indicates that it falls below the mean of the normative sample. z scores range from –3 to 3. In order to avoid negative sign and decimals, we can add a constant (generally 50) and multiply the value of z by another constant, 10. This transformation yield what are known as T scores. T scores can be directly calculated from raw scores as shown below :

$$T = 50 + 10\,(X - \bar{X})\ /S.D.$$

T score of 50 indicates average, values more than 50 indicate high scores, and values less than 50 indicate low scores. If the distribution of the raw scores is normal, z and T scores give information as to the percentage of normative sample which falls above and below a given z or T score :

z scores	–1	–2	–1	0	1	2	3
T scores	20	30	40	50	60	70	80
% of persons falling below	.1	2.3	15.9	50	84.1	97.7	99.9

Some less known transformations which are made with the choice of other additive and multiplying constants are Army General Classification Test Scores (AGCT), Colleague Entrance Examination Board Test Scores (CEEB), and Deviation IQ which are obtained as below:

AGCT = 20z + 100

CEEB = 100z + 500

Wechsler IQ = 100z + 100

S,B IQ (1960) = 16z + 100

Norms Based on Ordinal Position

Percentiles, Deciles, Normalized T scores, Stanine, and Sten are norms based on ordinal position of an individual in the normative sample.

Percentile : A percentile is any one of the ninety-nine point which divides a frequency distribution into 100 groups of equal size. Percentiles can be regarded as an individual's rank in a group of 100 subjects. In percentile norms P_{50} is the middle position (median) and P_{75} and P_{25} are indicative of high and low places in ranks. A score which falls beyond the range of scores of normative sample is assigned P_0 if it is less than the lowest score and P_{100} if it is more than highest score. But because it is not logical to assume that a person who is assigned P_0 is below every one and the person who is assigned P_{100} is above every one, Lyman (1963) recommended that it is better to use P_1 and P_{99} instead of P_0 and P_{100}, respectively. It is not difficult for a common man to understand the distinction between percentage and percentile scores if it is carefully explained to him. Moreover, percentile scores are universally applicable. They can be used with any age group and any type of test. However, their greatest disadvantage is that of inequality of units. If raw scores are normally distributed, their percentile equivalent near the centre (Mean/median of raw scores) are stretched while towards the extremes of raw scores they are contracted. For example, if median of a distribution is 40 (which is equivalent to P_{50}) a raw sore which is only 3 more than 40 may have a percentile equivalent of P_{60} but for giving rise to a difference of 10 percentiles between P_{15} and P_{25} a difference of 8 points of raw sores may be needed. The inequality of the percentile units is shown in the figure on the next page :

In spite of inequality of percentile scores one can have correct picture of such scores by plotting them on arithmetic probability paper in which vertical lines are spaced in the same way as percentile points.

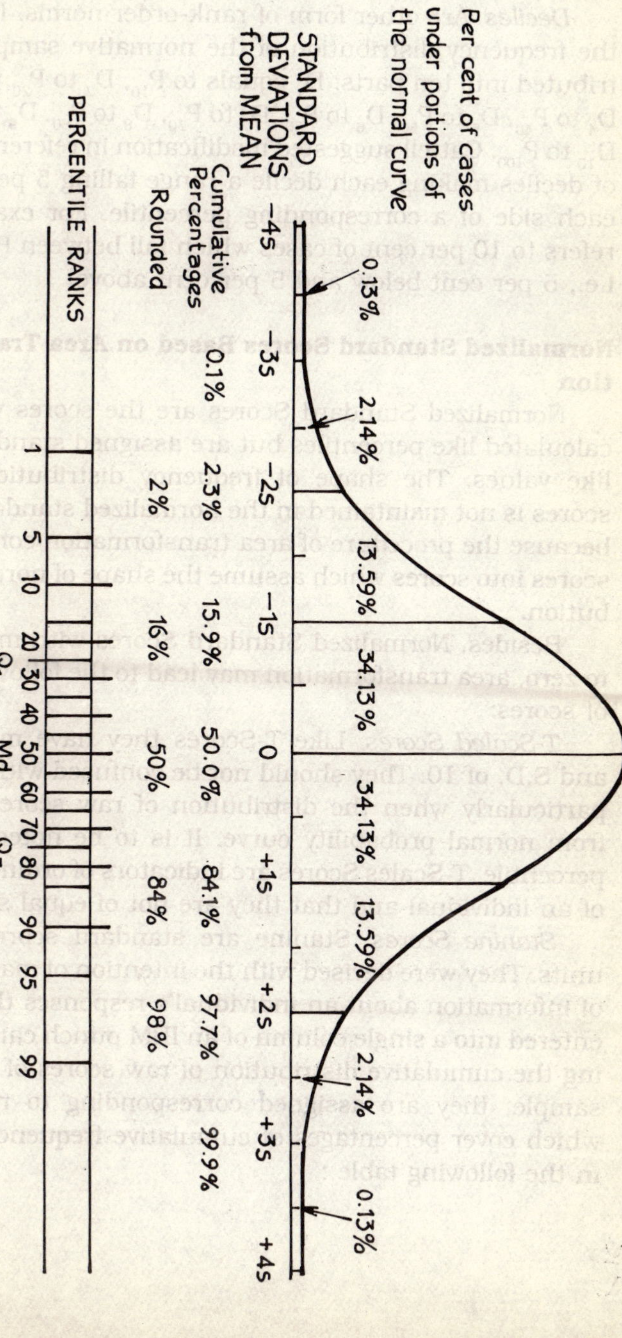

RELATIONSHIPS OF SELECTED SCORES IN A NORMAL DISTRIBUTION

Deciles. Are other form of rank-order norms. In Deciles the frequency distribution of the normative sample is distributed into ten parts: D_1 equals to P_{10}, D_2 to P_{20}, D_3 to P_{30}, D_4 to P_{40}, D_5 to P_{50}, D_6 to P_{60}, D_7 to P_{70}, D_8 to P_{80}, D_9 to P_{90} and D_{10} to P_{100}. Cattell suggested modification in reference points of deciles making each decile a range falling 5 per cent on each side of a corresponding percentile. For example, D_1 refers to 10 per cent of cases which fall between P_5 and P_{15}, i.e., 5 per cent below and 5 per cent above.

Normalized Standard Scores Based on Area Transformation

Normalized Standard Scores are the scores which are calculated like percentiles but are assigned standard-score like values. The shape of frequency distribution of raw scores is not maintained in the normalized standard scores because the procedure of area transformation converts raw scores into scores which assume the shape of normal distribution.

Besides, Normalized Standard Scores with mean equal to zero, area transformation may lead to the following kinds of scores:

T-Scaled Scores. Like T-Scores they have mean of 50 and S.D. of 10. They should not be confused with T-Scores particularly when the distribution of raw scores deviates from normal probability curve. It is to be noted that like percentile, T-Scales Scores are indicators of ordinal position of an individual and that they are not of equal steps.

Stanine Scores. Stanine are standard scores of nine units. They were devised with the intention of maximization of information about an individual's responses that can be entered into a single column of an IBM punch card. Obtaining the cumulative distribution of raw scores of normative sample, they are assigned corresponding to raw scores which cover percentages of cumulative frequencies shown in the following table :

	Lowest 4%	Next 7%	Next 12%	Next 17%	Middle 20%	Next 17%	Next 12%	Next 7%	Highest 4%
Stanine	1	2	3	4	5	6	7	8	9

Sten and C scores are similar to Stanine but the minimum and maximum value they assign are different. Sten are used for norms of scales developed at Cattell's Institute of Personality and Ability Testing. They provide for five normalize standard-score units on each side of mean. Each units is of the width of one-half standard deviation except stens of 1 and 10. The percentage of cumulative distribution covered up to different sten units is shown below :

	Lowest 2%	Next 5%	Next 9%	Next 15%	Low Middle 19%	High Middle 19%	Next 15%	Next 9%	Next 5%	Highest 2%
Sten	1	2	3	4	5	6	7	8	9	10

C-Scaled Scores are proposed by Guilford. They run from 0 to 10 and are calculated exactly as stanine but the assignment of scores to cumulative percentage of distribution is as follows :

	Lowest 1%	Next 3%	Next 7%	Next 12%	Next 17%	Middle 20%	Next 17%	Next 12%	Next 7%	Next 3%	Highest 1%
C	0	1	2	3	4	5	6	7	8	9	10

While converting an individuals raw scores into normative units, the assessor should not be only aware of the characteristics of the units used for reporting norms but also about the need of selection of proper normative (comparison) group with which score of the individual is to be compared. The selection of normative group is to be based on the considerations of the background of the individual as well as the purpose of testing. If the purpose is to know about an individual, he is to be compared with others who are of same age and cultural background. We may also compare an individual with a representative national sample. One may also use specific norms which are based on narrowly defined populations. The choice of specific norms depends on the purpose of assessment. Whatever kinds of norms are used it is always preferable to state the normative group for which they are develop. Specific norms may be for application to 'first-year engineering students', 'children living in rehabilitation centres', 'hospitalized psychiatric patients' etc. Local norms prepared on the bases of record available in an educational institution or industrial organization are also specific norms as they are based on narrowly defined populations.

Expectancy Tables and Expectancy Charts

Tables and charts showing the level of criterion behaviour or performance that one can expect from a subject who has obtained certain score are much useful for making sense out of assessment data particularly when the purpose of assessment is not only to describe the individual but to predict his behaviour and to take decision about him. An expectancy table contains the following information : class intervals of test scores, number of subjects in each interval, and cross categorization of subjects into criterion gradation corresponding to test-score intervals. An expectancy table using hypothetical data is presented below :

Test Number Percentage receiving each criterion grade Score of

Cases	Below		50	50-59	60-69	70-79	80-89	90+
65-69	48				18	20	35	27
60-64	54			5	25	30	25	15
55-59	103		11	23	29	35	2	
50-54	95	10	20	28	30	11	1	Below
54	89	30	45	20	8	2		

The expectancy table, like one given above, can be used for predicting the probabilities of an individual being placed in different criterion categories on the basis of his score on the assessment device. However, one can more rely on the probabilities when they are based on larger number of cases. In the above table interval 55-59 has as many subjects as 103 but class interval 65-69 has only 48 cases. Obviously, the prediction corresponding to class interval 55-59 shall be more dependable than prediction based on 65-69.

When criterion is dichotomized into pass-fail, successful-unsuccessful kind of categories, we can prepare expectancy charts showing percentage of pass/success corresponding to each score or score interval. Such a table is given below :

Staine	*Number of cases*	*Pass percentage*
1	2000	5
2	2000	7
3	2020	10
4	2025	15
5	1005	22
6	3002	38
7	3350	54
8	2003	68
9	20093	74

The above table may be used for finding the percentage of those who would not be able to pass/complete the training programme. This is given by subtracting from 100 the percentage of unsuccessful candidates among those who get certain Stanine score. For example, among those who got Stanine score of 1 the percentage of unsuccessful candidates would be 100–5 = 95.

More accurate prediction can be achieved by using a combination of other predictors in addition to the psychological test. This can be done by classifying the persons into categories formed by cross-classification according to age, sex, anxiety level, impulsiveness, etc. However, such an attempt becomes less and less rewarding if the number of persons who meet the specification of classification becomes lesser and lesser with the addition of the predictor variable. We know that with the decreasing number of subjects in categories the reliability of prediction is undermined.

Attention is to be drawn to the fact that we have to distinguish between $P(C_i/R_j)$ and $P(R_j/C_i)$. The first refers to the probability of a person being a member of the criterion group knowing his test responses (score). The second, $P(R_j/C_i)$ refers to the probability of obtaining certain score given the membership in a criterion group.

Profile

When scores of an individual on two or more tests/ subtests are available, it is useful to examine a pictorial representation of the scores so as to have an integrated understanding of his functioning. The study of a profile is based on the basic assumption that an individual functions as a whole and therefore, we should consider his scores in relation rather than in isolation with each other. The importance of the integrated configurational approach may be realized by the fact that behaviour of two persons with equally high scores on Depression Scale of MMPI would not be the same when one of them also has a high score on Psychopathic Deviation Scale but the other person got a low score.

There are two basic types of profile, specific and general. Specific profiles are devised for graphic representation of a particular test. The names of subscales or dimensions/ factors/ traits assessed by the tool are printed on the profile along with the space for raw scores and transformed scores. The profile may also contain the information of the normative group with which it can be used. For preparing profile of MMPI scales one has to use the different profile sheets for males and females.

A general profile is like a blank graph paper which has columns/ rows/ boxes for the identification data of the subject, particular of assessment device(s), space for raw scores and their transformed equivalents.

Lyman (1963) has given the characteristics of good profile. A good profile should have space for identification of subject, date of testing, name and form of test, recording of deviation in testing conditions, and information about the normative group. If norms are reported in percentile ranks, the space between the units near the median should be smaller than units near the extremes. The spacing is to be done keeping in view the areas under normal distribution. The manual and/or profile sheet should contain directions for the preparation of profile.

Since spatial differences between profile points can be

accentuated or diminished depending on scale used for representing the units of measurement (e.g., one T-score = 1 division or one T score = 5 divisions), visual inspection of differences in profile points does not convey correct information about the importance and significance of differences in profile points. Test manuals and/or special profile sheets usually mention the minimum numerical value of the difference that is to be considered significant. In DAT profile sheets, the spatial representation of scores is done in such a manner that vertical difference of one inch is an indication of significant difference. When no information is provided regarding the meaning and extent of difference, the means and standard deviations of two scales to be compared can be used for finding the minimum significant difference which is given by standard error of the difference calculated as below :

SE difference means = SE meas X + SE^2 meas Y

Where SE meas X and SE meas Y are standard errors of measurement in test x and y, respectively.

There have been attempts to make use of complete profiles for the description and prediction of an individual's behaviour. This is possible by obtaining a typical profile of a particular criterion group and then comparing an individual's profile with this typical profile. It is to be noted that profile comparison is not confined to finding differences in the scores of an individual on different scales included in profile and the corresponding scores on the typical profile. Such a comparison does not make use of all the variations between a given profile and the typical profile with which it is compared. Comparison of one profile with the other should consider the following kinds of differences which may exist between profiles to be compared :

1. *Elevation:* Refers to overall mean level of profile; it is indicated by the distance between the profile points as a whole from the reference line—the line representing either of the following : z value of 0, T value of 50, PR of 50.

2. *Scatter:* This refers to the variability of scores on the scales within profile around the over all mean of the profile.

It represents 'accentuation of shape'.

3. *Shape:* Refers to overall configuration of profile as determined by relative elevation among scales. Joining profile points, we get contours or shape of the curve. The profiles which is similar in respect of elevation scatter may have different shapes.

In order to eliminate the uncertainty of visual comparisons of profile different indicators of profile similarity are suggested:

1. Finding correlation between scores shown in the profiles to be compared appear to be a simple method of finding similarity between two profiles. However, correlation does not reflect differences in elevation as it is calculated using deviations from respective means (as in the case of product moment correlation) or converting scores into ranks. Irrespective of numerical values, if two sets of scores can be arranged in the same ascending or descending order, the correlation between the two sets would be perfect in spite of difference in elevation.

2. The D statistics originally proposed by Mahalonobis (1936) has been extensively used by Osgood and Suci (1952) for finding differences in the semantic profile of different concepts. The D statistics is based on the assumption that individual's scores can be regarded as points in the space created by coordinates equal to the number of scales/dimensions describing individuals in profile, i.e., number of profile points. This statistics takes into consideration differences of elevation, scatter and shape of profiles. It is very easy to calculate. The following example illustrates the procedure :

Individual	Scores on scales								
	A	B	C	D	E	F	G	H	I
Ishwar Lal	4	6	8	5	3	8	6	8	9
Ram Prakash	4	7	9	8	5	9	4	9	7
Difference (d)	0	1	1	3	2	1	2	1	2
d^2	0	1	1	9	4	1	4	1	4

$$\text{sum } d^2 = 25, \; D = \sqrt{d^2} = \sqrt{25} = 5$$

It is evident that differences between corresponding scores are found, squared and added and the square root of the total is taken to find value of D. The formula for calculation of D is:

$$Dk_{(iy)} = (a_{ji} - a_{jy})^2$$

Having obtained the value of D one has to decide that it is as small as to lead to the conclusion that the two profiles, which have been compared are similar. However, no definite criterion is available which may be helpful in decision of this kind. In addition to the problem of criterion, the following difficulties are also encountered in using D statistics :

1. The magnitude of the D is not comparable across different scaling metrics. The value of D obtained by using small units is different from that obtained when larger units are used for measuring the same thing which was measured by using small units.

2. The value of D does not take into consideration the number of dimensions involved in comparison.

3. The D statistics is based on the assumption that the profiles to be compared are made up of points located in the space created by orthogonal axes. That is, the variables in term of which comparison is being made, are independent. When variables are not really independent and this fact is ignored, large D value may be interpreted to be manifestation of differences in the profile points of two individuals in the total space while in reality the difference may be only in one dimension which is magnified by summing over correlated variables.

With the precautions implied in the above limitations, the D statistics can be used for finding the similarity of an individual with the typical profiles of different occupational and diagnostic groups. The typical profiles is obtained by using group means as profile points. That is typical profile is a graph of means of the group on the dimensions included in making a profile.

4. Pattern similarity coefficient (r_p) proposed by R.B. Cattell is claimed to be a better method of determining similarity between two profiles because :

1. r_p takes into account metrics and number of dimension involved in comparison;

2. Provides a convenient function which lies from +1 to –1 as does coefficient of correlation;

3. The significance of r_p can be determined.

In calculating value of r_p, the sum of d^2 is obtained in the same way as mentioned earlier. In addition to this we have to get the Median value of Chi Square for degree of freedom equal to the number of dimensions (k) involved in comparison. The formula for calculation r_p is as below :

$$r_p = \frac{E_k - \sum_{1}^{k} d^2}{E_k + \sum_{1}^{k} d^2}$$

Where k is number of dimensions involved in comparison, E_k = 2k, and k is the median of Chi Square values for k degree of freedom.

A r_p value of 1 indicates that two profiles under comparison have coinciding points, i.e., the two profiles are completely overlapping. A value of 0 indicates that corresponding points of profiles to be compared are as far a part as one would expect for any two points taken at random. The r_p value of –1 indicates that the corresponding profile points are at the opposite pole of distribution. Horn (1961) has provided a table which can be used for finding the significance of r_p for various numbers of orthogonal comparison. The table have columns for positive and negative r_p values corresponding to different values of k and probability levels.

While using r_p one should be careful about the kind of comparison he is making: Whether comparison is between two persons, two groups, or one person with a group? It may be noted that the last kind of comparison is of great importance in clinical diagnosis and personnel selection. One cannot be indifferent to the kind of comparison one is making because the standard error of r_p is related to standard deviation of the scores. When the profile of mean scores of one group is to be compared with such a profile of another group, we have to have the standard deviation (S.D.) of means of groups around the mean population of groups. Cattell et al. (1966) suggested that S.D. of the group means for the total population of groups may be estimated by using N+1 in the denominator. The logic of using N+1 in the denominator is that clinical and occupational groups are comprised of the individuals who are selected and homogeneous and for this reason within group variability is less than in the case of groups comprised of randomly selected persons. While making the proposal for estimating the S.D. from the S.D. of population of individuals and N the size of groups being compared, Cattell et al. (1970) point out that for accurate work there is no escape from the necessity of obtaining S.D. of means of groups.

In the absence of S.D. of group means, S.D. of individuals in the population of individuals is to be used in comparison of individual profile with profile of diagnostic or occupational groups. When an individual's profile is to compared with the profiles of different groups, r_p value for each comparison may be ranked and this ranking may be used for making decision about the person. Alternatively, "chances of success ratio" may be found for r_p cut off along with conventional probability level, e.g., 95 out of 100. This is done by comparing the fraction of persons in the occupation with the fraction of general population which reach or exceed a given r_p value. For most common individual to group comparison the value of ΣD^2 is also needed, where D is the difference between group means on each factor from general population mean, 5.5. The value of r_p can be obtained by formula:

$$r_p = \frac{(4K' + \Sigma D^2) - \Sigma d^2}{(4K' + \Sigma D^2) + \Sigma d^2}$$

Where K' is the median Chi-square with degree of freedom equal to number of factors.

A ready recknor given in Appendix 2 of Handbook of 16 PF may also be used for estimation of r_p.

As pointed out earlier, the advantage of r_p is that it is independent of influence of metric and number of dimensions being compared. Still the relation of r_p to d creates some problems because in calculating profile similarity of two persons each is "penalized" according to the square of his distance from the criterion, and without regard to direction. Ignoring the sign of d implies that the criterion is regarded as optimum while usually it is believed that performance on the criterion goes improving throughout the whole range of dimension.

The formula of r_p proposed above is applicable under certain circumstances. When the dimensions are oblique and when due to certain reasons unequal weights are to be assigned to variables we have to use r_n, the profile nearness coefficient.

Actuarial Prediction

Actuarial prediction is to be used when predictors are categorical. The method may be regarded as improved version of expectancy table. The method can also be used when the transformation of metric data into categories is deemed to be appropriate. It is an alternative methodology to multiple regression analysis to be discussed later in this chapter.

The actuarial predictions being considered just after the discussion of profile comparison because the D statistics is found to be of much help in developing the actuarial system of prediction. To understand the nature of actuarial system let us consider the situation where a number of personality measures are to be used for prediction of a number of criterion behaviour. Designating personality variables as R_1, R_2, R_3, R_4, etc., and Criterion behaviour as C_1, C_2, C_3, C_4, etc., our first task is to determine empirical relation between the two sets of variables. While considering the relationship between the two sets of variables it is important to draw attention to distinction between $P(C_i/R_j)$ and $P(R_j/C_i)$ and also to remind that they are not equal. Actuarial prediction makes use of $P(C_i/R_j)$ relation which tells us that given a particular pattern of test response, what is the probability that the individual whose pattern of response is given, is a member of a specific criterion group. The $P(R_j/C_i)$ kind of relation tells us that given membership in some criterion group what is the probability that the individual will get certain score on the predictor variable. This kind of relation is often reported as evidence of validity of the measuring instrument. However, as Dawes (1962) has pointed out, the two kind of relations are not mathematically equivalent, and for this reason the type of validity information presented in test manuals is misleading with respect to practical utility of the instrument.

Developing an Actuarial System

An actuarial system devised for general use is to be based on very large samples of the populations for which the system is being devised. A pre-existing data bank in which all kinds of informations about the psychiatric patients/ employees are stored may be much useful in developing actuarial system, because instead of collecting data we can make use of the data available in the data bank.

As one does not know in advance what kind of data would be useful in developing an actuarial system and because expenses involved in collection of fresh data are high, it is preferable to make the data bank as comprehensive as possible by putting on record every kind of information which was obtained from the client during routine interview and testing sessions. With the availability of funds and absence of data bank, data may be collected specifically for the purpose of developing actuarial system. The classes of data to be collected may be designated as :

1. Predictor variables; 2. Criterion data; 3. Personality descriptors and 4. Demographic and miscellaneous data.

Every actuarial system is to be initiated by deciding what is to be predicted, and what are predictor variables. Although an actuarial system may be devised for making one or two criterion discriminations, Wiggins (1973) recommend that it would be useful to collect data on other criterion designations, such as prognosis of recovery, responses to psychotherapy, length of hospitalization, etc. Even when the eventual categorization of criterion variable is to be broad, it is best to record the original criterion in finer categories (e.g., varieties of neurotic and schizophrenic reactions). Some of the important considerations involved in the selection of predictor variables are: availability, objectivity, reliability, multidimensionality, validity and theoretical relevance.

The words, phrases, adjectives, sentences that would be used in describing person who would be categorized on the basis of his responses on the predictor variables are known as personality descriptors. Such descriptors may be obtained with the help of direct observation of patient's behaviour by physicians, psychologists, nurses, and other attendants. Personality descriptors may be collected using adjective check lists, rating scales, and Q-sort descriptions. The members of the target population may themselves be asked to describe themselves with the help of Q-sort and other methods of self-description. Personality descriptors include symptoms and complaints of the patients which may be obtained with the help of a symptom check list and clinical reports. It may be noted that some personality descriptors are relatively simple to observe and record such as slow walking movement, personal temperament, going out of the ward, etc. Other personality descriptors are not open to direct observation but are to be inferred from behaviour, e.g., latent hostility or latent homosexuality.

As mentioned earlier it is always better to obtain demographic and other miscellaneous data while developing actuarial system because when the actuarial system is put to use, the availability of demographic information such as age, place of birth, sex, marital and socio-economic status etc. of the taxonomic groups would enable us to match the individual to be diagnosed/described with the appropriate groups. Our reliance on the actuarial system would depend on the close resemblance of the individual and the taxonomic group. It is, therefore, necessary to discuss the procedure of taxonomic classification.

Taxonomic Classification

An important step in developing actuarial prediction system is to classify individuals into homogeneous and mutually exclusive groups. This classification is done on the basis of subjects' scores on the predictor variables. The classification may be simple or complex. A classification is simple if it depends on few variables. The simplest classification using MMPI would be categorization of subjects on the basis of their highest scale scores. A complex classification take into consideration a large number of variables simultaneously. While deciding the basis of classification (and thus the level of complexity), one has to make a comprise between specificity (group homogeneity and independence) and reliability (sufficient number of subjects in groups). With increasing complexity specificity is on increase but one may not get sufficient number of subjects for the taxonomic groups. Taxonomic grouping can be done a priori basis; it can also be done using statistical devices like D or r_p.

The decision to use a priori or empirical/statistical criterion for taxonomic classification of profiles involves the dilemma of ignoring known or assumed to be known predictor-criterion relationships on the one hand and precluding the use of undiscovered relations on the other. Some other problems with a priori classification of profiles are:

1. Lack of homogeneity within class; 2. lack of mutual exclusiveness of profile classes; 3. small frequencies of the occurrence of such profiles. These problems do not occur when statistical methods are used to arrive at taxonomic classification. Steps involved in the statistical classification of profiles for the purpose of developing an actuarial system are as below:

Collection of profiles and Identification of potential nuclear groups

Suppose we have to develop an actuarial system using MMPI clinical scale as predictors. We start with the collecting of a large number of profiles of members of population for which the system is to be developed.

Having collected a large number of such, say 1000, profiles, we obtain D values for each of the possible 1000 × 99/2 = 49500 comparisons. We also calculate standard deviation of scores of all the ten clinical scales, square the each S.D. and find the total as illustrated below:

Scale :	1	2	3	4	5	6	7	8	9	10
S.D.	10	11	13	12.2	14.2	9.8	10.2	11.1	14.2	11.4 2
S.D.	100	121	169	148.8	201.6	96.0	104.0	132.2	201.6	130.0

The value of sum of $S.D^2$ (1404.2) is used as the criterion for deciding similarity/dissimilarity between two profiles to be compared. If ½ ΣSD^2 is used as minimum definition of profile dissimilarity, profiles which have D^2 less than that are regarded as similar in the selection of potential nucleus groups. Having calculated Ds and determined the criterion we can from the groups of similar profiles. For each of the 1000 profiles, we find the profile whose D^2 from that profile does not exceeds 702.

For this a chart is prepared in which first column contains the names of all the persons whose profiles are found to be in the criterion range, the second column contains the list of profiles which are found to be similar to the profile named in the first column, and the third column has the number of profiles which are found to be similar to the profile given in the first column profiles are ordered in terms of number of similar profiles with which they are associated. The record sheet is like the one given below:

Profile	Similar profiles (Within 702 points of the profile listed in the first column)	Total number of similar profiles
Razdan	Srivastava, Gopi, Anu... etc.	260
Ashok	Farhat, Anand, Rakesh....etc.	245
Yadav	Fernandis, Singh, Prakash....etc.	180
Nisar	Bahadur, Srivastava, Chadha....etc.	139
Malik		0

There will be as many as 1000 rows in the record sheet corresponding to number of persons.

The profile of Razdan shall be taken to be first nuclear group because this profile is associated with the largest numbers of other profile as can be seen from the last column. Having selected the first group we have to eliminate from other rows the names of persons whose profiles are also listed there. For example, Srivastav's profile appears again in the row of Nisar; it will be deleted from there. The purpose of doing so is to have mutually exclusive nuclear groups. The same procedure is repeated with the profile which is next in terms of number of similar profiles. With the repetition of the procedure we are left with a smaller number of mutually exclusive groups, say 50. Some of these groups may have large number of profiles while other groups may have as few as 2 profiles.

Identification of Prototype Profiles

The next step in developing actuarial system is to make the potentially nuclear groups which are homogeneous, mutually exclusive, and as maximally dissimilar to each other as possible. The number of profile which are left, for example 50, after the completion of the previous step are now compared with one another with respect to D^2 value of each nuclear profile in the total group. The table given below shows a portion of 50 × 50 matrix. The entries are D^2 differences between the profiles involved.

	Razdan	Ashok	Yadav	Nisar	Agarwal
Razdan	0	2634	2397	1189	4973
Ashok	2634	0	2645	3209	2372
Yadav	2397	2645	0	1975	1894
Nisar	1189	3209	1975	0	2015
Agarwal	4973	2372	1894	2015	0
Column sum	11193	10860	8911	8388	11254

Defining profile dissimilarity as the value of D^2 exceeding the value of sum of D^2, we eliminate from each row the profile with value less than this value. Using Column sum as an index of dissimilarity, we begin with Razdan's profile which is most dissimilar to other potential nuclear profiles. In the first row we find that difference of Razdan's profile with the profiles of Nisar is less than 1274. This two entry shall be eliminated from Razdan's row and the row of Nisar is also eliminated from the matrix. The procedure of eliminating profiles which are too similar to other nuclear groups is continued with next dissimilar potential nuclear profile. Doing this we are left with potential nuclear profiles groups which are not only maximally distinct with others but are also lesser in numbers due to elimination of groups like Nisar's and Yadav's. Out of 50 profiles we may be left with, for example 27 groups.

Elimination of Small Prototype Groups and Augmentation of Prototype Groups

In the process of classification of profiles one has to make compromise between two contradictory requirements ensuring homogeneity and distinctiveness which are necessary for purity and usefulness of classification. If a taxonomic system can be useful for 1 per cent or 2 per cent of population, it would be of little use for 98 per cent of people because their profile would not be found similar to any one and would remain uninterpreted. A decision is, therefore, to be taken to eliminate prototypes which are associated with less than a given number of profiles, for example 12. For the remaining prototype profile, mean value on all the ten scales for all similar profiles associated with that prototype are found. The means give the average profile of the prototype groups and are used for the purpose of augmenting prototype groups. This is done by finding other profiles which are similar to the representative prototype profiles. Using each set of ten averages the D value is obtained by finding differences in corresponding scores of the profiles which are not included in any of the prototype groups. As the similarity of prototype profiles is also to be ensured, a more rigorous criterion, e.g., 1/4 sigma D may be used for finding the profiles which are similar to a given prototype. New averages are obtained using the scores which were already in the prototype and which are included now. The process of profile comparison is repeated using the new averages of prototype groups on the one hand and unclassified profiles on the other. This time the criterion of similarity may be relaxed even more. The procedure may continue until the prototype groups are sufficiently augmented.

Construction of Actuarial Tables

In the construction of actuarial tables criterion data,

personality descriptors, and demographic data associated with each profile group are separated into different files. For each file the frequency of occurrence of different categories of criterion and other data are tabulated. These frequencies may be converted into percentage within each prototype. The percentages can directly be read as probabilities. We can make such kind of statements as, "the probability that Mr. Bhargava whose profile is similar to prototype I, will receive the psychiatric diagnosis of Manic-depression is .7". In order to escape from a Barnum type description of personality, it is important to indicate the departure of a given percentage from the base line. The relative frequency of occurrence of categories of criterion data in the entire sample is taken to be the base line for assessing the departure. If a criterion information/personality description is found to occur in 78 per cent of cases, the information/ personality descriptor is not of much use in differentiating one individual from others. Astericks and algebraic signs may be used to identify the percentages which are significantly below or above the base line, i.e., percentage in the entire sample. Marks and Seeman (1963) used +, ++, +++, signs to indicate deviations above and –, – –, – – – to indicate deviations below the basal percentage.

It is worth while to describe some of the procedures used in obtaining personality descriptors for different types of profiles. For the Marks-Seeman system the primary source of personality descriptors were 108 Q-sort items. Taking a person classified to have one particular type of profile, the professional staff familiar with the person was asked to place each Q-sort item in one of the nine categories indicating its degree of applicability to the person. The mean placement of Q-sort items was found for each of the persons. The personality descriptions of nine to ten persons having the same kind of profile were intercorrelated and five persons who were more similar psychologically were selected as defining group for that profile. The mean placement of Q-sort items was found for each of the 16 types of profiles. Three staff psychologists rated 225 items selected from case histories, hospital records, and therapy notes for different defining groups.

Mark-Seeman system is based on a priori classification of profiles. The rules which they used for classification of profiles into prototype groups is being mentioned as an example of a priori classification : A profile will be classified as 2-7-8 type if the following conditions are met :

Rules

1. D, Pt and Sc>70
2. D-HS>15
3. D-Sc < 15
4. Pt -Pd>10
5. Pt-Pa>10
6. Sc - Pt<5
7. Pt and Sc > Hs and Hy
8. Ma < 70
9. Si >70
10. L and K <70; F<80

Actuarial system can be used for the prediction of fixed as well as free criteria. When the system is used for placing the individuals in fixed categories of social, clinical, or economic importance—such as aggressiveness, depression, job success, etc. — the prediction is of fixed criteria. When actuarial system is used for providing general personality description without reference to some external socially useful fixed categorizations, the prediction is of the nature of free criteria. It may be noted that the elaborations of personality characterization would depend upon how many personality descriptors were originally collected and how many out of them were found to be associated with a given profile. If a computer is fed with the programme of classification of profiles and the personality descriptors associated with different kinds of profiles, it can write psychological report selecting declarative sentences for its memory.

Multiple Prediction

We can make use multiple regression equation for the prediction of the criterion which is also quantified. The need to use more than one variable in prediction of a criterion arises when the criterion is to complex and a single variable is able to predict only a portion of the criterion variance as indicated by much difference between the actual and predicted scores. It may be noted that the maximum amount of criterion variance which a single variable can predict is equal to the square of coefficient of correlation and even as high correlation of a predictor with a criterion as .8 would explain 64 per cent of criterion variance. To encompass remaining 36 per cent of variance other predictors are to be used whose number would depend upon their correlation with the criterion, intercorrelation among them, and the level of accuracy desired in prediction.

Multiple-regression equation makes use of summation of weighted predictor variables to predict the criterion variable. That is, the basic multiple regression model assumes that versions of the criterion variables accounted by each predator variable can be added to have total variance accounted by all the predictors put together.

Like simple bivariate regression equation, multiple regression provides the regression coefficients for each of the variables which are being used in the prediction of a criterion:

$$Y = b_1 X_1 + b_2 X_2 + b_3 X_3 \ldots\ldots\ldots + b_n X_n$$

When a large number of predictors are to be used for the prediction of a criterion, their regression coefficients, beta, can be obtained by using prepackaged computer programmes which use the following formula for finding the beta coefficients:

$$\beta = R^{-1}.C$$

Where R is the matrix of intercorrelation among predictor and C is the vector of correlation of predictors with the criterion.

Having obtained the beta coefficients it is possible to predict the criterion setting regression equation either in standard score form or in raw score form for any number of predictors, m.

When a large number of predictors are used for the prediction of a criterion it is found that they do not equally contribute in the prediction of the criterion. This is indicated by their beta coefficients which differ in magnitude. When some beta coefficients are large while other are small it is important to select some of the useful predictors and discard others due to following reasons :

1. It would involve less expenditure to assess individuals in respect of lesser number of variables.

2. It is easier to interpret the composite which is made up of smaller number of variable than that which is made up of a large number of variables.

3. A regression equation comprising few variable is more stable, i.e., free of impact of chance factors, than an equation made up of a large number of variables.

The procedure for selection of more effective predictors from among the original set of predictors known as stepwise multiplication correlation. Stepwise multiple correlation may follow step-up or step-down approach. In step-up approach we start prediction using the variable which is found to have highest correlation with the criterion and then add variable with next highest correlation with criterion. This is followed by determining the improvement in the accuracy of prediction. This process of adding one variable at time in the regression equation is continued till it is found that further addition of a predictor does not improve the prediction. In step-down procedure instead of adding variables one by one we remove from the regression equation the variable which has lowest beta weight in the multiple equation in which all the variable were used. One by one variables from the multiple equation are taken away and the loses of accuracy in the prediction is studied every time. The procedure is stopped when the removal of a variable lead to significant decrease of the value of R.

The task of prediction of a criterion with the help of a set of scores on measures of personality is not completed with the making of regression equation, calculation of R and finding the most suitable predictors. We have to find how much stable is the R for other samples. McNemar (1969, p. 205) has given a formula for finding the degree of shrinkage of R when we apply regression equation to a new sample:

$$R^{-2} = 1 - (1 - R^2)\ \frac{N - 1}{N - m}$$

The procedure of determining the stability of regression equation to a new sample is known as cross-validation.

Often cross-validation is planned simultaneously with the programme of developing multiple regression equation. The original sample is broken into two parts and the data obtained from one part of the sample is used for determining beta weights and data from the other part of the sample is used for cross validation. However, data collected once for both developing regression equation and cross-validation may be influenced by the situational or temporary factors which may not be present at other occasions. In double-cross validation two regression equations are developed making use of the data of two parts of a sample. Each regression equation is then validated using the data of the part of the sample which was not used for the development of regression equation.

Moderator Variables

The multiple-regression model is based on the mathematical assumption that the criterion variable can be best estimated by additive combination of weighted predictors. This model is not appropriate when special configurations of predictor variables are associated with unique values of the criterion variables.

Let us take a simple example to explain the situation to which we are referring. Let there be three variables y, x_1, and x_2, y being the criterion and x_1, x_2 the predictors. Finding product moment correlation between x_1 and y we may find that its value is as low as .10. However, when the sample is divided into high and low groups on the basis of its scores on the other variable x_2, the correlation between x_1 and y calculated for high and low groups are found to be .35 and –.05. This finding indicate that the relationship between the two variables x_1 and y is dependent upon the values of x_2. When such a situation arises in analysis of variance it is referred as interaction between the variables x_1 and x_2.

Saunder (1956) coined the term moderator variable to refer to the variable on which the predictive validity of some psychological variables is dependent. The term occurs in the context of differential predictability phenomenon demonstrated by Frederiksen and Melville (1954) when they tried to predict grade-point average in engineering school with the help Engineering scale of Strong Vocational Interest Blank. For a group of 154 engineering freshmen at Princeton University, the correlation between the Engineering scale and grade-point average was found to be .10. However, when the group of freshmen were divided into compulsive and non-compulsive subgroups on the basis of their scores on Strong Accountant scale, the relationship between the predictor and the criterion for compulsive and non-compulsive groups were found to be -.01 and .25, respectively. It was argued that compulsiveness influences the relationship between the predictor and criterion. In compulsive students the relationship between the two variables is obscured by the fact that compulsive tendencies interfere with the expression of motivation in performance. The relationship is higher for noncompulsive students because they are free of such inefficient tendencies.

Moderator variables for specific prediction situation may be developed using a method proposed by Ghiselli (1960). A regression equation is set to predict criterion variable with the help of a single predictor and the absolute value of D, the difference between the predicted (y') and actual criterion (y) scores is obtained which is $y'-y$. The subjects are then divided into high—and low—predictable groups and item analysis is carried out to identify the items which can discriminate between the two groups. The items which are found to discriminate are cross-validated by determining their ability to make discrimination in new samples.

It is to be pointed out that due to assumption of additive of contribution of predictive variables in multiple-regression analysis, moderator variables cannot be included in the equation when the relationship between x_1 and y varies directly as a function of x_2, we have substitute liner-multiple equation by an expression like one suggested by Saunder (1956):

$$y = b_1x_1 + b_2x_2 + b_3x_1x_2$$

The expression is known as linear joint function (Ezekil and Fox, 1959). While the phenomenon of moderation of relationship between the predictor and criterion has been demonstrated in a large number of studies, the utility of linear-joint-function model in improvement of prediction of the criterion is at best suggestive and at best needs further evidence to be considered to be well demonstrated.

In attempt to improve the prediction of the criterion variable, the use of more complex functions involving higher order expressions is also suggested. Examples of such expressions are squared-joint-function relationship and second-order parabolic joint function. The expressions are:

$$f = b_1 x_1 + b_2 x_2 + b_3 x_1 x_2^2 + b_4 x_1^2 x_2$$

$$f = b_1 x_1 + b_2 x_2 + b_3 x_1 x_2 + b_4 x_1 x_2^2 + b_5 x_1^2 x_2$$

There is no limit to complexity of functional relations that can be used in the prediction of criterion. Wiggin (1973) observed that for making use of more complex models in prediction of a given criterion we should have at our disposal well articulated theories of personality organization so as to enable us to make an appropriate choice of model of prediction from among the myriad possibilities that exist. The following observation of Ward also warns us against the undeliberated use of complex models : "If the relationship that are represented by the equations actually exist in the population, the more complex equations might not maintain better predictive efficiency on subsequent samples." (Ward, p. 10). Ward's observation was in the context of the reports that the complex models do not remain effective when applied to an independent sample. However, the observation is also relevant to the initial decision to use complex equation.

Suppressor Variables

While discussing the use of personality variables in the prediction of a criterion it is mentioned that best predictors to be used in multiple regression equation are those which have high correlation with the criterion and have low intercorrelation among themselves. Horst (1941) drawn attention to the 'suppressors variables' which can help in improving prediction of a criterion in a way different from the good predictors having the two characteristics mentioned above. Suppressor variables are those variables which are not correlated with the criterion but they are correlated with the predictors in such a manner that they are helpful in taking away unwanted 'baggage'. The unwanted baggage is checked by overlapping of the suppressor variable with the portion of the variance of the predictor which is unrelated to the criterion and hence is useless. In a regression equation using one predictor and one suppressor variable the extra baggage is shed through subtraction term :

$$y = b_1 x_1 - b_2 x_2$$

Since the variance contributed by personality variables in the prediction of a criterion is vitiated by the sources of response distortions and response styles, measures of variance response sets and response style are expected to be good suppressor variables. Dicken (1963) and Goldberg, Rorer, and Green (1970) conducted studies to determine the effect of suppression of social desirability and other response styles on improvement of prediction of certain criteria with the help of California Personality Inventory (CPI). No evidence of successful suppression of acquiescence of stylistic variance was obtained.

The above discussion of different methods of utilization of personality data was confined to applied situations like educational and vocational guidance, personnel selection in industrial and military organizations, diagnosis and classification of human malfunctioning, etc. Besides such applied uses, personality assessment is also needed when research is to be conducted on factors contributing towards sources of individual differences, personality organization, personality dynamics, personality change, cross-cultural differences and other problems in which data is to be obtained with the help of personality assessment devices. Personality assessment may also be needed when within group (error variance) is to be minimized by assigning subjects to different experimental groups which are similar to each other in respect of the variable to be controlled.

Bibliography

Adorno, T. W., Frankel-Brunswik, E., Levinson, D.J., and Sanford, R.N. (1950), *The Authoritarian Personality*, New York : Harper.

Alf, E.F., and Dorfman, D.D.(1967), The classification of individual into two criterion groups on the basis of a discontinuous pay off function, *Psychometrica*, 32 : 115-123.

Allen, J.G. (1981), The clinical psychologist as a diagnostic consultant, *Bulletin of Meninger Clinic*, 45 : 247-258.

Allport, G.W., and Odbert, H.S. (1936), Trait names : A psychological study, *Psychological Monographs*, 47 (Whole no. 211).

Allport, G.W. (1937), *Personality*, New York : Holt.

Allport, G.W., and Pettigrew, T. (1957), Cultural influence on the perception of movement : the tapezoidal illusion among Zulus, *Journal of Abnormal and Social Psychology*, 55 : 104-113.

Allport, G.W. (1961), *Patterns and growth in personality*, New York: Holt, Rinehart, and Wilson.

Amrine, M. (1965), The 1965 congressional inquiry into testing : a commentry, *American Psychologist*, 20 : 859-870.

Anastasi, A. (1982). *Psychological testing*, New York : Macmillan (5th edition).

Arthur, A.Z. (1966), A decision making approach to psychological assessment in the clinic, *Journal of Consulting Psychology*, 44: 272-276.

Arthur, A.Z., and Freemantle, A. (1966), Extreme response bias and associative commonality, *Psychonomic Sci*, 5 : 103-107.

Asthana, H.S. (1950), Hindustani adjustment inventory, *Education*, 29 : 17-20.

Bell, J.M. (1977), Stressful life events and coping methods in mental illness and wellness behaviour, *Nursing Research*, 26: 136-141.

Bechtold, H.P. (1959), Construct validity : a critique, *American Psychologist*, 14 : 619-628.

Bennett, G.K., Seashore, H.G. and Wesman, A.G. (1974), *Fifth edition manual for the Differential Aptitude Tests, Forms S and T*, New York : Psychological Corporation.

Bentler, P.M. (1969), Semantic space is (approximately) bipolar, *Journal of Psychology*, 71 : 33-40.

Berg, I.A. (1955), Response bias and Personality : The Deviation hypothesis, *Journal of Psychology*, 40 : 60-71.

Berg, I.A. (1957), Deviation responses and deviant people : the formulation of the deviation hypothesis, *Journal of Consulting Psychology*, 4 : 154-161.

Berg, I.A. (1959), The unimportance of test item content. In B.M. Bass and I.A. Berg (Eds.), *Objective approach to personality assessment* , Princeton : Van Nastrand, 1959.

Berg, I.A. (1961), Measuring deviant behaviour by means of deviant response sets. In I.A. Berg and B.M. Bass (Eds.), *Conformity and deviation*, New York : Harper.

Berg, I.A. (1967), The deviant hypothesis : broad statement of its assumption and postulates. In I.A. Berg (Ed.), *Response set in personality assessment*, Chicago : Adline, 146-190.

Berg, I.A., Hunt, W.A. and Barnes E.A. (1949), *The Perceptual Reaction Test*, Evanstone, III. : I.A. Berg.

Berry, J.W. (1969), On cross-cultural comparability, *International Journal of Psychology*, 4 : 119-128.

Berry, J.W., and Dasen, P.R. (1974), Introduction : History and method in cross-cultural study of cognition. In J.W. Berry and P.R. Dasen (Eds.), *Culture and cognition : reading in cross cultural psychology*, London : Methuen, 1-20.

Berry, J.W. (1980), Introduction to Methodology, In H.C. Triandis and J.W. Berry. (Eds.), *Handbook of cross-cultural psychology: vol. 2, methodology*, Boston : Allyn and Bacon.

Block, J. (1965), *The challenge of response sets*, New York: Appelton Century Crofts.

Brenghelman, J. C. (1959), Differences in questionnaire responses between English and German nationals, *Acta Psychologic*, 16: 339-355.

Brim, O.J., and Hoff, D.P. (1957), Individual and situational differences in desire for certainty, *Journal of Abnormal and Social Psychology*, 54: 225-229.

Brislin, R. (1970), Back translation for cross-cultural research, *Journal of Cross-Cultural Psychology*, 1: 185-216.

Brislin, R., Lonner, W., and Thorndike, R. (1973), *Cross-cultural research methods*, New York: Wiley.

Brodman, K., Erdman, A.J., and Wolf, M.G. (1949), *Manual of CMI Health Questionnaire*, New York: Cornell University Medical College.

Brogden, H.E., and Taylor, E.R. (1950), The dollor criterion—applying the cost accounting concept to criterion construction, *Personnel Psychology*, 3: 133-154.

Brown, M.N. (1950), Evaluating and scoring the Minnesota Multiphasic "Cannot Say" items, *Journal of Clinical Psychology*, 6: 180-184.

Buchwald, A.M. (1961), Verbal utterance as data, In H. Feigal and G.Maxwell (Eds.), *Current issues in philosophy of science*, New York: Holt.

Burgess, E.W. (1928), Factors determining success or failure on parole. In A.A. Bruce (Ed.), *The working of indeterminate sentence law and parole system in illinois*, Illinois: Illinois Board of Parole, 205-249.

Burt, C. (1939), Factor analysis of emotional traits, *Character and Personality*, 7: 238-254; 285-299.

Butcher, J.N., Keller, L.S., and Bacon, S.F. (1985), Current development and future direction in computerized personality assessment, *Journal of Consulting and Clinical Psychology*, 53: 803-825.

Butcher, J.N., and Tellegan, A. (1966), Objections to MMPI items, *Journal of Consulting Psychology*, 30: 527-534.

Campbell, D. (1968), A cooperative multinational opinion exchange, *Journal of Social Issues*, 24: 245-258.

Campbell, D., Brislin, R., Stewart, V., and Werner, O. (1970), Back translation techniques in cross-cultural research, *Paper submitted to the International Journal of Psychology*, (referred by Brislin 1970).

Campbell, D.T. (1960), Recommendations for APA test standards regarding construct, trait, and discriminant validity, *American Psychologist*, 15: 546-553.

Campbell, D.T., and Fisk, D.W. (1959), Convergent and discriminant validity by the multitrait multimethod matrix, *Psychological Bulletin*, 56: 81-105.

Canter, F.M. (1963), Simulation on the California Psychological Inventory and the adjustment of the simulator, *Journal of Consulting Psychology*, 27: 252-256.

Carhuff, R.R., Barnett, L., and McCall, J.N. (1965), *The counsellor's handbook: scale and profile interpretation of MMPI*, Urbana, Ill: R.W. Parkinson and Associates.

Carp, A.L., and Shavzin, A.R. (1950), The susceptibility to falsification of the Rorschach psychodiagnostic technique, *Journal of Consulting Psychology*, 14: 230-233.

Carr, H.A., and Kingsbury (1938), The concept of trait, *Psychological Review*, 45: 497-524.

Carrol, J. (1966), Quelques measures subjectives en psychologie: frequencies des mots, significativite et qualite de truduction, *Bulletin de psychologic*, 19 : 530-592.

Casagrande, J. (1954), The ends of translation, *International Journal of American Linguistics*, 20 : 335-340.

Cattell, R.B. (1946), *The description and measurement of personality*, New York : World Books, Younker-on-Hudson.

Cattell, R.B. (1947), Confirmation and clarification of the primary personality factors, *Psychometrica*, 12 : 197-220.

Cattell, R.B. (1948), Primary factors in the realm of objective tests, *Journal of Personality*, 16 : 459-487.

Cattell, R.B. (1950), *Personality : A systematic, theoretical, and factual study*, New York : McGraw-Hill.

Cattell, R.B. (1957), *Personality and motivation : structure and measurement*, New York : World Book.

Cattell, R.B. (1964), Validity and Reliability : A proposed more basic sets of the concepts, *Journal of Educational Psychology*, 55 : 1-22.

Cattell, R.B. (1966), The scree test for number of factors, *Multivariate Behavioral Research*, 1 : 140-161.

Cattell, R.B., Coulter, M.A., and Tsujioka, B. (1966), The taxonomic recognition of types and functional emergents. In R.B. Cattle (Ed.), *Handbook of Multivariate Experimental Psychology*, Chicago : Rand McNally.

Cattell, R.B., and Jaspers, J. (1967), A general plasmode (No. 30-10-5-2) for factor analytic exercise and research. *Multivariate Behavioral Research Monograph*, 67-3, 1-212.

Cattell R.B., Eber, H.W., and Tatasuoka, M. (1970), *Handbook of the Sixteen Personality Factors Questionnaire*, Campaign Ill.: Institute of Personality and Ability Testing.

Chapman, J.L. (1967), Illusory correlation in observational report, *Journal of Verbal Learning and Verbal Behavior*, 6 : 151-155.

Chaudhry, U. (1964), *An Indian modification of the children's apperception test*, New Delhi : Mansayan.

Christie, R., Havel, J., and Seinderg, B. (1958), Is the F Scale irreversible ? *Journal of Abnormal and Social Psychology*, 14: 230-233.

Cofer, C.N., Chance, J.E., and Judson A.J. (1949), A study of malingering on MMPI, *Journal of Psychology*, 27 : 491-499.

Cole, M., and Sribner, S. (1974), *Culture and thought*, New York : Wiley.

Cowen, M.N., and Stiller, A. (1959), The social desirability of trait descriptive terms : order and context effects, *Canadian Journal of Psychology*, 13 : 193-199

Craver, C.S., and Scheier, M.F. (1981), *Attention and self regulation: A control theory approach to human behaviour*, New York: Springer-Verlag.

Craver, C.S., and Scheier, M.F. (1983), A control theory model of normal behaviour and implications for problems in self-management. In P.C. Kendall (Ed.), *Advances in cognitive behavioral research and therapy* (Vol. 2), New York: Academic Press, 127-194.

Craver, S.C. Scheier, M.F., and Weintraub, J.K. (1989), Assessing coping strategies : a theoretically based approach, *Journal of Personality and Social Psychology*, 56 : 267-283.

Cronbach, L.J. (1941), An experimental comparison of the multiple true-false and multiple-choice tests, *Journal of Educational Psychology*, 32 : 533-543.

Cronbach, L.J. (1942), Studies of acquiescence as a factor in true-false tests, *Journal of Educational Psychology*, 33 : 401-415.

Cronbach, L.J. (1946), Response sets and test validity, *Educational and Psychological Measurement*, 6 : 475-494.

Cronbach, L.J. (1950), Further evidence on response sets and test design, *Educational and Psychological Measurement*, 10 : 3-31.

Cronbach, L.J. (1955), Processes affecting score on 'understanding of others' and assumed similarity, *Psychological Bulletin*, 53 : 177-193.

Cronbach, L.J., and Meehl, P.E. (1955), Construct validity in psychological tests, *Psychological Bulletin*, 52 : 281-302.

Cronbach, L.J. (1958), Proposals leading to analytical treatment of social perception scores. In R. Tagiuri and L. Petrallo (Eds.), *Person perception and interpersonal behaviour*, Stanford, California : Stanford Press, 359-379.

Cronbach, L.J., and Gleser, G.C. (1965), *Psychological tests and personnel decision*, (2nd edition), Urbana : University of Illinois Press.

Crown, D.P., and Marlowe, D. (1964), The approval motive, *Studies in evaluative dependence*, New York : Wiley.

Dahlstorm, W.G. (1969), Invasion of privacy : how legitimate is the current concern over this issue? In J.N. Butcher (Ed.), *MMPI : Research developments and clinical applications,* New York : McGraw-Hill.

Dahlstorm, W.G., and Welsh, G.S. (1960), An MMPI Handbook : *A guide to use in clinical practice and research,* Minneapolis: University of Minnesota Press.

Dahlstorm, W.G.,Welsh, G.S., and Dahlstorm, L.E. (1972), *An MMPI Handbook : Vol. 1, Clinical interpretation,* Minneapolis: University of Minnesota Press.

Dana, R.H. (1984), Personality assessment : Practice and teaching for next decade, *Journal of Personality Assessment,* 48 : 46-57.

Das, G. (1961), Standardization of Maudsley Personality Inventory on an Indian Population, *Journal of Psychological Research,* 5 : 7-9.

Dawes, R.M. (1962), A note on base rate and psychometric efficiency, *Journal of Consulting Psychology,* 26 : 422-424.

De, B. Significant studies in the quantitative assessment of the diagnostic validity of WAT, *Bihar University Journal,* 2.

De, B. Stimulus words as complex indicators in diagnostic free association, *Journal of Education and Psychology,* 15 : 152-162.

Dhapola, T.S. (1967), Adjustment and extroversion-neuroticism, *Indian Psychological Review,* 3 : 147-150.

Dicken, C.F. (1959), Simulated pattern on the Edwards Personal Preference Schedule, *Journal of Applied Psychology,* 43 : 372-378.

Dicken, C. (1963), Good Impression, social desirability, and acquiescence as suppressor variables, *Educational and Psychological Measurement,* 23 : 699-720.

Dillon, W.R., and Goodstein, M. (1984), *Multivariate analysis: methods and applications,* New York : John Wiley.

Duff, F.L. (1965), Item subtlety in personality inventory scales, *Journal of Consulting Psychology,* 29 : 565-570.

Dutt, N.K. (1967), *Adaptation of Maudsley Personality Inventory,* Varanasi : Rupa Psychological Centre.

Ebbinghaus, H. (1897), Uber eine neue Methode zur prufung geistiger Fahigkeiten und ihre Anwendung bei Schulkindern, *Z. angewand. Psychol.,* 13 : 401-459.

Ebel, R.L.L. (1965), *Measuring educational achievement,* Englewood Chiffs, N.J : Prentice-Hall.

Ebel, R.L.L. (1967), The relation of item discrimination to test reliability, *Journal of Educational Measurement,* 4 : 125-128.

Eber, H.W. (1964), Recent advances in automated interpretation of MMPI, Paper presented at 6th annual MMPI Symposium, Minneapolis.

Edwards, A.L. (1953), The relationship between judged desirability of a trait and the probability, *Journal of Applied Psychology,* 37 : 90-93.

Edwards, A.L. (1957), *The social desirability variable in personality assessment and research,* New York : Dryden.

Edwards, A.L. (1959), *Edwards personal preference schedule,* New York: Psychological Corporation.

Edwards, A.L. (1969), *Techniques of attitude scale construction,* Bombay : Vakil, Feffer, and Simons.

Edwards, A.L. (1970), *The measurement of personality traits by scales and inventories,* New York : Holt, Rinehart and Winston.

Edwards, A.L., and Diers, C.J. (1962), Social desirability and the factorial structure of MMPI, *Educational and Psychological Measurement,* 2 : 501-509.

Edwards, A.L., and Walker, J.N. (1961), A short form of the MMPI: the S.D. Scale, *Psychological Reports,* 8 : 485-486.

Edwards, A.L., and Walsh, J.N. (1964), Response sets in standard and experimental personality scales, *American Educational Research Journal,* 1 : 52-61.

Elder, J.W. (1973), Problems of cross-cultural methodology, In M. Armed and A.D. Grimshav (Eds.), *Comparative sociological research : methodological problems and strategies,* New York: Wily.

Eysenck, H.J. (1947), *Dimensions of personality,* London : Kegan Paul.

Eysenck, H.J. (1950), Criterion analysis : an application of the hypothetico-deductive method to factor analysis, *Psychological Review,* 57 : 38-53.

Eysenck, H.J. (1952), *The scientific study of personality,* London: Routledge and Kegan Paul.

Eysenck, H.J. (1959), *Manual of M.P.I.,* London : University of London Press.

Eysenck, H.J., and Eysenck, S.B.G. (1975), *Manual of Eysenck Personality Questionnaire,* London : Hodder and Stonghter.

Eysenck, S.B.G. and Eysenck, H.J. (1964), *Manual of the Eysenck Personality Inventory,* London : University of London Press.

Eysenck, H.J., and Eysenck, S.B.G. (1980), *Reference Manual for Eysenck's Personality Questionnaire*, London: London University Press.

Ezekiel, M., and Fox, K.A. (1959), *Methods of correlation and regression analysis*, (3rd edition), New York : Wily.

Feldman, M.J., and Gralay, J.L. (1954), The effects of an experimental set to simulate abnormality in group Rorschach performance, *Journal of Projective Techniques.*, 18 : 326-334.

Ferguson, G.A. (1951), A note on the Kuder-Richardson formula, *Educational and Psychological Measurement*, 11 : 612-615.

Findly, W.G. (1956), Rationale for the evaluation of item discrimination statistics, *Educational and Psychological Measurement*, 16 : 175-180.

Fink, R. (1963), Interviewer training and supervision in a survey of Laos, *International Social Science Journal*, 15 : 21-34.

Flanagan, J.C. (1939), General consideration in the selection of estimating the product moment coefficient from data at the tail of the distribution, *Journal of Educational Psychology*, 30: 674-680.

Flesch, R. (1949), The art of readable writing, New York.

Forsberg, I.A. (1938), Rorschach reactions under varied instructions, *Rorschach Research Exchange*, 3: 12-30.

Frank, L.K. (1936), Projective methods for the study of personality, *Journal of Psychology*, 8, 389-413.

Frederiksen, N., and Melville, D. (1954), Differential predictability in the use of test scores, *Educational and Psychological Measurement*, 14 : 647-656.

Frick, B.G. (1956), Response set as a suppressor variable in the OAIS and MMPI, *Journal of Consulting Psychology*, 20: 161-169.

Frutcher, B. (1967), *Introduction to factor analysis*, New Delhi: East-West Press.

Gage, N.L., Leavitt, G.S., and Stone, G.C. (1956), The intermediary key in the analysis of interpersonal perception, *Psychological Bulletin*, 53 : 238-266.

Gallagher, C.E. (1965), Opening remarks. In Testimony before house special sub committee on an invasion of privacy of the committee in government operations, *American Psychologist*, 20 : 955-988.

Galton, F. (1879), Psychometric experiments, *Brain*, 2: 149-162.

Gambhiranand, Swami (1984), *Bhagwatgita, With the commentory of Shankaracharya*, Translated by Swami Gambhiranand,

Advaita Ashram, Calcutta.

Garrett, H.E. (1962), *Statistics in psychology and education*, Bombay : Allied Pacific.

Geer, J.H. (1959), The development of a scale to measure fear, *Behavior Research and Therapy*, 3 : 45-54.

Ghiselli, E.E. (1960), Differentiation of individuals in terms of their predictability, *Journal of Applied Psychology*, 40: 374-377.

Gilbert, J.A. (1897), Research upon children and college students, *Iowa Univ. Stud. Psychol.*, 1 : 1-39.

Gilbert, L.A., and Holohan, C.K. (1979), Conflict between student and other life roles. *A comparison of high and low effective copers*, Unpublished paper.

Goffman, E. (1963), *Stigma*, London : Penguin Books.

Goldberg, L.R. (1963), A model of item ambiguity in personality assessment, *Educational and Psychological Measurement*, 23: 467-492.

Goldberg, L.R. (1970), Man versus model of man : a rationale plus some evidence, for a method of improving on clinical inference, *Psychological Bulletin*, 73 : 523-536.

Goldberg, L.R., Rorer, L.G., and Greene, M.M. (1970), The usefulness of stylistic scales as potential suppressor or moderator variables in prediction from CPI, *Oregon Research Institute Research Bulletin*, 10 : No. 3.

Goldberg, L.R., and Slovic, P. (1967), Importance of item content : an analysis of a corollary of the deviation hypothesis, *Journal of Consulting Psychology*, 145 : 462-472.

Goldfried, M.R., and Sprafkin, J.N. (1974), *Behavioral Personality Assessment* , Morristown, N.J. : General Learning Press.

Gough, H.G. (1954), Some common misconceptions about neuroticism, *Journal of Consulting Psychology*, 18 : 287-292.

Gough, H.G. (1957), California Psychological Inventory : Manual, Palo Alto : Consulting Psychologist Press (revised 1964).

Grayson, H.M., and Olinger, L.B. (1957), Simulation of "normalcy" by psychiatric patients on the MMPI, *Journal of Consulting Psychology*, 21 : 73-77.

Guilford, J.P. (1940), *An inventory of factors STDCR*, Beverly Hill, California : Sheridan Supply Co.

Guilford, J.P. (1941), The phi coefficient and chi square as indices of item validity, *Psychometrica*, 6 : 11-19.

Guilford, J.P. (1954), *Psychometric Methods*, New York: McGraw-Hill.

Guilford, J.P. (1959), *Personality*, New York: McGraw-Hill.

Guilford, J.P. (1954), *Psychometric Methods*, Bombay: Tata McGraw-Hill.

Guilford, J.P., and Martin, H.G. (1943 a), *Personnel Inventory : Manual of direction and norms*, Beverly Hills, California : Sheridan Supply Co.

Guilford, J.P., and Martin, H.G. (1943 b), *The Guilford Martin inventory of factors GAMIN, Manual of directions and norms*, Beverly Hills, California, Sheridan Supply Co.

Guilford, J.B., and Zimmerman W.S. (1949), The Guilford Zimmerman *Temperament Survey : Manual of instructions and interpretations*, Beverly Hills, California: Sheridon Supply Co.

Guion, R.M. (1965), *Personnel Testing*, New York: McGraw-Hill.

Gynther, M.D., Burkhart, B.R., and Hanovitz, C. (1979), Do face valid items have more predictive validity than subtle items ? The case of MMPI Pd scale, *Journal of Consulting and Clinical Psychology*, 47 : 295-300.

Hamilton, D.L. (1968), Personality attributes associated with extreme response style, *Psychological Bulletin*, 69, 192-203.

Hanley, C. (1956), S. Social desirability and response to items from the three MMPI scales D, Sc, and K, *Journal of Applied Psychology*, 40 : 324-328.

Hanley, C. (1957), Deriving a measure of test-taking defensiveness, *Journal of Consulting Psychology*, 21 : 391-397.

Harris, J.G., Jr. and Baxter, J.C. (1965), Ambiguity in MMPI, *Journal of Consulting Psychology*, 29 : 112-118.

Hartshorne, H., and May, M.A. (1928), *Studies in deceit*, New York: MacMillan.

Hasan, Q., and Khan, S.R. (1983), Dimensions of Gandhian (Nonviolent) Personality, *Psychological Research*, 2 : 100-106.

Hasan, Q., and Khan, D. (1978), Sources of response distortions on Sinha's Anxiety Scale, *Manas*, 25 : 1-11.

Hasan, Q., and Sadiq (1981), J. MMPI Hs and Pa scales : Social desirability, item endorsement, and authoritarianism, *Indian Journal of Clinical Psychology*, 8 : 49-55.

Hase, H.D. and Goldberg, I.R. (1967), The comparative validity of different strategies of deriving personality inventory scales, *Psychological Bulletin*, 67: 231-248.

Hathaway, S.R. (1964), MMPI: Professional use by professional people, *American Psychologist*, 19 : 204-210.

Hathaway, S.R. (1976), Foreword. In R.D. Fowler, *The clinical use of automated MMPI*, Nutley, N.J. : Hoffman-La Roche.

Hathaway, S.R., and McKinley J.C. (1943), *The Minnesota Multiphasic Personality Schedule, Minneapolis* : University of Minnesota Press.

Hathaway S.R., and McKinley, J.C. (1951), *The Minnesota Multiphasic Personality Inventory Manual,* New York : Psychological Corporation.

Hathaway, S.R., and Momachesi E.D. (1961), *An atlas of MMPI profiles, Minneapolis* : University of Minnesota Press.

Heilbrun, A.B. (1963), Revision of the MMPI K correction procedure for improved detection of maladjustment in a normal college population, *Journal of Consulting Psychology,* 25 : 161-165.

Henry, E.M., and Rotter, J.B. (1956), Situational influences on Rorschach responses, *Journal of Consulting Psychology,* 20: 457-462.

Herson, M. (1973), Self-assessment of fear, Behavior Therapy, 4: 241-257.

Hesterly, S.O. (1963), Deviant response patterns as a function of chronological age, *Journal of Consulting Psychology,* 27: 210-214.

Heymans, G., and Wiersma E. (1906), Beitrage zur spezidllen psychologic anf Grund einer Massenunterschung, *Zeitschrift fur psychologie,* 43 : 81-127; 258-301.

Hoffman, P.J. (1960), The paramorphic representation of clinical judgement, *Psychological Bulletin,* 57 : 77-80.

Holden, R.R., and Jackson, D.N. (1979), Item subtlety and face validity in personality assessment, *Journal of Consulting and Clinical Psychology,* 47 : 454-468.

Holmes, T.H., and Rahe, R.H. (1967), The Social Readjustment Rating Scale, *Journal of Psychometric Research,* 11: 213-218.

Holt, R.R. (1958), Clinical and statistical prediction : A reformulation and some new data, *Journal of Abnormal and Social Psychology,* 56 : 1-12.

Holzberg, J.D., and Alessi, S., Reliability of shortened MMPI, *Journal of Consulting Psychology,* 13, 288-292.

Horn, I.J. (1965), A rationale and test for the number of factors in factor analysis, *Psychometrica,* 30 : 179.

Horst, P. (1941), *The prediction of personal adjustment,* New York: Social Science Research Council.

Irvine, S. (1968), *Human behavior in Africa : some research problems noted while compiling source material,* Paper presented to the East Africa Institute of Social Research Workshop in Social Psychology, New York City.

Jackson D.N. (1967a), Review of J. Block "The Challenge of response set," *Educational and Psychological Measurement*, 27: 207-219.

Jackson, D.N. (1970b), *Personality Research From Manual*, Goshen, N.Y. : Research Psychologist Press.

Jackson, J.M. (1949), A sample and more rigorous technique for scale analysis, In *A manual for scale analysis*, Part II, Montreal : McGill University.

Jackson, D.N., and Messic, S. (1957), A note on ethnocentrism and acquiescent response sets, *Journal of Abnormal and Social Psychology*, 54 : 132-134.

Jackson, D.N., and Messic, S. (1958), Content and style in personality assessment, *Psychological Bulletin*, 55 : 243-252.

Jain, U. (1979), *Extreme response style*, New Delhi : National Publishing House.

Jalota, S. (1965), A Study of Maudsley Personality Inventory (in Hindi and Punjabi versions), *Indian Psychological Review*, 2: 29-30.

Jones, J.W. (1980), *The staff burnout scale for health professionals,*, Chicago : London House, Management Consultants.

Jones, R.R., and Goldberg, I.R. (1967), Interrelationship among personality scale parameters : item response stability and scale reliability, *Educational and Psychological Measurement*, 27 : 323-333.

Joshi, M.C., and Singh, B. (1963), *Hindi adaptation of some MMPI Scales*, Department of Psychology, Banaras Hindu University, Varanasi.

Jung, C.G. (1910), The association method, *American Journal of Psychology*, 2 : 219-269.

Kaiser, H.F. (1958), Varimax criterion for analytic rotation in factor analysis, *Psychometrica*, ting but also

Kapoor, S.D. (1963), A comparative study of the personality questionnaire items presented in the first and second person, *Manas*, 10 : 25-34.

Karson, S., and O'Dell, J.W. (1975), A new automated interpretation system for 16 PF, *Journal of Personality Assessment*, 39: 256-260.

Kelly, L.E. (1969), *The assessment of human characteristics*, New Delhi : Prentice-Hall.

Kelly, T.L., The selection of upper and lower groups for the validation of test items, *Journal of Educational Psychology*, 30, 17-24.

Kenney, D.T. (1956), The influence of social desirability on discrepancy measures between real and ideal self, *Journal of Consulting Psychology,* 20 : 315-318.

Kestenbaum, J.M., and Hammersla, J. (1976), Filler items and social desirability in Rotter's Locus of Control scale, *Journal of Personality Assessment,* 40, 162-168.

Klientmuntz, B. (1963), MMPI decision rules for the identification of college maladjustment : a digital computer approach, *Psychological Monograph, 77* (14, whole no. 477).

Kobasa, S.C. (1979), Stressful life events, personality, and health: an inquiry into Hardiness, *Journal of Personality and Social Psychology,* 37 : 1-11.

Korchin, S.J. (1986), *Modern Clinical Psychology,* Delhi : CBS Publishers (First Indian Edition).

Krishnan, B. Need for a validity scale in personality inventories, *Psychological Studies,* 1961, 4 : 55-60.

Krishnan, B. (1964), A note on research work in the Department of Psychology, University of Mysore, In *Psychological Research in India,* Varanasi : Tara Press, 156-157.

Kuder, G.F., and Richardson, M.W. (1937), The theory of estimation of test reliability, *Psychometrica,* 2 : 151-160.

Kureshi, A. (1971), *AAPS Motive Test,* Varanasi : Rupa Psychological Corporation.

Lacher, D. (1974a), *The MMPI : Clinical assessment and automated interpretation,* Los Angeles : Western Psychological Services.

Lacher, D. (1974b), Accuracy of an automated interpretation system, *Journal of Consulting and Clinical Psychology,* 42: 267-273.

Lanyon, R.I. (1967), Simulation of normal and psychopathic MMPI personality patterns, *Journal of Consulting Psychology,* 31 : 94-97.

Lanyon, R.I. (1968), *A handbook of MMPI group profiles,* Minneapolis: University of Minnesota Press.

Lanyon, R.I., and Goodstein, L.D. (1971), *Personality assessment,* New York : John Wiley.

Lazarus, R.S. (1966), *Psychological stress and coping process,* New York : McGraw-Hill.

Lazarus, R.S., and Folkman, S. (1984), *Stress appraisal and coping,* New York : Springer.

Leatherman, M., and Dana, R.H. (1982), *Burnout in college population : Life experience and personality correlates,* Paper presented at 10th annual conference in Personality and Social Psychology, Fayette Vilie, A.R.

Lentz, T.F. (1938), Acquiescence as a factor in measurement of personality, *Psychological Bulletin*, 36, 659.

Lindquist, E.F. (1951), *Educational Measurement*, Washington, D.C: American Council on Education.

Loevinger, J. (1947), A systematic approach to the construction and evaluation of tests of ability, *Psychological Monographs*, 61 : No. 4 (Whole No. 285).

Loevinger, J. (1957), Objective tests as instruments of Psychological theory, *Psychological Reports*, 3: 635-694, Monograph No. 9.

Longacre, R. (1958), Items in Context — their bearing on translation theory, *Language*, 84: 482-491.

Loo, R.A. (1979), Psychometric investigations of the Eysenck Personality Questionnaire, *Journal of Personality Assessment*, 43: 54-58.

Lorge, I. (1967), The fundamental nature of measurement, In D.N. Jackson and S. Messick (Eds.), *Problems in human assessment*, New York : McGraw-Hill, 43-56.

Lyman H.B. (1963), *Test scores and what they mean, Englewood Cliffs*, N.J. : Prentice-Hall.

Machover, K. (1949), *Personality projection in the drawings of human figure, Springfield, Ill.* : Thompson.

MacKinnon, D.W. (1958), An assessment study of air force officers: Part V. *Summary and applications*. Wright Air Development Centre Technical Report No. 91 (v). Personnel Laboratory, Lackland Air Force Base, Texas, (December 1958).

MacNamara, J. (1967), The bilingual linguistic performance, a psychological overview, *The Journal of Social Issues*, 23 (2), 56-75.

Mahalanobis, P.A. (1936), On the generalized distance in statistics, *Proc. National Inst. Sci. Industry*, 12 : 49-55.

Mair, M. (1988), Psychology of telling story, *International Journal of Personal Construct*, 1 : 125-138.

Malik, A.K. (1986), Personality evaluation : Development of a Multiphasic measure, New Delhi, Jainson Publications.

Maloney, M.P., and Ward, M.P. (1976), *Psychological Assessment: A computer approach*. New York : Oxford University Press.

Mark, P.A., and Seeman, W. (1963), *The actuarial description of personality: an altas for the use with the MMPI*, Baltimore: Williams and Wilkins.

Mandler, G. (1967), Organization and memory, In K.W. Spence and J.T. Spence (Eds.) , *Psychology of learning and motivation*, vol. 1, New York : Academic Press.

Maslach, C., and Jackson, S.E. (1981), Measurement of experienced burn out, *Journal of Occupational Behavior*, 2 : 99-113.

Matarazzo, J.M. (1983), Computerized psychological testing, *Science*, 221-323.

McCoy, W.J. (1977), Further impressions of psychologists ambivalence towards tests, *Hospital and Community Psychiatry*, 28: 544.

McNemar, Q. (1962), *Psychological statistics*, New York : John Wiley.

Meehl, P.E. (1945), The dynamics of structured personality tests, *Journal of Clinical Psychology*, 1 : 296-303.

Meehl, P.E. (1954), *Clinical versus statistical prediction, A theoretical analysis and review of the evidence*, Minneapolis : University of Minnesota Press.

Meehl, P.E. (1956), Wanted a good cookbook, *American Psychologist*, 11 : 263-272.

Meehl, P.E., and Hathaway, S.R. (1946), The K factors as a suppressor variable in the MMPI, *Journal of Applied Psychology*, 30 : 525-564.

Meehl, P.E., and Rosen, A. (1955), Antecedent probability and the efficiency of psychometric signs, patterns, or cutting scores, *Psychological Bulletin*, 52 : 194-216.

Meredith, G.M. (1966), Stereotypic desirability profiles for 16 PF Questionnaire, *Psychological Reports*, 23 : 1173-1174.

Messick, S., and Jackson, D.N. (1961), Desirability scale values and dispersions for MMPI items, *Psychological Reports*, 8 : 404-414.

Messick, S. (1980), Text validity and the ethics of assessment, *American Psychologist*, 35 : 1012-1029.

Miller, G. (1953), What is information measurement? *American Psychologist*, 9 : 3-11.

Miller, G.A. (1956), The magic number seven plus or minus two: Some limitations in our capacity for processing information, *Psychological Review*, *63* : 81-89.

Miller, G., and Beebe-Center, T. (1956), Some Psychological methods for evaluating the quality of translation, *Mechanical Translation*, 3 : 73-80.

Million, T. (1983), The DSM-III: An insider's perspective, *American Psychologist*, 38 : 804-814.

Mischel, W. (1968), *Personality and assessment*, New York : Wiley.

Mischel, W. (1969), Continuity and change in personality, *American Psychologist*, 24 : 1012-1018.

Mischel, W. (1977), On the future of personality measurement, *American Psychologist*, 32 : 246-253.

Mohan, J. Eysenck, H.J., and Eysenck, S.C.G. (1987), The Eysenck Personality Questionnaire : an Indian experience, *Personality and Group Behaviour*, 70 : 67-69.

Mohan, V., and Sandhu, S. (1986), Development of scale to measure Sattavic, Rajsick, and Tamsic Guna, *Journal of Indian Academy of Applied Psychology*, 12: 46-52.

Moreland, K.L. (1983), *A comparison of validity of two MMPI interpretation system : A preliminary report*, paper presented at 18th annual MMPI symposium, Minneapolis.

Morris, B.S. (1949), Officer selection in British Army, 1942-1945, *Occupational Psychology*, 23: 219-234.

Moiser, C.L., and McQuitty, J.V. (1940), Methods of item validation and abacs for item test correlation and critical ratio of upper-lower difference, *Psychometrica*, 5 : 57-65.

Murray, M.A. (1938), *Exploration in Personality*, New York : Oxford University Press.

Murray, H.A. (1943), *Thematic Apperception Test Manual*, Cambridge, Massachusetts : Harvard University Press.

Muthaiya, B.C., and Gnana Kanan, I. (1973), *Developmental Personnel*, Hyderabad : N.I.C.D.

National Committee on Test Standards, (1966), *Standards for educational and psychological test manuals*, APA (Abriged form reprinted in D.A. Payne and R.F. Morris (Eds.), *Educational and Psychological measurement*, New Delhi : Oxford IBH, 1972.

Nida, E. (1976), A framework for analysis and evaluation of theories of translation, In R. Brislin (Ed.) , *Translation : application and research*, New York : Wisley/Halsted, 47-91.

Norman, W.T. (1963a), Relative importance of item content, *Journal of Consulting Psychology*, 27 : 166-174.

Norman, W.T. (1963b), On estimating psychological relationship: social desirability and self-reports, *Psychological Bulletin*, 67: 273-299.

O'Donovan, D. (1965), Rating extremity : Pathology or meaningfulness? *Psychological Review, 72* : 358-372.

Obsone, D.A. (1970), A moderator variable approach to MMPI validity, *Journal of Clinical Psychology*, 26 : 486-490.

Ortar, G., (1963), Is a verbal test cross-cultural? *Scripta Hierosolymitana* (Hebrew University), 13, 219-235.

Orr, P.L., and Dana, R.H. (1982), Life events, resistance resources, and health status of social case workers, *Journal of Sociology and Social Welfare*, 9 : 245-257.

Osgood, C.E., and Suci, G.S. (1952), A measure of relation determined by both mean difference and profile information, *Psychological Bulletin*, 49 : 251-262.

Pareek, U. (1965), Reliability of the adult form of Indian adaptation of the Rosenweig's P.F. study, *Indian Journal of Psychology*, 40 : 67-72.

Peabody, D., (1966), Authoritarian scales and response bias, *Psychological Bulletin*, 65, 11-23.

Peak, H., Muney, B., and Clay, M., Opposite structures, defenses and attitudes, *Psychological Monographs*, 74 (8, Whole No. 495).

Perry, N.C., and Michael W.B. (1951), The estimation of a coefficient for an entire criterion group from phi coefficient calculated from the use of extreme tails of normal distribution of criterion scores, *Educational and Psychological Measurement*, 11 : 629-638.

Pervin, L.A. (1970), *Personality : theory, assessment and research*, New York : John Wiley.

Philips, H. (1960), Problems of translation and meaning in fieldwork, *Human Organization*, 18 : 184-192.

Pike, R. (1954), *Language in relation to a united theory of the structure of human behaviour*, Glendale : Summer Institution of Linguistics.

Prasad, K., and Asthana H.S. (1947), An experimental study of meaning by the Rorschach method, *Indian Journal of Psychology*, 23 : 55-58.

Rempel, P.B. (1958), The use of multivariate statistical analysis of MMPI scores in classification of delinquents and non-delinquents high school boys, *Journal of Consulting Psychology*, 22: 17-23.

Rempel, P.B. (1960), Analysis of MMPI data for classification purpose by multivariate statistical techniques, *Journal of Experimental Education*, 28 : 219-228.

Richardson, M.W. (1936), Notes on the rationale of item analysis, *Psychometrica*, 1 : 69-76.

Richert, E.L. (1965), Native reaction as a guide to meaningful translation, In J. Beekman (Ed.), *Notes on translation with drill*, California : Summer Institute of Linguistics, 1965.

Robinson, E.S. (1933), The psychology of public education, *American Journal of Public Health*, 23 : 1-25.

Roid, G.N., and Gorsuch, R.L. (1984), Development and clinical use of test-interpretive programs on micro computers. In M.D. SchWatz (Ed.), Using computer in clinical practice, New York : Haworth.

Rorer, L.G. (1965), The great response style myth, *Psychological Bulletin*, 63 : 61-82.

Rorer, L.G., Hoffman, P.J., and Hsieh, K.C., (1966), Utilities as base rate multipliers in the determination of optimum cutting scores for the discrimination of groups of unequal size and variance, *Journal of Applied Psychology*, 50, 364-368.

Rosenwald, G.C. (1965), Physician and psychodiagnosis, *Psychiatry Quarterly*, 39 : 16-31.

Rosenwig, S. (1950), Levels of behavior in psychodiagnosis with special reference to the Picture Frustration Study, *American Journal of Orthopsychiatry*, 20 : 63-72.

Rulon, P.J. (1939), A simplified procedure for determining the reliability of a test by split-halves, *Harvard Educational Review*, 9 : 99-103.

Sarbin, T.R. (1968), Ontology recapitulates philosophy: The mystic nature of anxiety, *American Psychologist*, 23 : 411-418.

Sarason, I.G., Johnson, J.H. and Siegel, J.M. (1978), Assessing the impact of life changes : development of life experience survey, *Journal of Consulting Psychology*, 46 : 932-946.

Saunder, D.R. (1956), Moderator variable in prediction, *Educational and Psychological Measurement*, 16 : 209-222.

Sawyer, J. (1966), Measurement and prediction, clinical and statistical, *Psychological Bulletin*, 170-200.

Scheier, M.F., and Craver, C.S., (1988), A model of behavioral self-regulation: Translating intention into action, In L. Berkowitz (Ed.), *Advances in experimental Social Psychology*, (Vol. 2), New York: Academic Press.

Schmidt, F.L., Hunter, J.E. and Urry, V.W. (1976), Statistical power in criterion related validation studies, *Journal of Applied Psychology*, 61 : 473-485.

Seeman, W. (1952), Subtlety in structured personality tests, *Journal of Consulting Psychology*, 16 : 278-283.

Sechrest, L. (1963), Incremental Validity : a recommendation, *Educational and Psychological Measurement*, 23 : 153-158.

Sen, A. (1949), A study of Rorchach test, *British Journal of Psychology*, 19 : 142-143.

Shaffer, J.W. (1963), A new acquiescence scale for MMPI, *Journal of Clinical Psychology,* 19, 412-415.

Shanker, U. (1956), Rorschach responses of a group of juvenile thieves, *Indian Journal of Psychology,* 31 : 15-20.

Shanmugam, T.E. (1959), The verbal projection stories of delinquent boys, *Psychological Studies,* 2 : 15-20.

Sharma, M.R. (1977), Kautilya and Management, *Indian Management,* July, 3-9.

Sharp, S.E. (1899), Individual Psychology; a study in psychological methods, *American Journal of Psychology,* 10, 329-391.

Simoneit, M. (1940), Zur charakterlogischen Auswertung von Reaktionpruefungen, *Archive fuerdie gesamate Psychologie,* 83 : 357-384.

Sines, L.K., and Silver, R.J. (1963), An index of psychopathology (Ip) derived from clinicians' judgements of MMPI profile, *Journal of Clinical Psychology,* 19 : 324-326.

Sinha, J. (1968), The n-ach/n-cooperation underlimited/ unlimited resource conditions, *Journal of Experimental Social Psychology,* 4 : 223-246.

Spranger, E. (1928), *Types of men.* (trans. by P.J.W. Pigors) Halle: Nilmeyer.

Strahan R.F., and Wilson, D.W. (1976), Buffer items, insight, and Marlow-Crowne Social Desirability Scale, *Journal of Personality Assessment,* 40 : 320-323.

Stern, G.G., Stein, M.I. and Bloom, B.S. (1956), *Methods in personality assessment,* Glencoe, Ill.: Free Press.

Stones, M.J. (1982), The microgrid: A micro computer version of the repgrid, *Candian Psychology,* 23 : 102-104.

Sundberg, N.D. Snowdown, L.R. and Reynolds, H.M. (1978), Toward assessment of personal competence in life situations, In M.R. Rosenweig and I.W. Porter (Eds.), *Annual Review of Psychology,* 29 : 179-221.

Tallent, N. (1958), On individualizing in psychologist's clinical evaluation, *Journal of Clinical Psychology,* 14 : 243-244.

Tallent, N. (1983), Psychological report writing (2nd ed.), Englewood Cliffs, N J : Prentice-Hall.

Tallent, N. (1987), Computer generated psychological reports : a look on the modern psychometric machine, *Journal of Personality Assessment,* 51 : 95-105.

Tarone, E., Cohen, A.D., and Dumas, G. (1983), A closer look at some inter language terminology : a framework for communication strategies, In Claus French and Gabriele Kasper (Eds.),

Strategis in inter language communication, London : Longman, 4-14.

Taylor, H.C., and Russell, J.C. (1939), The relationship of validity coefficients to practical effectiveness of tests in selection: Discussion and tables, *Journal of Applied Psychology,* 23: 565-578.

Thorndike, E.L. (1903), *Educational Psychology,* New York : Teachers' College.

Thurstone, L.L. (1947), *Multiple factor analysis, a development and expansion of vector of mind,* Chicago: University of Chicago Press.

Thurstone, L.L. (1949), *Thurstone Temperamental Schedule,* Chicago : Science Research Association.

Thurstone, L.L. (1951), *The dimension of temperament Psychometrica,* 16 : 11-20.

Treisman, A. (1965), The effect of redundancy and familiarity on translation and repeating back a foreign and native language, *British Journal of Psychology,* 56 : 369-379.

Triandis, H.C. Malpass, R.S., and Davidson, A. (1972), Cross-Cultural Psychology, *Biennial Review of Anthropology.*

Valez-Diaz, A., and Ganzalez-Regosa, F. (1987), The Spanish Version of the Clinical Analysis Questionnaire : A precautionary note, *Journal of Personality Assessment,* 51 : 414-416.

Veradi, T. (1983), Strategies of target language learner communication : Message adjustment. In Cluse French and Gabriele Kasper (Eds.), *Strategies in interlanguage communication,* London : Longman, 79-99.

Verma, S.K., and Wig, N.N. (1976), P.G.I. Health Questionnaire N-2 : Construction and initial tryouts, *Indian Journal of Clinical Psychology,* 3 : 135-142.

Verma, S.K., and Wig, N.N. (1977), P.G.I. Health Questionnaire N-2 : item behavior in clinical population, *ISPT Journal of Research,* 1 : 37-46.

Vernon, P.E. (1948), Indices of item consistency and validity, *British Journal of Psychology,* Statistical Section, 1 : 152-166.

Vernon, P.E., and Allport, G.W. (1931), A test for personal value, *Journal of Abnormal and Social Psychology,* 26 : 231-248.

Ward, J.H., Jr. (1954), An application of linear and curvilinear joint function regression in psychological prediction. *Research Bulletin,* 54-86, Air Force Personnel Training Research Centre, Lackland Air Force Base Texas (referred by Wiggins, 1973).

Webb, E. (1915), Character and intelligence, *British Journal of Psychology*, Monograph Suppliment, III.

Wesley, F., and Karr, C. (1966), Problems in establishing norms of cross-cultural comparisons, *International Journal of Psychology*, 1 : 257-262.

White, B.J., and Harvey, O.J. (1965), Effects of personality and own stand on judgement and production of statement about a central issue, *Journal of Experimental Social Psycology*, 1: 334-347.

White, B.W., and Saltz, E. (1957), The measurement of reproductibility, *Psychological Bulletin* (reprinted in D.N. Jackson and S. Messick (Eds.), Problems of Human Assessment, New York : McGraw-Hill, 1967).

Wig, N.N., and Verma , S.K. (1978), *Construction and standardization of P.G. I. Health Questionnaire, Agra* : Agra Psychological Cell.

Wiggins, J.S. (1962), Strategic, method, and stylistic variance in MMPI, *Psychological Bulletin*, 59 : 224-242.

Wiggins, J.S. (1964), An MMPI item characteristic deck, *Educational and Psychological Measurement*, 24 : 137-141.

Wiggins, J.S. (1973), *Personality and prediction: principles of personality assessment*, Readin, Massachusetts: Addison-Wesley.

Williams, K.L. (1965), Checking translation for wrong meaning. In J. Beekman (Ed.), *Notes on translation with drills*, California: Summer Institute, 38-43.

Wober, M. (1957), Towards an understanding of the Kiganda concept of intelligence, In J.W. Berry and P.R. Dasan (Eds.), *Cross Cultural Cognition*, London : Methuen.

Woodworth, R.S. (1917), *Personal data sheet*, Chicago : Stoelting.

Zax, D.H., and Lowy, D.C. (1964), Extreme response tendencies as a function of emotional adjustment, *Journal of Abnormal and Social Psychology*, 69 : 654-657.

Zimmer, H. (1954), Self-acceptance and its relation to conflict, *Journal of Counselling Psychology*, 18 : 447-449.

Zubin, J. (1950), Test construction and methodology, In R.E. Harris, J.G. Miller, G.A. Munch, L.J. Stone, H-L. Teuber, and J. Zubin (Eds.), *Recent advances in diagnostic psychological testing*, Springfield, Ill. : Chares C. Thomas.

Zukerman, M., Eisen, Babra (1962), Relationship of acquiescence and extreme response set of authoritarianism and dependency, *Psychological Reports*, 10 : 95-102.

Author Index

Adorno, T.W., 80
Alessi, S., 118
Alf, E.F., 54
Allen, J.G., 36
Allport, G.W., 15, 18, 20, 22, 45, 81, 143, 246
Amrine, M., 64
Anastasi, A., 180, 252
Arthur, A.Z., 54, 202
Asthana, H.S., 59

Barnes, E.A., 198
Barnett, L., 123
Baxter, J.C., 50
Bechtold, H.P., 191
Beebe-Center, T., 246
Bennett, G.K., 185
Bentler, P.M., 197
Berg, I.A., 101, 198-200, 216
Berry, J.W., 228-30
Block, J., 125, 207
Brengelman, J.C., 201
Brim, O.J., 202
Brislin, R., 242-43, 245, 247, 251
Broadman, K., 126
Brogden, H.E., 184
Brown, M.N., 219
Buchwald, A.M., 100
Burgess, E.W., 51
Bukhart, B.R., 213
Burt, C., 48
Butcher, J.N., 50

Campbell, D., 40, 94, 242-43
Carkhuff, R.R., 123
Carp, A.L., 211
Carr, H.A., 21, 62
Carrol, J., 246
Casagranda, J., 241
Cattell, R.B., 22, 28-29, 39, 48, 59, 126, 136, 139, 141-42,147, 149-56, 176, 253
Chance, J.E., 218
Chowdhry, U., 59
Christe, R., 197
Chapman, J.L., 66
Cofer, C.N., 218
Cole, M., 224
Cohen, A.D., 234
Cowen, M.N., 50
Craver, S.C., 90, 92
Cronbach, L.J., 52, 77, 93, 179, 186, 191, 195
Crowne, D.P., 217-18

Dahlstorm, W.G., 112
Dahlstorm, L.E., 66
Dana, G., 61-62
Das, G., 59
Dasen, P.R., 228
Davidson, A., 227

Dawes, R.M., 268
De, B., 59
Dhapola, T.S., 59
Dicken, C.F., 209, 282
Dier, C.J., 206
Dillon, W.R., 135, 137
Dorfman, D.D., 54
Duff, F.L., 79, 213
Dumas, G., 234
Dutt, N.K., 59

Ebbinghaus, H. 44
Ebel, R.L.L., 168
Eber, H.W., 59, 142, 147, 149-56
Edwards, A.L., 49-50, 76, 79, 83, 104, 196, 205, 217, 289
Elder, J.W., 236-37
Erdman, A.J., 126
Eysenck, H.J., 38, 48, 138-39, 141, 157-61, 188
Eysenck, S.B.G., 157-61
Ezekil, M., 281

Feldman, M.J., 211
Ferguson, G.A., 179
Findley, W.G., 168
Fink, R., 244
Fisk, D.W., 40, 47, 149, 190
Flangan, J.C., 128, 171
Flesch, R., 250
Folkman, S., 90
Forsberg, I.A., 210
Fox, K.A., 281
Frank, L.K., 44
Frederiksen, N., 280
Freemantle, A., 202
Frick, B.G., 216
Frutcher, B., 131

Gage, N.L., 190
Gallagher, C.E., 66
Galton, F., 43
Gambhiranand Swami, 90
Garrett, H.E., 170
Geer, J.G., 73
Gilbert, J.A., 44
Gilbert, L.A., 62
Gleser, G.C., 54
Gonzalez-Regosa, F., 233
Gorsuch, R.L., 56
Goffman, E., 208
Goldberg, L.R., 50, 52, 56, 79, 108, 282
Goldfried, M.R., 32
Goodstein, L.D., 37, 65, 140
Goodstein, D., 135, 137
Gorsuch, R.L., 56
Gough, H.G., 49, 209, 218
Grayson, H.M., 210
Guilford, J.P., 20, 24, 48, 84, 131, 141, 164-65, 168
Gynther, M.D., 213

Hamilton, D.L., 201
Hammersla, J., 214
Hanley, C., 205, 216
Harris, J.G., 50
Hartshorne, H., 112
Harvey, O.J., 202
Hasan, Q., 60
Hanovitz, C., 213
Hathway, S.R., 113, 117, 124
Havel, J., 197
Hersen, M., 73
Hesterly, S.O., 202
Lazarus, R.S., 90
Heymans, G., 47
Hoffman, P.J., 52, 54
Holden, R.R., 105, 213
Holmes, T.H., 62
Hoff, D.P., 202
Holohan, C.K., 62
Horn, I.J., 137, 266

Holzberg, J.D., 118
Horst, P., 281
Hsieh, K.C., 54
Hunt, W.A., 198
Hunter, J.E., 185

Irvin, S., 232

Jackson, D.N., 49, 96, 105, 194, 196-97, 206, 213
Jackson, J.M., 172
Jackson, S.E., 62
Jain, U., 203
Jalota, S., 59
Johnson, J.H., 62
Jones, J.W., 62
Joshi, M.C., 59
Judson, A.J., 218
Jung, C.G., 44

Kaiser, H.F., 136
Kapor, S.D., 59
Karr, C., 232
Karson, S., 55
Kelly, E.L., 33, 35, 46
Kelly, T.L., 167
Kenny, D.T., 205
Kestebaum, J.M., 214
Kingsbury, 21
Khan, D., 60
Khan, S.R., 60
Klientmuntz, B., 56
Kobasa, S.C., 62
Krishnan, B., 59
Kuder, G.F., 74, 165
Kureshi, A., 59

Lacher, D., 58
Lanyon, R.I., 37, 65
Lentz, T.F., 195
Lindquist, E.F., 173
Loevinger, J., 80, 93, 172, 180, 186
Longacre, R., 242
Lonner, W., 242
Lorge, I., 33, 195
Lyman, H.B., 262

Machover, K., 70
MacKinnon, D.W., 47
MacNamara, J., 246
Mahalonobis, P.A., 264
Mair, M., 61
Malik, A.K., 59, 89
Maloney, M.P., 36
Malpass, R.S., 227
Mark, P.A., 275
Marlowe, D., 217-18
Martin, H.G., 84, 141
Mandler, G., 31
Maslach, C., 62
May, M.A., 112
McCall, J.N., 123
McCoy, W.J., 37
McKinley, J.C., 110, 117
McQuitty, J.V., 170
McNemar, Q., 88
Meehl, P.E., 42, 53-54, 77, 80, 93, 100, 113, 123, 186, 191
Melville, D., 280
Meredith, G.M., 150
Messick, S., 194, 197, 206
Mischel, W.B., 30-31, 63, 66
Miller, G., 242
Miller, G.A., 31
Million, T., 62
Mischel, W., 60-61
Momachesi, E.D., 123
Moreland, K.L., 58
Morris, B.S., 46
Moiser, C.L., 170
Murray, H.A., 44, 49, 70, 81
Muthayya, B.C., 59

Nida, E., 240
Norman, W.T., 79, 107

Obsone, D.A., 218
Obdert, H.S., 143
Olinger, L.B., 210
O'Donovon, D., 202
Osgood, C.E., 264

Pareekh, U., 59
Peabody, D., 201
Peak, H., 201
Pervin, L.A., 18, 79
Pettigrew, T., 246
Phillips, H., 242
Prasad, K., 59

Rahe, R.H., 62
Rempel, P.B., 122
Reynold, H.M., 37, 253
Richardson, M.W., 74, 165
Riohert, E.L., 239
Rorer, L.G., 194, 197, 207, 282
Rorschach, H., 44
Rosenwald, G.C., 36
Rosen, A., 53
Rosenweig, S., 37
Rulon, P.J., 178
Russell, J.C., 53

Sarbin, T.R., 191
Sandhu, S., 89
Saunder, D.R., 279-80
Sawyer, J., 52
Scheier, M.F., 90, 92
Schafer, R., 36
Schmidt, F.L., 185
Scribner, S., 224
Seashore, H.G., 185
Seeman, W., 106, 213, 275
Seidnerg, B., 197
Sechrest, L., 53
Sen, A., 59
Shaffer, J.W., 217
Shanker, U., 59
Shanmugam, T.E., 59
Sharma, M.R., 41
Shavzin, A.R., 211
Siegal, J.M., 62
Silver, R.J., 121
Simoneit, M., 45
Sines, L.K., 54, 121
Sinha, J., 231
Slovic, P., 79, 108
Snowden, L.R., 37, 253
Sprafkin, J.N., 32
Spranger, E., 80
Stewart, V., 243
Strahan, R.F., 215
Stern, G.G., 102
Stiller, A., 50
Stone, G.C., 190
Suci, G.S., 264
Super, 37
Sundberg, N.D., 37, 253

Tallent, N., 35, 42, 57-58
Tarone, E., 234
Tatsuoka, M., 142, 147, 149-53, 155-56
Taylore, E.R., 84
Taylor, H.C., 53, 84
Tellegen, A., 50
Triandis, H.C., 223, 227
Thorndike, E.L., 242
Thurstone, L.L., 137

Urry, V.W., 185

Valez-Diaz, A., 233
Veradi, T., 234
Verma, S.K., 59, 125-26
Vernon, P.E., 45-46, 81

Walker, J.M., 205
Walsh, J.M., 206

Ward, M.P., 36
Webb, E., 48
Weintraub, J.K., 90, 92
Welsh, G.S., 112
Werner, O., 243
Wesley, F., 232
Wesman, A.G., 185
Wiersma, E., 47
Wig, M.M., 59, 125
Wiggins, N.N., 47, 50, 70, 79, 102, 107, 216, 269
Williams, K.L., 237-38
Wilson, D.W., 215
Wober, M., 229
Woodworth, R.S., 71
Wolf, M.G., 126

Zax, D.H., 202
Zimmer, H., 205
Zimmerman, W.S., 141
Zubin, J., 38
Zukerman, M., 202

Subject Index

Abac, biserial r, 171
phi coefficient, 170
point-biserial r, 171
tetrachoric r, 169-70
Acquiescence, *see* also Response styles
acceptance, 197
agreement, 197
dealing with, 216
definition of, 194
detection of
in MMPI, 195-96, 217
Actuarial prediction, 50, 268
a priori classification
asymmetry of inferences, 268
and automoted clinical prediction, 55-56
construction of tables for, 274-75
data for preparation of, 268-69
nature of, 268
personality descriptors for, 269-70
Alabama programme, *see* computer based interpretation
Allport Vernon Study of values, 45, 80-81
Alpha coefficient, 179
Analysis of personality
proposals for, 20
Analytic approach, 109
Anti-test attitudes, 60-62
Approximate system analysis (ASA), 234
Arthashastra, 41
Aspects of existence
eigenwelt (one self), 18
mitwelt (others), 18
unwelt (society), 18
Astronomy, 42
Aunt Fanny error, 42
Assessment, *see* also Personality Assessment
and contemporary life, 62
behavioural, 33
(of) burn outs, 62
classification of devices, 37-39
constructivist, 61
(of) coping strategies, 62, 90-91
criticism of, 65-66
distinction from measurement, 35-37
importance of, 45-47
important uses of, 70
immorality of, 64, 66-67
inaccuracy of, 64-65
live in, 45
measurement and assess-

ment, 33-34
media of, 37-40
Mischel's condemnation of, 61
(of) positive characteristics, 62
purpose of, 41
Role in decision making, 253
(of) stress, 62
unwarranted applications of, 65

Barnum effect, 42
Base rate, 52
b coefficient, *see* Regression weight
Behavioural Assessment, 32-33
distinctive feature of, 32
variables focused in, 32-33
Bell Adjustment Inventory
Indian version of, 59
Borderline personality, 62

California F scale, 200
California Psychological, 48
Inventory, 210
Categorical predictors, 268
Children personality Questionnaire, 142-43
Clinical prediction, 50-53
Clinical modelled strategies assumptions of, 56
Coefficient of homogeneity, 180
Common variance, 132
Communalities
estimation of, 132
Communication in foreign language strategies of, 233-35
Computer Applications,
test development, 54-55
test administration, 54-55
test interpretation, 54-55
(CBTI), 55-58
Computerbased test interpretation, 55-58
Albama programe, 55
Butcher's programe, 55
Caldwell's programe, 55
Eber's programe for 16 PF, 55
Lacher's programe, 55, 58
shortcomings of, 58
validity of, 57
Computer outputs, 56-57
clinical-actuarial, 57
clinical modelled, 56
descriptive, 56
Computer synthesis, 149
Consistency of a test, 175
Constructivist Assessment, 61
Construct Validity, 185
Campbells recommendations about, 187-89
consideration, item domain, 93-94
structural, 94-95
Meehl's definition of, 186
method of determining, 182
group differences, 187
factor analysis, 187
study of internal structure, 188
study of change over occasion, 188
Cope scale, 90-93
factors measured by, 90
validity of, 93
Coping, 90
emotion focused, 90-93
problem focused, 90-93
Criterion

implicit, 109
explicit, 109
external, 99
Criterion behaviour, 107
Criterion variance, 103
Correspondence
approach, 70
of response and mental interior, 99
Cross-classification, 261
Cross-cultural assessment
problems of equivalence in, 224
problems of meaning in, 224
Cross Cultural Research, 226-27
Cross Validation, 104
Culture-syntonic measures, 224
Decentering in translation, 244
Deviation
absolute and relative, 101
critical and non-critical, 100
Deviation hypothesis 100, 198-99
Deviation response style, 199
Diagnostic system
revision of, 62
Differential accuracy, 52
Differential reliability
index, 49, 97

Early Personality Questionnaire, 143
Edwards Personal Preference Schedule (EPPS), 81-84
features of, 81
profile stability, 83
validity of, 76, 84
Empirical assessment, 69
item ambiguity in, 105
item pool, 105
Emic-etic distinction, 230-31
Endorsement frequency
Equivalence, importance of, 227-30
empirical demonstration, 228
kinds of, 228-30
Errors, in measurement
Constant, 173
Sources of, 175
Error variance, 132, 173
Expectancy tables
information contained in, 260
use in prediction
of categorical data, 260
Eysenck Personality Inventory, 159
Eysenck Personality Questionnaire, 157-62

Factor analysis
applications of, 47
comparability of methods of, 134
components of variance: common, error, specific, 132
confirmatory and exploratory, 133
criterion analysis, 139
criterion column, 139
criterion groups, 139
rotation of factors, 137-38
types of, 133
Factor analytic approach to assessment, 129-62
Factor scales: 141
Eysenck Personality Inventory, 159

Eysenck Personality Questionnaire, 157-62
Guilford-Zemmermab Temperament Survey, 48, 141
GAMIN, 141
Sixteen PF Questionnaire, 141-57
STDGR, 141
Thurstone Temperament Schedule, 141
Faking, 208
control of, in EPPS, 212
in MMPI, 113
False positive and false negative, 113, 209
Forced-choice format, 49, 212

Geer fear survey, 73
Generalizability
across methods, trait indices, 175-76
and coefficient of reliability, 175-76

Habit (S-R), as unit of personality, 29-30
Homogeneity
as reliability, 178
of item content, 73-74
Horn's procedure, in factor analysis, 137
Hypochondriasis (Hs) scale, 114
Hypothetico-deductive method, 139
Hysteria scale, 114

Illusory correlation, 65
Improper usage of assessment devices, 64-69
base rate, 52, 64
illusory correlation, 65
inadequate criteria, 65
minority groups, bias against, 65
unwarranted applications, 65
Individual in a group, standing of, 254
Institute of Personality Assessment and Research, 46
Instrumental point view, 100
Invalid use of personality tests, *see* improper usage, 64-68
Invasion of privacy
confidentiality, 66
inviolacy, 66
MMPI and personnel selection, 65
reasons for concern, 65
Item ambiguity, 105
Item analysis, 163-172
Item content, importance of, 78, 102, 107-8
Item difficulty, 163
Item discrimination, 163-69
Item editing, 72
Item homogeneity, 180
Item subtlety, 105-6
Item total relation, 169
Item variance, sources of, 79

Jackson plus percentage, 172
Jodhpur Multiphasic Personality Inventory, 84-89
evaluation, 89
item analysis, 85
reliability, 86
psychoneurosis scales, 84
psychosis scales, 84-85
psychosomatic scales, 85
validity, 85-87

Judgmental accuracy, components of Judgemental process, 56-57
automatization of, 56
mathematical models, 56

Kent-Rosnoff list, 44
Klientmuntz decision rules, 56
Kuder-Richardson formula, 74,179

L-data, 39
factors in, 144, 149
L-scale, also *see* MMPI
and test taking attitude, 112
impact on primed profiles, 11
Ok score, 111
L 6, 113

Maudsley Personality Questionnaire, 48
Measurement
assignment of numbers in, 26-27
distinction from assessment intensive and extensive, 26-27
redundency in, 130
Million Clinical Multiaxical Inventory (MCMI), 62
Minnesota Multiphasic Personality Inventory (MMPI)
acquiescence in, 195-96
actuarial atlas, 123-24
clinical scales, 114-15
code books, 123-24
derivation of scales, 115-17
interpretation of scores, 118-19
item language, 124
normative sample of, 124
profile coding, Hathway and Welsh, 122-23
psychiatric anchorage of, 124
purpose of, 110
reliability of, 117
salient features of, 110
Moderater variables
development of, 280
Motivational distortions, also *see* response distortions
dealing with, 211
detection of, 215-16
sources of, 194
suppression of, 220
Multidimensional scales, 48
Multiphasic scales, 48-49
Multitrait-Multimethod metrix, 190
Multiple prediction, 276-79
regression coefficients, 277
selection of predictors, 277-78
stepwise multiple correlation, 278

Needs
manifest, 49
measured by EPPS, 81-83
Murray's list, 81
Nomological network, 79

Office of Strategic Services (OSS), 46

Paramorphic representation, 52
Persona, meaning of, 15-16
Personal Data Sheet, 44
Personal Equation, 43

Personality
as an aggregate, 16
as individuality, 16-17
as layer of dispositions, 17
as mode of adjustment, 17
as pervasive pattern, 17
definition of:
Allport's, 17
Allport's revised, 18
Jurist, 16
Pervin's implications for measurement, 18-19
philosophical, 16
sociological, 16
theological, 16
Personality assessment
approaches to, 50
contemporary life and changes in practice, 61-64
comparison of approaches, 49
criteria of classification, 38-39
immoral usage, 66-67
inaccuracy of usage, 64-65
methods of, 30
Personality data
importance of transformation, 253-54
transformation in Z, 255 and
ordinal position, 256
Personality descriptors, 269
Personality Research Form
content saturation, 96
step in construction, 96-97
Personality Questionnaires, developed in India, criticism, 60
P.G.I. Health Questionnaire
item analysis, 127-28
purpose, 126
reliability, 127-28
validity, 128
Phi-coefficient, 170
Picture Reaction Test (PRT), 199
Point-biserial Correlation, 171
Prediction
classification of methods, 153-55
use of complex functions in, 281
Predictive Validity, 183-84
Profiles
kinds of, 262
good profiles, 262
prototype, 273-74
Profile Classification
a priori, 271
statistical, 271
steps in, 270-71
Profile Comparison
aspects of, 263
individual-group, 266
Profile similarity
indicators of, 264-67
correlation, 264
D statistics, 264-65
pattern similarity, 265
coefficient of (rp) 266-67
Projective hypothesis, 44
Pseudo scientific assessment
astrology, 42
astronomy, 42
palmistry, 42
phrenology, 42

Rational item pool, 69
Rational-theoretical assessment
awareness of mental set, 70

correspondence of item-content and response
item pool, 69-70
reliability, 96
self-awareness, 78
validity, 76-77
Reliability,
definition, 172-73
effect of test length on, 177
equivalent form, 177
error variance, 173-75
factor influencing, 174-75
hit index, 172
in generalizability theory, 175-76
inter-item consistency, 178-81
kinds of, 176-80
Kuder-Richardsm (K-R) formula, 178
Spearman-Brown formula, 177
split-half, 177
test-retest, 176
Regression equation, 276-78
r_p, *see* profile similarity coefficient
Response distortions
Contamination sources, 149
detection of, 215-16
overcoming of, 218-19
response set, 203-11
response style, 200-3

Second stratum factors, 148
Selection ratio, 52-53
Sensitivity testing, 43
Sixteen Personality Factors Questionnaire, 48
Social desirability
and item endorsement, 204-5
dealing with, 25
in EPPS, 25-26, 212
in MMPI, 17-20, 212-13
measures of, 205
scale values (SDSVS), 204
Source traits, 22
Source of variance in test scores
Specific variance, 132, 173-76
Statistical prediction, 50-52
Standard of performance, 102
Stress models, 90
Stimulas-response units, 29-30
Subsystem validation, 229
Suppressor Variables, 281-82
Surface traits, 22

Target language, 234-35
Technical recommendation for psychological tests, 186
Test scores:
construct-referenced meaning, 224
criterion-referenced meaning, 224
test taking attitude, *see* L scale, 112
Tetrachoric correlation (rt), 169
abac for, 170
Thematic Apperception Test, 41
rational assumptions in, 70
Theoretical approach to assessment, 70
Theoretical item pool, 72
Traits
arguments against, 30-31
classification, 23-24
discovery of:
clinical method, 22-23
common sense, 23

experimental method, 22
surface and source, 22
Properties of, 24-27
durability & flexibility, 26
functional fluctuation, 25, 27
general traits, 23
generality, 26
scalability, 25
universality, 25
implications for
measurement, 26-27
Translation
and cross-cultural
assessment, 232-33
good translation, 246-50
back translation, 243-44
decentering in, 244
errors in 233, 237-39
equivalence of, 233
methods of, 240
multistage iteration in, 244
original language,
quality of, 241-42
Types
continuous, 28
discontinuous, 28
meaning of, 28
Method of Identification of:
arbitrary standards, 29
clinical methods, 29
statistical methods, 29

Unitary traits, 129
Universal Index of personality factors, 140, 147
Utility in decision making:
coefficient of, 53-54
Validity
administrative, 186
concurrent, 183-84
construct, 185-91
content, 183
variation in, 186
Values
Allport Vernon Scale, 80-81
Spranger's classification, 80
Variance,
common, 132
error, 132, 173
random, 173
sources of, 173
specific, 132
total, 132
true score, 6, 13
Veterans Administration Selection Research Project, 47

War Office Boards (WoBs), 45
Woodworth Personal Data Sheet, 44
Word Association, 44